Oklahoma Project for
Discourse and Theory

THE AUTONOMOUS
MALE OF ADAM SMITH

THE AUTONOMOUS MALE OF ADAM SMITH

by Stewart Justman

University of Oklahoma Press
Norman and London

By Stewart Justman

The Hidden Text of Mill's Liberty (Lanham, Md., 1991)
The Autonomous Male of Adam Smith (Norman, 1993)

Library of Congress Cataloging-in-Publication Data

Justman, Stewart.
    The autonomous male of Adam Smith / by Stewart Justman.
       p.   cm.—(Oklahoma project for discourse and theory ; v. 14)
    Includes bibliographical references (p.   ) and index.
    ISBN 0-8061-2542-X (alk. paper)
    1. Smith, Adam, 1723-1790—Contributions in sex role. 2. Smith,
Adam, 1723-1790. Theory of moral sentiments. 3. Sex role.
I. Title. II. Series.
HQ1075.J87   1993
305.3—dc20   93-9258
                                           CIP

The Autonomous Male of Adam Smith is Volume 14 of the Oklahoma Project for Discourse and Theory.

The paper in this book meets the guidelines for permanence and durability of the Committee on Production Guidelines for Book Longevity of the Council on Library Resources, Inc. ∞

1 2 3 4 5 6 7 8 9 10

We still feel within us, and we cherish and cultivate, those inbred sentiments which are the faithful guardians, the active monitors of our duty, the true supporters of all liberal and manly morals.

—*Edmund Burke,* Reflections on the Revolution in France

Contents

Series Editors' Foreword

The Oklahoma Project for Discourse & Theory is a series of interdisciplinary texts whose purpose is to explore the cultural institutions that constitute the human sciences, to see them in relation to one another, and, perhaps above all, to see them as products of particular discursive practices. To this end, we hope that the Oklahoma Project will promote dialogue within and across traditional disciplines—psychology, philology, linguistics, history, art history, aesthetics, logic, political economy, religion, philosophy, anthropology, communications, and the like—in texts that theoretically are located across disciplines. In recent years, in a host of new and traditional areas, there has been great interest in such discursive and theoretical frameworks. Yet we conceive of the Oklahoma Project as going beyond local inquiries, providing a larger forum for interdiscursive theoretical discussions and dialogue.

Our agenda in previous books and certainly in this one has been to present through the University of Oklahoma Press a series of critical volumes that set up a theoretical encounter among disciplines, an interchange not limited to literature but covering virtually the whole range of the human sciences. It is a critical series with an important reference in literary studies—thus mirroring the modern development of discourse theory—but including all approaches, other than quantitative studies, open to semiotic and post-semiotic analysis and to the wider concerns of cultural studies. Regardless of its particular domain, each book in the series will investigate characteristically post-Freudian, post-Saussurean, and post-Marxist questions about culture and the discourses that constitute different cultural phenomena. The Oklahoma Project is a sustained dialogue intended to make a significant contribution to the contemporary understanding of the human sciences in the contexts of cultural theory and cultural studies.

The title of the series reflects, of course, its home base, the University of Oklahoma. But it also signals in a significant way the particularity of the *local* functions within historical and conceptual frameworks for understanding culture. *Oklahoma* is a haunting place-name in American culture. A Choctaw phrase meaning "red people," it goes back to the Treaty of Dancing Rabbit Creek in Mississippi in 1830. For Franz Kafka, it conjured up the idea of America itself, both the indigenous Indian peoples of North America and the vertiginous space of the vast plains. It is also the place-name, the "American" starting point, with which Wallace Stevens begins his *Collected Poems*. Historically, too, it is a place in which American territorial and political expansion was reenacted in a single day in a retracing called the Oklahoma land run. Geographically, it is the heartland of the continent.

As such—in the interdisciplinary Oklahoma Project for Discourse & Theory—we are hoping to describe, above all, multifaceted *interests* within and across various studies of discourse and culture. Such interests are akin to what Kierkegaard calls the "in-between" aspect of experience, the "inter esse," and, perhaps more pertinently, what Nietzsche describes as the always *political* functioning of concepts, art works, and language—the functioning of power as well as knowledge in discourse and theory. Such politics, occasioning dialogue and bringing together powerfully struggling and often unarticulated positions, disciplines, and assumptions, is always local, always particular. In some ways, such interests function in broad feminist critiques of language, theory, and culture as well as microphilosophical and microhistorical critiques of the definitions of truth and art existing within ideologies of "disinterested" meaning. They function in the interested examination of particular disciplines and general disciplinary histories. They function (to allude to two of our early titles) in the very interests of theory and the particularity of the postmodern age in which many of us find ourselves. In such interested particulars, we believe, the human sciences are articulated. We hope that the books of the Oklahoma Project will provide sites of such interest and that in them, individually and collectively, the monologues of traditional scholarly discourse will become heteroglosses, just as such place-names as *Oklahoma* and such commonplace words and concepts as *discourse* and *theory* can become sites for the dialogue and play of culture.

ROBERT CON DAVIS
RONALD SCHLEIFER

Norman, Oklahoma

Acknowledgments

Thanks are due to Oxford University Press for permission to quote from its 1976 edition of the *Theory of Moral Sentiments,* which the 1982 Liberty Classics edition reproduces. Thanks are owed as well to the Interlibrary Loan Office of the University of Montana Library for so helpfully attending to taxing requests. Ken Lockridge, bursting with ideas, both inspired and informed me; the comradeship of Gerry Brenner, Robert Johnstone, and Doug Purl, fellow freethinkers, sustained me. Kim Wiar of the University of Oklahoma Press stood by this manuscript through all of its trials and transformations, and extended to me the best of all courtesies, freedom. To Lissy, finally, deep gratitude.

THE AUTONOMOUS
MALE OF ADAM SMITH

CHAPTER I

Introduction

Women are taught dependence, men independence. Women are taught submission, men assertion. Women learn to be emotional, men rational. Women, but not men, are expected to pity. Women are confined to the domestic realm, while men venture hardily into public affairs. So we are accustomed to think.

As crude as these simplicities are, they are widely believed and find credit even in serious scholarship. Many scholars, it is true, would argue that the gender distinctions just cited are the product of a particular social formation, often called bourgeois society, but few seem to dispute the antitheses themselves. Yet the antithesis of public-rational man and private-emotional woman finds poor support in the work that is the closest thing to an authorized version of the morality of bourgeois society, Adam Smith's *Theory of Moral Sentiments*. As Smith's *Wealth of Nations* stands as the classic exposition of the case for free trade, so the *Theory of Moral Sentiments* investigates the moral bonds holding together the commercial way of life. And contrary to our attribution of reason to men, the *Theory* argues that reason plays a paltry role in the affairs of men in commercial society compared to such subrational forces as habit and sympathy. The latter, according to Smith, is the binding force of the commercial order—a principle whose workings are deeper, swifter, and surer than reason. The ways of sympathy have so little to do with reason (says Smith) that even when reason bids us resist an unjust ruler, we find ourselves unwilling to do so, such is our habit of sympathizing with our own masters—and on this habit, perfectly irrational as it is, political order depends.

If sympathy is a natural force of attraction like gravity, economic pursuits are like motion; in turn they are motivated less by reason than by irrational longings and habit (a variant of Hume's maxim that reason does not propel to action). Like the feudal magnates who senselessly frittered away their power and patrimony in the love of ornaments—a story Smith tells with superb irony in the *Wealth of Nations*—the men of commercial society seek goods that are worthless on any rational assessment. Commercial society is so busy because men struggle like the proverbially vain "wives of aldermen" to show better than their fellows, the author's wording setting up an unexpected resemblance between men and women.[1] But while women are satirized for their frivolity or condemned for their excessive desires, it seems that men's boundless desire for frivolous goods keeps laborers employed and so actually secures the political order. Perhaps because capitalism lives and trades on "vices" long imputed to women— such as limitless desire and the projection of false but alluring images—Adam Smith finds that the men of commercial society act like aldermen's wives, admire fops who are less males than unsexed "things," and give themselves up to their ruling passion of vanity, the folly of "weak" minds.[2] Partly in order to spare himself and his readers the uneasy implications of his own vision of an effeminate society, Adam Smith draws on the heavily masculine idiom of stoicism, so I will argue. We can form an idea of how provocative *The Theory of Moral Sentiments* could have been by reading Mary Wollstonecraft's indictment, in the *Vindication of the Rights of Woman*, of a society depraved by luxurious women and womanish men.[3]

The reader of *The Theory of Moral Sentiments* finds, then, that the men of commercial society are impelled by the faulty reason and wandering desire, the vanity and love of ornament that moralists of all persuasions censured in women. To be sure, the illicit appetites of women were in some degree projections of men— men like the Homeric chiefs who adorned their female slaves and proclaimed their own wealth by their numbers,[4] and the modern successors of those chiefs. The vain woman displays herself and not her proprietor; in all likelihood it is because she poses so evocatively the threat of insubordination and riot that the male imagination dwells on this figure so fantastically. In Adam Smith's time luxury in fact distinguished not women but the aristocracy, which employed it as a spectacle of power, an instrument of rule. What then permitted moralists to speak as though vanity and luxury were peculiarly female vices when everyone could see, and any number said, that men were vain and luxurious themselves? The fallacy of essence. The fallacy of essence enables it to be said that while men may happen to be vain and luxurious, women are these things essentially, by nature—much as Adam Smith's friend Hume alleges that all of us are shortsighted all the time, but women peculiarly so. "All human creatures, especially of the female sex," he says, "are apt to over-look remote motives in favour of any present temptation."[5] It is not that men are any less subject to moral shortsightedness, for Hume argues that men's passions "*always* plead in favour of whatever is near and contiguous."[6] All the same, Hume is willing to say that this defect of judgment specially concerns women: "especially . . . the female sex." Thus the superiority of men is saved.

By the same token, however, the fallacy of essence implies that when men are vain and ostentatious, they take on what are essentially traits of women. They become effeminate. Because the ruling passion of the men of commercial society, according to Adam Smith, is vanity, those men stand constantly in risk of effeminacy—the effeminacy decried by numberless writers high and low as the worst of the depraving effects of commerce. For example, in his celebrated *Estimate of the Manners and Principles of the Times,* published close upon the first edition of the *Moral Sentiments,* John Brown argues with tireless iteration that England has sunk to a condition of "vain, luxurious, and selfish EFFEMINACY."[7] Smith himself employs the same language to describe consumer goods as that used by earlier critics of women's love of consumption. He calls such things baubles, trinkets, trifles, toys. In part, it is Smith's defense of consumer society in spite of his contempt for its highest prizes, and in spite of his conservative temperament, that makes his thought so interesting.

With his love of display, Smithian man imitates the ways of the aristocracy, but in the author's eyes his model is just as bad as though he were imitating women; after all, it is not inherited, aristocratic wealth that builds up the stores of the nation and improves society. Such, in fact, is the association of courts with women (famous for their "empire" over men), that in all probability Adam Smith would have seen the aristocracy itself as effeminate, just as men of his time identified public, or showy, women with the aristocratic regime and its corrupt splendor.[8] Observe, for example, the clear gender-coding of Smith's statement that "the external graces, the frivolous accomplishments of that impertinent and foolish thing called a man of fashion, are commonly more admired than the solid and masculine virtues of a warrior, a statesman, a philosopher, or a legislator" (*TMS*, p. 63). I argue that in *The Theory of Moral Sentiments* these figures of masculinity are mere props—plaster casts of antique heroes—dignifying a way of life wherein men are not called in any numbers to be warriors (for Smith rejects the idea of a citizen militia) or to take any part in legislation, but *are* called to trade, an activity not on the list of masculine enterprises.[9] The "solid and masculine" virtues provide the semblance of a solid foundation to a theory of society that otherwise rests on such dubious practices as conformism and the emulation of the rich, practices exposed by Smith's own successor in the liberty tradition, John Stuart Mill. Adam Smith "glorifies conformity" to social norms.[10]

So deep is the association of women with luxury and corrupt display that in our own century exponents of architectural modernism were still declaiming against a "depraved, feminine tendency toward kitsch."[11] So too lasted the association of women with the corruption of courts and capitals. It was in this spirit that Werner Sombart, who cites Adam Smith, once argued that courtesans "gave life at court its distinctive character," while the court in turn set standards of ostentation for society in general to imitate.[12] Smithian man is an imitator; he matches his behavior to that of others, although as a rule Adam Smith considers this a benign process governed by the marvelous mechanism called sympathy. Smith also believes, however, that sympathy corrupts. It draws us into an identification with the great and the glittering, whose part we like to take. (So it is that the man of fashion, a sort of human bauble, is "commonly . . . admired.") As he imitates his social betters in the hope of shining like them, Smithian man corrupts himself[13] and indulges in the vanity that was endlessly denounced in women, especially the women of high society.

As with vanity, so with luxury. Craving luxury goods not for the meager pleasure they afford in themselves but for the gaping admiration they arouse in others, Smithian man partakes of the corruption that for centuries was another word for luxury. But the original sin of luxury was "committed by 'the woman,'" Eve; through luxury, the depraved desire imputed to the daughters of Eve spreads, infecting—many said, effeminating—men. Perhaps the worst of it is that luxury and capitalism seem made for one another. Reputedly, luxury grows to encompass entire nations,[14] while capitalism widens the market for luxury goods, playing right into the expansionary tendencies of luxury itself. As theorists increasingly recognized by Adam Smith's time, a commercial society both stimulates and thrives on "imaginary wants"—wants that are without limit and cannot be quenched; traditionally, however, desires that swell on being satisfied and threaten to be all-consuming had been ascribed to women, famed for their unreason.[15] Not everyone welcomed the notion of a society whose mainspring was excessive desire, and as though to preempt objections, Smith impressed classical values dear to the critics of luxury into the service of commercial society. His moral model of stern and humane virtues in balance casts a Roman aura over the *Moral Sentiments*. More particularly, he portrays the industriousness, frugality, and steady habits of the prudent man as a kind of lesser stoicism— stoicism on a human scale. As the sun illumines the moon, so the stoic virtue of self-command lends a "sober lustre" to the minor virtues of prudence (*TMS*, p. 242). By the exercise of self-command, the prudent man overcomes the human tendency to give in to "any present temptation" and tames self-love into something decent and socially presentable. By analogy with his doctrine of tempering rude passions, Adam Smith has tempered a rude stoicism and brought it down to the level at which people can go along with it; he has fitted stoicism to the requirements of commercial society. "The moral quality of prudence," that cardinal Smithian virtue, "depends on its association with the Stoic virtue of self-command."[16] Thus the author fortifies the manhood of Smithian man, who otherwise bears a distinct family resemblance to woman, both in his vanity and corruption on the one hand and his propriety on the other.

It is notorious that men have long perceived women dually—for example, as madonnas and whores. (Moreover, men have projected the contradiction of their perceptions onto women themselves, calling it women's unreason.) Smithian man possesses a dual existence too, sharing in the general "corruption of . . . moral sentiments" (*TMS*, p. 61) while nevertheless leading a morally decorous life of frugality and hard work. In the latter, seemlier aspect, the aspect in which he is best known, Smithian man is the counterpart of a woman—a proper woman, dutiful, inoffensive, retiring. The "public man / private woman" antithesis hardly prepares us for this Smithian figure, for, as Adam Smith remarks explicitly, the prudent man wants no part of public business. His abstention from public life gives him a kind of fictitious superiority to women confined not by choice but by fiat in the private sphere. And while the antithesis of public man and private woman prompts us to think of women whose field of concern is narrow and men whose field of concern is broad, the theorists of the Scottish Enlightenment were convinced that men act with blinders on and "have not the capacity to contemplate larger 'objects,' " so "frail" is their rationality.[17] Hence, for example, the shortsightedness that in the opinion of Hume belongs to everyone, even men. In the feebleness of his reason and the littleness of his concerns, in the "weakness of his powers" and "the narrowness of his comprehension" (*TMS*, p. 237), Smithian man resembles the image—*his* image—of the bourgeois woman.

In turn, the prudent tradesman, with his "inferior" virtues (*TMS*, p. 304), exemplifies the man of limited views, as propriety itself— conformity with average moral standards—is portrayed by Smith as markedly inferior to the more dazzling virtues (*TMS*, p. 25). Unable to see as far as the public interest but performing the "smallest" duties (*TMS*, p. 237) with faultless exactitude, the prudent man is the mirror image of the woman deemed unfit to hold political views and called to the chaste performance of her duties.[18] The resemblance between the prudent man and the proper woman Smith leaves implied. No such restraint inhibits his discussion of the lower-class man, depicted by Smith as miserably lacking in courage and political capacity, a "mutilated and deformed" being, a man unmanned.[19] Evidently a class double standard spares the bourgeois the humiliation that Adam Smith feels free to mete out to the laborer. (In a related example of favoritism, John Brown excoriates the effeminacy of Britain and yet spares the middle ranks.) But the resemblance of the prudent man and the proper woman holds good whether the author wishes to veil it or not. In the words of Defoe, "The credit of a tradesman . . . is the same thing in its nature as the virtue of a lady."[20]

Nor is the prudent male an incidental figure in Adam Smith's theory of society, for it is precisely his humble and tireless efforts that build up the wealth of the nation. The leading figure of Smithian society, then, does not venture hardily into the public world—his prudence forbids it—just as he does not make rational judgments about the good. (The Smithian doctrine of the poverty of reason anticipates the bias of romanticism, although it is commoner to trace that bias back to Burke than to Smith, his intellectual associate.) In these respects as in his modesty, propriety, even submissiveness,[21] Smithian man answers his own image of woman. As Burke associates beauty with the lovely gradual swells of a woman's body, so the prudent man gradually swells the wealth of the nation, his efforts possessing the irresistible effect so commonly imputed to women. As propriety keeps women chaste in spite of their inclination "to over-look remote motives," so propriety keeps the prudent man decent in spite of his weak regard for the public good.[22] As in Smith's own account the careful wife fails in none of her duties in spite of her lack of affection for her husband (*TMS*, p. 162), so the prudent man faultlessly observes the little rules of propriety in spite of his lack of social affections. As merchants can get along "without any mutual love or affection" (*TMS*, p. 86), in a sort of loveless marriage, so the dutiful wife does not need feeling. Both the proper woman and the prudent man are apt to lack ardor—and both, let it be said, represent types or norms rather than literal beings.[23]

All of the resemblances just cited illustrate capitalism's unsettling effect on tradition, in the present case the venerable tradition of male supremacy. I am persuaded by Max Weber's argument that capitalism works against tradition. And yet in order to justify itself, it may cling to the very values it negates, as when robber barons tried to make themselves look like hereditary grandees, or when today's zealots of the market speak touchingly in the name of "traditional values." Adam Smith himself strives to liberate commerce from traditional restrictions but founds his moral theory on a principle that binds us together as mysteriously and inarguably as tradition itself, the principle of sympathy. Sometimes, says Smith, we join in with the passions of others before we know what we are sympathizing with—an analogue of the conservative belief that we are parties to tradition without necessarily knowing how the tradition got started.[24] While he advocates novel economic doctrines, Smith's theory conjures up men who are joined as if by tradition and trouble themselves as little about political questions as tradition-bound subjects who think government is not their concern. Traditionally, government was viewed "as a phenomenon as spontaneous, as devoid of human central planning, and as receiving as much guidance from providence, as language, or as the development of knowledge in general."[25] In the thought of Adam Smith, the economy takes on a providential design deeper than human wisdom. In attempting to naturalize laissez-faire, in playing up unreasoned responses like sympathy, in opposing central planning, and certainly in contemplating slow change, Smith in effect reinstates tradition in an analysis that is untraditional itself. As he unfolds his moral theory, similarly, Smith appeals to old values, notably stoic values, to lend gravitas and stability to new ways. He employs the traditional language of male supremacy to make up for the prudent man's lack of such traditional goods as reason, nobility, generosity, and in fact self-mastery. In other words, Adam Smith adheres to the tradition of male supremacy that his own theory reduces to the status of a prejudice, as the celebrated rationalization of the world is said to have reduced "patriarchal or feudal" values to irrational vestiges of the past.[26]

Although committed on the whole to that new thing under the sun, commercial society, Smith was temperamentally conservative, and no evidence suggests that he wanted to discard so customary and consoling a fiction as the superiority of men. Much as the skepticism of Hume accepts as customary usage what it cannot accept as a verdict of reason, so the wry philosophy of Adam Smith endorses the gender prejudices of his culture while leaving them without a basis in reason. At least that is its effect. (In Smithian society, for example, education fills the heads of men, not women, with fluff.)[27] No doubt Smith never intended to erode the distinction between able men and feeble women, but he himself held that our actions often escape our intentions. And intentionally or not, his own theory of the evolution of society distinctly implies that patriarchy itself has lost its basis.

Among the traditions cut by capitalism, Adam Smith would list the very passing on of patrimonial estates. With the manufacture and marketing of luxury goods, he argues, men for the first time gain the opportunity to squander the revenue that used to remain in the family for generations on end. They leap at the chance to bankrupt themselves for the sake of "trinkets and baubles, fitter to be the play-things of children than the serious pursuits of men."[28] Having thus unmanned themselves and unknowingly propelled history to a higher phase, all in order to adorn their persons, they leave their sons without a patrimony. So it is that families of substance, families "such as have possessed some considerable estate from father to son for many successive generations, are very rare in commercial societies."[29] In Smith's terms, the height of patriarchy was reached long ago when shepherds of formidable authority and ancient lineage ruled over their clans.[30] In those biblical ages the institution of patriarchy was grounded in a way of life wherein luxury goods were few and wealth hard to consume. Commercial society, by contrast, deals in luxury goods and makes consumption a way of life, while its shifting fashions, paper fortunes, and portable forms of wealth (so portable that merchants can always pick up and leave their country of residence if they like) undermine the permanence that patriarchy claims. In Smith's Scotland, not the commercial centers but the backward Highlands tribes exemplified patriarchy;[31] sociologically speaking, his theory of the progress toward commercial civilization supposes the weakening of patriarchal rule. Smith's analysis of a commercial society that emerges as the rich dissolve their own patrimonies— an event he views with a kind of celestial smile—leaves the paternal order as groundless as Hume left customary beliefs and as Bentham left the prejudices supporting the British political system.

So corrosive is Smith's skepticism that it leaves the political order foundationless. It turns out that the established order is "founded" on the merest trick of the imagination—subjects' habit of glorifying their rulers in their own minds (*TMS*, p. 52). In *The Theory of Moral Sentiments,* Adam Smith calls into question so much that is basic to commercial society, including the worth of the things men covet, that there is no reason why his irony should have somehow stopped short of throwing doubt on the superiority of men themselves. Thus his theory that men are deceived for their own good into pursuing worthless goals destroys the male claim to superiority over women who (many Victorians were to say) need shielding from harsh truths and whose dangerous energies (many traditional misogynists had said) need to be tied up in harmless pursuits. Once the ruling passion of commercial society has been reduced to vanity, and vain men have been scolded for their "superficial weakness and trivial folly" (*TMS*, p. 115), which is the very idiom that Mary Wollstonecraft uses for corrupt women, not much separates men and women morally. The implied analogy between men and women in Smithian society goes farther yet. Women were called good if they dutifully attended to domestic concerns, and impudent and dangerous if they made a public display of themselves; Smithian men are good as long as they accumulate wealth by the socially approved habits of frugality and diligence, but when they intrude into public affairs, they are apt to become the vile "merchants and manufacturers" Smith execrates in the *Wealth of Nations* for seducing the nation and perverting public policy. If the bad woman corrupts and the good woman radiates "influence," influence and corruption were alternative terms for the process by which the crown managed parliament in the age of Adam Smith,[32] as they alternately describe the improving effect exercised by Smithian man in his sympathetic aspect and the tainted sentiments of the same figure in his baser mode.

In spite of his certainly conventional attitudes, then, Smith's analysis portrays men as analogues of women, casting doubt on their celebrated superiority. If Smithian man weren't somehow deficient in manhood, the author wouldn't have corrected the deficiency in revisions of *The Theory of Moral Sentiments* by installing "the man within" (e.g., p. 137), or conscience, as a kind of superior self; if Smithian man were a man to all appearances, he wouldn't have to be shown to be a man inwardly. Injecting men with stoic manhood also means injecting them with resignation, a virtue that helps stabilize a society based, if that is the word, on deference to the unworthy and deceits of the imagination. In the first two chapters I reflect on Adam Smith's use of the language of stoicism both to fortify the manhood of men and to quiet political passions, passions all the more dangerous, perhaps, as traditions lose their ground and come to be seen and spoken of as prejudice and habit. Having entered Christian thought upon the collapse of the polis (the center of value in the ancient world),[33] stoicism lends itself to Smith's efforts to depoliticize men—to make "self-government" (*TMS*, p. 23) entirely a matter of mastery of the passions.

Not with all his heart, however, did Adam Smith break with the classical paradigm of men as actors in public life. The republican tinge of his values—his worry over the loss of martial spirit, his contempt for the court, his eye for what he called corruption, his reverence for the figure of the Legislator, his agrarianism, his honorific view of the landlord superior to Fortune's injuries and changes, his citations of Cicero (identified with republican virtue), his regard for the public good, indeed his stoic leanings[34]—this itself helps to explain his reluctance to admit that his own theory embarrasses the distinction between men and women; for the republican tradition was deeply biased in favor of men, like its political models, the ancient republics. Like a republican, Smith celebrates "the men who were capable of atchieving such great actions" as founding colonies; significantly, however, he adds that these manly deeds redound little to the honor of Europe, whose policy toward the colonies was mean and shortsighted from the beginning.[35] In *The Theory of Moral Sentiments* Smith sings of great actions and heroic manliness but is perhaps more concerned with common prudence, which depending on your perspective looks either like meanness and small views, or like seemliness and probity.[36] In either case the prudent man is the protagonist of commercial society.

In coming pages I argue that Smith infuses the prudent modern with a degree of ancient virtue, with stoicism, in order to make up for the lack of manhood that his theory hints at so suggestively. I say "so suggestively" because if the good woman at the time was defined as being "even-tempered, patient, modest, and prudent,"[37] these are the very virtues that almost all interpreters of Smith agree he hoped commercial society would bring out in men. (From the beginning, for example, his *Theory of Moral Sentiments* emphasizes even temper—the tuning of the emotions to a point neither too high nor too low.) Indeed, sympathy itself, the binding force of the Smithian universe, was "closely associated" with the feminine at the time Smith wrote.[38] In the spirit of republicanism, Adam Smith once said outright that commercial society makes men "effeminate and dastardly."[39] For sound reasons, however, he was unwilling to reject that society, and in *The Theory of Moral Sentiments* he presents the same "effeminate and dastardly" male under a more eulogistic description. Dastardliness becomes prudence, and effeminacy a proper demeanor and an aversion to public life.

If the resemblance of the prudent man to the good woman, as veiled as it is, humbles men, even more disturbing is the resemblance of the same man in another of his aspects to the vain, corrupt woman. Ironist though he was, Smith could not endure the thought that commercial society rests on just those vices of vanity and corruption so loudly and unanimously imputed to women—that the commercial way of life is actually founded on what he himself called the corruption of our moral sentiments. It is manly stoicism, especially emphasized in the last edition of *The Theory of Moral Sentiments,* that gives the author's theory of commercial society the "solid" foundation it otherwise might seem to lack. In Adam Smith's Newtonian vision of the moral universe, stoicism supplies gravitas, gravity. Without it, Smithian men would be weightless, like the inanities they covet and the vapid illusions they dedicate themselves to. As, in the mind of Edmund Burke, British liberty "carries an imposing and majestic aspect" by reason of its noble ancestry,[40] so the stoic is the noble, if rude and distant, ancestor of Smith's modern. Some one hundred years after the final edition of the *Theory,* a French theorist would argue that it was time to emancipate the discussion of luxury from the influence of archaic ideals, including stoicism, hostile to wealth. In Adam Smith's *Theory* it is as though the young ideology of commerce were not yet ready to stand on its own, for it relies equivocally on archaic virtue. Conservative in temper, Smith had no wish to cast off all at once "the enormous weight of the past" bearing on any discussion of the seductive power of luxury.[41]

If the crucial issue of debate in the Scottish Enlightenment was how "ethical life [read: male virtue] was to be preserved in the age of industry and refinement,"[42] Adam Smith's preservative was stoicism, an antique set of values of such wide appeal in the eighteenth century that its votaries included both the orthodox Samuel Johnson and the infidel Voltaire.[43] Stoicism has something for everyone, it seems. In the moral theory of Adam Smith, it has something for the average prudent man. A notionally stoic self-command keeps Smithian man from losing himself to the seductive appeals of luxury—a vice traditionally personified as a woman[44]—and preserves him from the depravity of moral sentiments that is general in commercial society. As luxury was traditionally the capital sin, the sin that contained all others, so to Adam Smith's mind self-command is the capital virtue, the virtue that enables all others. "Self-command is not only itself a great virtue, but from it all the other virtues seem to derive their principal lustre" (*TMS*, p. 241).

However, the stoicism of Smithian man is a fiction. The insecurity that keeps him in motion simply rules out stoicism. "Obsessive and anxious," plagued with "uneasiness,"[45] Smithian man is in truth the very opposite of a stoic. Smithian prudence may be ennobled by its "association" with stoic virtue, but association is based on fancy or habit, not reason. The stark contradiction between stoic apathy and the pursuit of happiness must be one of those incongruities "at times almost amounting to self-contradiction" which we are assured do not matter much in the *Moral Sentiments*.[46] I take the conventional view that contradictions matter, and am interested in Smith's use of verbal patches to cover them. Smith himself concludes that stoicism has little application to the business of life—a judgment that doesn't stop him from reflecting a little of the "lustre" of the stoic virtues onto the man of business, now seen by a Burkean fiction as the distant descendant of an illustrious ancestor, a modern ennobled by ancient lineage.[47] (As though to confirm how poorly stoicism really comports with commercial pursuits, certain French theorists of the early years of this century took up with stoic values precisely "to combat the ethic of material self-interest preached by liberal economists.")[48] By composing his moral theory in the language of a middling stoicism, Adam Smith implies that the values of traditional humanism are somehow upheld in modern commercial society. In the moral theory of Adam Smith, the language of Roman virtue is a shining anachronism, an unmoving star by means of which the author navigates the dangers posed by his own view of men as devoted pursuers of trivial goods.

In the Smithian world, Cicero's maxim of "well ordered behavior"[49] becomes the art of suiting one's behavior to one's company. Roman self-mastery becomes the tempering of the passions. The stoic concept of natural law becomes the laws securing property in the "system of natural liberty."[50] As, according to stoic precept, people's "moral state" depends on themselves alone, so in the world of natural liberty our economic state theoretically depends on our own efforts.[51] The stoic prescription of "fatigue and industry" turns into the bourgeois maxim of work.[52] The stoic's invulnerability to fortune becomes the financial invulnerability of the thriving tradesman whom "nothing can hurt . . . but himself; if he comes into any mischiefs, they are of his own choosing."[53] In all, the Smithian actor is infused with a kind of belated or sentimental stoicism that asks him to "moderate" his urges (*TMS*, p. 292) and that serves to moralize the characteristic pursuits of commercial society, such as diligent labor and social emulation—moralizes, too, that even emotional temperature which theorists both before and after Max Weber identified as part of the work-discipline of the commercial order. Where Nietzsche rages against "the tuning down of the affects to a harmless mean,"[54] Adam Smith approves the calibration of the passions "to a certain mediocrity" (*TMS*, p. 27). And this muting of the passions, evidence of the celebrated calming effects of commerce,[55] makes men appear the masters of themselves. As Joseph Addison prescribed to his readers "a strong steady masculine piety" (a slogan of little meaning),[56] so Adam Smith employs the stoic principle to fortify his argument and give it a masculine foundation. That one of the founding texts of commercial society is itself founded squarely on a fiction of manhood can only have confused ethical debates like those *The Theory of Moral Sentiments* arose from in the first place—debates already muddled by the identification of virility with virtue.

Does *The Theory of Moral Sentiments* set out one man's vision of society or a vision widely shared? Considering that six editions of the *Theory* were published during Adam Smith's lifetime; that many other commentators concurred that both men and women in commercial society were driven by envious emulation and the love of display; considering that the *Theory* constantly speaks of what "we" do—speaks in the name of a moral consensus—it seems Smith indeed spoke for views widely held. In his philosophical capacity Smith sometimes gives "common sense" an ironic twist, but it is his standard of appeal in the end. His uncommon acuity and cool philosophical reserve make him all the more persuasive, perhaps, as a spokesman for shared beliefs. That he gives an original turn to "common sense" means that the falsity of his distinction between men and women reflects in some sense on the gender codes of commercial society itself. *The Theory of Moral Sentiments* matters if only for what it reveals about those codes. Additionally, though, Smith's understanding of the spectacle of power helps to explain the survival of old habits of deference in the commercial order,[57] as his theory of male narcissism prefigures the "culture of narcissism" of our own commercial society. In the thought of Adam Smith, men partake of the vanity and corruption indelibly associated with women by long tradition—a tradition extending from the biblical harlot in spectacular attire, through the Wife of Bath and Milton's Dalila, both of them also spectacular in nature, to Pope's Belinda, a sort of minor monarch of a commercial empire. The love of display so insistently imputed to women becomes in Adam Smith a male trait, the trait that more than any other keeps commercial society in motion.

As we reflect on the drowning of reality by image in the consumer culture of today, we would do well to recall the imagistic mentality of Smithian man, a member of the first consumer society to appear on earth, that of eighteenth-century England.[58] The consumer syndrome analyzed by Stuart Ewen in *All Consuming Images*—the fascination with deceptive appearances, the induction of dream states, the hypnotic allure of spectacle, the anxious imitation of elites—is all but explicit in the theory of Adam Smith.[59] Written into *The Theory of Moral Sentiments* is the comforting belief that men outrank women in spite of their weak reason, their "imaginary wants," their corrupted sentiments, their grotesque illogic (exemplified in mercantilism), their hunger to be gazed at in admiration—traits identified with women by the same customary practices, the same "habitual associations"[60] that Adam Smith, like Hume, considered the court of last resort in social and political questions.

Some might say that Smith's *Theory of Moral Sentiments* is really not fraught with implications for commercial society; that its analysis of moral habits shouldn't be taken for a reliable description of the ways of men; that it is more prescriptive than descriptive; that in any case it is just what it says it is, a theory, nothing more. To some degree this objection holds. Thus political participation in some loose sense of the term was probably broader, even among otherwise "prudent" men, than Adam Smith's moralism allows.[61] Smith does not endorse the radical agitation of the late years of the eighteenth century in England, a subject on which he seems to say silently what Coleridge would say in a moment of anger: political contests sow discord, exasperate passions, debauch morals.[62] Smith prefers harmonious sentiments to acrimony, and yet he shares many positions with the radicals, notably a decided antiaristocratic bias and advocacy of frugality and free trade. Such is the common ground between Smith and the radicals that Isaac Kramnick was led to list Smith among those seeking the overthrow of the social hierarchy—this in spite of Smith's explicit defense of that very structure (*TMS*, p. 226).[63] Presumably it was Smith's hope that the reform of society and the installation of middle-class values could be accomplished with a minimum of heat and upheaval. As an inheritor of Locke, he probably shared that theorist's sense of the unfruitfulness of verbal disputes, and his language of propriety and decorum casts men not as pushy upstarts or battling disputants but as harmonizers with the status quo. I imagine that like his economic values, Smith's preference for concord was shared by many. Smith considered that men do best to attend quietly to their own business, to perform to the duties of their station. So fundamental were notions like this that it would be capricious to set them down as the theories of some solitary thinker.

Again, from the fact that stoicism colors Smith's moral theory it does not follow that men at the time were really stoic, but it is likely that many shared the idealization of manliness and the distrust of pitched or political passions that inform Smith's use of the stoic idiom. When I speak of Smithian man, then, I have in mind not an empty abstraction but an ideal type in the sense in which C. Wright Mills and before him Max Weber employed this notion— a figure in whom leading traits of his kind are summed up. Certainly *The Theory of Moral Sentiments* is an idealized model, yet we can't do without models. The competition between classical and commercial models in Smith's own time, investigated by J. G. A. Pocock, was no academic matter but charged with consequence, if only because the former was the only paradigm the Western tradition afforded of men as actors in public life. As we might expect of a figure as interesting as Adam Smith, his loyalties in the matter of ancients and moderns went both ways. The effect of his theory is at once to outmode classical values and to lend some of their prestige to the new ideology of commerce—prestige it wouldn't need if models didn't matter. Even so solid a thing as a house must be built on some theory, some model, of social relations; builders may or may not subscribe to the theory that adults need separate sleeping quarters from children, for example, and as they judge, so they build. While society is not built as methodically as a house, models or theories are still needed if construction is to go forward. Theory informs reality; it is not off to one side.

That in itself doesn't establish that Adam Smith's theory, *The Theory of Moral Sentiments,* entered into social reality. Nevertheless, something like Smith's theory of prudence must be taken up by groups committed to the diligent accumulation of wealth and, moreover, to the proposition that society is borne forward by every man's religious attention to his own business. So, too, the moralizing of the private sphere—evidenced both in the sanctification of the domestic woman and in Smith's defense of the private interests of men acting in a nonpolitical capacity—was no theorist's dream but a social fact of defining importance in what is called the bourgeois order. Similarly, if we subtract the accent of irony from Smith's theory of consumption-for-display, we find it agrees with many other accounts of the workings of "emulation" in his time. In fact, merchandisers played consciously on the craving of social inferiors to show like the rich—precisely the adulation of wealth that Smith found to be the way of the world. As Neil McKendrick has made stunningly clear, the consumer culture of today, with its incessant hype, hyperbole, self-mockery, and fixation on health and beauty, descends directly from marketing techniques that made their first appearance in England during the life of Adam Smith.

Although it indeed sees into the commercial way of life, the *Moral Sentiments* has little to say about clubs, actively sympathetic to political radicalism, peopled by middle-class men who otherwise espouse Smithian values.[64] Smithian man is no kind of radical. Shying away from both clubs and controversy, submitting by habit, radiating an improving influence into the world, keeping out of public affairs (for that is what is meant by minding one's own business), Smith's prudent man, the producer of wealth, is the counterpart of the good woman of prescriptive literature. Indulging as consumer in the sweet pleasures of vanity and display, he resembles the bad woman whom men complain of eternally. Either way, the male of Smithian society has more in common with his own image of woman than he, or Adam Smith himself, cares to admit. The distinction between men and women in the thinking of Adam Smith is wholly specious and artificial, prefiguring "the artificiality of the binary logic" of Victorian thinking about the sexes.[65] In a way, the Victorian woman said to hold "a nation's moral wealth" in her keeping[66] follows from Smith's theory of the wealth of nations, as the Victorian notion of a sexual division of labor evolves from the Smithian division of labor; the shift from traditional representations of the wantonness and instability of woman to the domestic woman of the Victorian ideal is the concern of my third chapter.

If the prudent man responsible for the wealth of the nation is modest and proper and shies away from controversy instinctively, the good woman is called on to watch over and as it were secure the goods of the male in the commercial phase of civilization, in a distinct reversal of her proverbial role as consumer of man's substance and sexual betrayer. During the life of Adam Smith, the terms "consume" and "luxury" were cleansed of some—not all—of the foul associations they had gathered over the centuries, as indeed was the reputation of women, long identified with voracious orality and corrupt desire. The expurgation of the term "luxury" is well illustrated by Smith's own comment that when he classes goods like beer and wine as luxuries he does not mean "by this appellation to throw the smallest degree of reproach upon the temperate use of them."[67] (If "luxury" hadn't been a term of reproach, Smith would never have had to issue this disclaimer.) Much as the concept of luxury, as a vice that ruins nations, was somewhat relaxed to allow for the innocent enjoyments of the middle class, so the age-old image of the luxurious (lustful) woman, ruinous to men, made way for the heavily expurgated image of the domestic woman of middle-class virtue. A purveyor of that image used a thoroughly Smithian metaphor when she wrote that women are "the minor wheels and secret springs of the great machine of human life and action," just as her aesthetic of the fit and proper and becoming, and her idealization of "fellowship of feeling" tally closely with Smith's.[68]

Expurgated like luxury was "consumption," a term traditionally evoking thoughts of depraved extravagance (and particularly the depraved extravagance of women). That key word of the eighteenth century, "taste," is after all an eating metaphor. "Taste" is consumption moralized. According to Smith's teacher, Francis Hutcheson, we judge of goodness and badness by our sixth sense, the moral sense, in the same way we judge of a plum by our sense of taste; the act of consumption becomes, of all things, a model of moral judgment.[69] What another might have considered a paradigm of sensual indulgence—the savoring of a fruit, with all of its biblical overtones—Hutcheson moralizes. Adam Smith departed from Hutcheson in some respects, but for him too consumption stands at the center of things. "Consumption is the sole end and purpose of all production."[70] Here the word "consumption" reads like a purely denotative term, acquitted of the sensationally bad meanings it had long carried. The desensationalizing of words like "luxury" and "consumption," which by our time have become neutral terms in a dismal science, anticipates Bentham's campaign to neutralize evocative terms employed by the enemies of reform like red flags of danger. In time, neutrality of language becomes the mark of the bureaucrats and technicians who give consumer society its "rationality." Splitting means and ends, instrumental reason arises in turn from the distinct splitting of the functions of production and consumption both in fact and in theory at the time of the emergence of the discourse of political economy.[71]

With the enhancement of the role and repute of consumption in Adam Smith's time, and with the conversion of luxuries into decencies, goes a change in the culturally official image of women who preside over the home where consumption itself is centered. As in his culture, so in the writings of Smith himself we find evidence of a shift away from traditional antifeminism, which dwells feverishly on the "luxury" of women, to a norm of domesticity celebrating the constancy and virtue of woman in her role as consumer. In order for wealth to be accumulated in a steady and predictable, or Smithian manner, woman cannot be the despoiler of man and his goods that she had so long, and so loudly, been claimed to be. In order for men to achieve that great desideratum, "the enjoyment of such possessions as we have acquir'd by our industry and good fortune,"[72] they cannot marry someone whose nature it is to run riot. And in order for long labor to issue in the enjoyment of possessions, it cannot be viewed as the curse of toil that was laid on mankind as a penalty for the crime of Eve.[73] I theorize that a dual process known as improvement—the same process studied by the thinkers of the Scottish Enlightenment—taught men taste and propriety, conformity and seemliness; as it also instituted the culturally official norm of the domestic woman, who is nothing like the whorish figure of woman so prominent in medieval and Renaissance culture. (By the same token, however, the expurgation of the image of woman means that traditional rude imagery survives at some level. It does not drop out of currency altogether.)

As the constant passion for gain vanquishes the more blustery passions of man's nature, according to theorists of "improvement," so the domestic woman, with her sweet constancy, comes to be seen as possessing an all-conquering weakness.[74] In her gentleness she marks the high point of the ideology of the "douceur," the gentleness, of commerce.[75] Adam Smith's man of commerce, for his part, improves society gently, by his good manners, by imperceptibly building up the wealth of the nation, and by absenting himself from public questions. In his modesty, invisibility, inoffensiveness, decency, quietness, and submission, in his vestal habits and indeed his admiration of social superiors, the prudent man bears out the observation that "intellectual and psychological submissiveness is the prevalent attitude among men *and* women" in a hierarchical society.[76] His speech "perfectly inoffensive," he is "an exact observer" of all the proprieties. He submits by habit to his own equals. In all, the prudent man—the agent of progress whose constancy prevails over the designs of monopolists and politicians—bears himself with what can only be called a frigid moral chastity.[77] He does not "reason and dispute" with superiors (*TMS,* p. 53), because when people reason and dispute, the habits of deference fray, and in the end those habits and nothing else keep the political order standing. Besides, he simply doesn't possess much reason: so says Adam Smith.[78] Given to "waking dreams" and states of enchantment,[79] Smithian man is less likely to go in for the political rationalism of Mary Wollstonecraft than to embrace the lovely illusions defended by her opponent Burke. In the realm of taste, too, he opposes what is leveling in tendency. His aesthetic likes are represented by the reviewers who bayed their disapproval of Wordsworth for the impropriety of his subjects and for his inversion of traditional rankings. The Smithian model of steady labor and consonant sentiments discourages dispute in favor of more improving endeavors. Roughly speaking, no sooner was this model enshrined in the 1790 edition of the *Moral Sentiments* than it was disputed itself: as Smith justified the corruption of moral sentiments in the interests of order, agitation for political reform heated up. And when Kant said that the French Revolution "finds, in the minds of all spectators, a sympathy very near to enthusiasm,"[80] it was as if the tranquillity of the Smithian model of sympathy had been shattered.

Neither Whig nor Tory, Adam Smith was a conservative who believed in progress. As a conservative he recommended a species of "stoic" quietude that in principle conserves the manhood of men and secures the polity against the dangers of upheaval while progress nevertheless occurs. In particular, the removal of impediments to economic pursuits, what comes to be called laissez-faire, enables progress. The work of Adam Smith, which so well exemplifies the thinking of the Scottish Enlightenment, is thus like a matrix in which principles later differentiated as liberal and conservative are held in unity.[81] This conceptual richness helps to account for the deep influence of the Scottish Enlightenment on the American founders. Scottish ideas are written into the American republic from the beginning,[82] and it seems to me likely that Smithian notions continue to influence both liberals and conservatives, and continue to nurture the belief that progress takes place when people give it no thought—when they just do their job. The neo-Smithian F. A. Hayek cites the maxim that "civilization advances by extending the number of important operations we can perform without thinking about them."[83] The aim of this study, inconsistent as it may be with the advance of civilization, is to stir thought.

CHAPTER 2

Stoic Values in *The Theory of Moral Sentiments*

If Americans are asked what they mean by freedom, they will say something like "Freedom means doing what you like" or "You are free if you can act without constraint" or "You are free if government has no authority over what you do." In other words, to be free means to be unhindered, to act at will. Freedom as a kind of exemption from interference: this notion is both popularly held and officially inscribed in our political culture. In scholarly discussion, the freedom of exemption is often given the awkward name of "negative liberty," as in Isaiah Berlin's influential essay on "Two Concepts of Liberty," where we read that liberty in this sense "is simply the area within which a man can act unobstructed by others. If I am prevented from doing what I could otherwise do, I am to that degree unfree; and if this area is contracted by other men beyond a certain minimum, I can be described as being coerced, or, it may be, enslaved."[1] The author goes on to distinguish negative from "positive liberty," a notion distinctly alien to us children of liberalism. Positive liberty is the liberty of being in charge of oneself, whether this means snuffing out ignoble desires (like a stoic who wills virtue) or identifying with one's own political masters (as people might identify with, and feel free through, a strongman who tramples their liberty to do as they like).

No doubt the difference between positive and negative liberty is no merely verbal matter, but full of political consequence. Nevertheless, the distinction between the two liberties—one negative, one positive; one familiar, one forbidding; one clear, one seemingly an abuse of words—may lead us to think that these ideas don't mix. They do. When John Stuart Mill protested the tyranny of public opinion, he wasn't really pleading for more negative liberty, since Victorians were already at liberty to defy their neighbors; they simply lacked the nerve to do so, being hostage to their own timidity and conformism. In decrying an oppression "enslaving the soul itself,"[2] Mill meant that people had lost charge of their own selves and become the thralls of their fears (not thralls of the state). That is, he argued implicitly from the tradition of positive liberty. Indeed, if stoicism belongs to that tradition, Mill admired the stoics of ancient Rome. In *On Liberty* itself he pays a felt tribute to the stoic Marcus Aurelius.

Adam Smith too felt for the stoics a kind of veneration. No one can be more closely identified than Smith with the doctrine of noninterference, the doctrine that to this day defines for us in liberal society what it is to be free, and yet Smith responded deeply to stoic principles that belong without doubt to the tradition of positive liberty. Those principles are written into his *Theory of Moral Sentiments*—published in editions both before and after the *Wealth of Nations,* for Smith was first and last a moral philosopher—where they provide, as I will argue, a kind of false foundation to his analysis. In order to buttress his argument for negative liberty, the author grounded it on stoic principles from the more august, and distinctly masculine, positive liberty tradition.

Stoicism—masculine self-mastery—serves to shore up Adam Smith's analysis of morality, for (as will be seen) without its dignifying presence in *The Theory of Moral Sentiments,* it might well appear that the author had turned the male actor into a composite of female stereotypes: a person careful to please, held to exacting standards of propriety and blamelessness, vain, fantastic, and apt to squander what faulty rationality s/he possesses in the love of baubles and show. Like a good woman, Adam Smith's prudent man faithfully performs small duties; like a bad woman, the infamous "merchants and manufacturers" of the *Wealth of Nations* intrude into the public sphere, confuse the minds of men with their specious appeals, and pervert the public good. I mean to say that some mixture of genuine insight and sheer prejudice led Adam Smith to picture the men of commercial society not as the rational agents they are commonly thought to be, but almost as proverbially dual women, at once creatures of error and patterns of propriety. Thus he likens men both to women crazed with vanity (*TMS*, p. 57) and to women exact in the performance of their duties (*TMS*, p. 162). Of these two types he clearly prefers the second. It is said that Edmund Burke employed a "feminine paradigm" of men submissive and obedient.[3] So did Adam Smith, who shared Burke's belief in free trade and reprobation of the spirit of system, and whose *Theory of Moral Sentiments* Burke praised in the highest terms.

I theorize that it was in part to avert the shaming implications of his own "feminine paradigm" that Adam Smith exalted the stoic principle of self-command in his *Theory of Moral Sentiments*, especially in its last edition. If the *Wealth of Nations* and *The Theory of Moral Sentiments* can be taken together as a kind of philosophical charter of the commercial way of life (and there is every evidence that the author himself paired them thus), then we can say that in establishing negative liberty, Adam Smith drew heavily on the masculine idiom of positive liberty from the tradition of classical humanism, a tradition after all more venerable than the quite new ideology of commerce. The Puritans indeed had been able to make out industry and frugality to be a sacred duty; deeply wary of the threat to political order posed by the Puritans and their "enthusiasm," Adam Smith grounds industry and frugality not in religious ardor but in a cool stoicism—a stoicism teaching submission to the order of things. In the sense that it prescribed self-denial without bringing in Puritan zealotry, stoicism came in handy for Adam Smith, but it was more than a mere device or convenience. He really honored the stoic ideal. Evidently Smith was reluctant to dismiss classical values and turn the day over to the commercial actor with his minor virtues, defective autonomy, mean purposes,[4] and probable corruption. Even those moderns who, like Smith, were prepared to argue that human nature flourished in commercial society as it could not in the harsh austerity of the ancient world—even they remained attached to the ancient image of masculine virtue, the kind of virtue possessed by the stoic of *The Theory of Moral Sentiments*.[5] To put this in another way, Adam Smith was loath to dissolve the classical ideal of virtue into good manners and sheer seemliness, even if that is certainly the tendency of his own moral theory.[6]

In a moment we will take up the question of why trade was seen to soften old values, at once grand and harsh by the standards of commercial society. In the course of that discussion it will become clear that in contrast to the common understanding of men as rational and self-directing, Adam Smith pictures the men of his consumer society as socially directed, highly irrational in their judgments, and deficient in conscious agency. First let me try to establish that the language of stoicism does in fact color Adam Smith's analysis of morality.

In a letter written not long after the publication of the first edition of the *Moral Sentiments,* Smith cites "the great lesson of Stoical magnanimity and firmness." Years later he extolled these very virtues in the man he considered the best who ever lived, David Hume: in dying, Hume displayed an astonishing "magnanimity and firmness."[7] From the fact that he saw the incomparable Hume as a stoic, we may gauge Adam Smith's feeling for the stoic ideal. Indeed, at one point in the *Moral Sentiments,* the author remarks that stoicism has inspired men to perform "actions of the most heroic magnanimity and most extensive benevolence" (*TMS,* p. 293). Next to this, surely, any other set of virtues can be but second best, or, as Smith designates the virtues of prudence, "inferior" (*TMS,* p. 304).

Stoicism makes for greatness of soul—magnanimity, that virtue of ancient lineage—and inspires men to act for the greater good. It teaches men to despise false goods, meaning anything other than virtue itself. It exhorts them to remain the masters of themselves and bear all with bravery and equanimity. The stoic emancipates himself from all unruly desires, all desires but the desire for virtue, as in this vignette from Isaiah Berlin's discussion of positive liberty: "The tyrant threatens me with the destruction of my property, with imprisonment, with the exile or death of those I love. But if I no longer feel attached to property, no longer care whether or not I am in prison, if I have killed within myself my natural affections, then he cannot bend me to his will."[8] These words could have been penned by Adam Smith himself, for in his review of moral theories he presents a felt account of the stoic doctrine that places our happiness "altogether in our own power, and under our own direction," no matter how we are circumstanced (*TMS,* p. 279). Perfectly possessed of himself, the stoic

is master of all his passions, [and] does not dread any circumstance in which the Superintendant of the universe may think proper to place him. The bounty of that divine Being has provided him with virtues which render him superior to every situation. If it is pleasure, he has temperance to refrain from it; if it is pain, he has constancy to bear it; if it is danger or death, he has magnanimity and fortitude to despise it. (*TMS*, p. 278)

Nor does stoicism hold an incidental place in Adam Smith's thought. It holds a place of honor. Smith's library is said to have been "full of Stoic texts," and as the editors of the Glasgow edition of his works state, "Stoic philosophy is the primary influence on Smith's ethical thought."[9] In the stoic supremely the master of himself, Adam Smith evidently found a counterweight to moderns who lose themselves in the pursuit of contemptible goods, like the kind of showy eminence that wealth brings.

Luxury and love of display—vices habitually imputed to women before, during, and after the lifetime of Adam Smith—are the very key to Smith's system, being responsible in his view, as in the view of others at the time, for the rise and continuance of commercial society itself. Much as the feudal landlord once dissipated his patrimony and power in the love of sheer trumpery ("a pair of diamond buckles, perhaps"), so the economic actor of commercial society struggles blindly to achieve the equally vacuous good, status. And if the landlord spent his authority, the economic actor spends his autonomy—his authority over himself. Without the stabilizing presence of manly values in *The Theory of Moral Sentiments,* the actors of commercial society, with their childish judgments and corrupt tastes and aroused vanity, might all too clearly resemble their own image of women.[10] Already described as a woman is the man of wealth who spends his fortune on "little ornaments of dress."[11] Similarly the man whose vanity "forc[es] itself upon the notice of every wandering eye" (TMS, p. 62), which is the language traditionally used to censure public or straying women. Similarly the "weak man" who seeks unmerited praise, as men so commonly do.[12] Such imputations of unmanliness were after all common enough in the moral literature of the period, such as John Brown's *Estimate of the Manners and Principles of the Times* (1757–58), which drums on the theme of effeminacy. In his very *Sermons to Young Women* (1765), James Fordyce laments "the effeminate, trifling, and dissolute character of the age."[13] Because commercial society is open to these accusations, and perhaps too because he is so keenly aware of men's mindless love of the merest "trinkets" (*TMS*, p. 181), Adam Smith infuses his defense of the commercial way of life with the rhetoric of resolution (as opposed to dissolution) and sobriety (as opposed to trifling).

We would not have expected the philosopher of free trade to be enrolled in a disparate tradition of liberty going back to antiquity, but so he is. Adam Smith sees in the stoic, with his impressive self-mastery, all of the autonomy that seems lacking in the actors of a commercial age taken up with the love of false goods. Thus stoic values crown Adam Smith's analysis of moral life, ennobling his argument as a Latin inscription on a public building lends dignity and grandeur.[14] If this implies that those values, for all their nobility, play a rhetorical or honorific role in *The Theory of Moral Sentiments,* that is just what I mean. For as Smith himself recognized, the stoic ideal of self-mastery is so demanding and remote that it can't really play much of a part in a commercial society where people busily pursue a fantasy of happiness and govern their actions by common prudence rather than the magnificent maxims of fortitude.[15] In other words, the presence of stoicism in *The Theory of Moral Sentiments* indexes the absence of the stoic principle in the affairs of life. It seems that the closest thing to a stoic way of life that modern society affords is landowning. Thus in the *Wealth of Nations,* Adam Smith describes the landlord as possessing a kind of Boethian invulnerability and peace of mind. Knowing that his capital is "much less liable to accidents" than the trader's, the landlord has that sense of being superior to Fortune's injuries which is so much talked of by the stoic tradition. He is "really a master, and independent of all the world."[16] Such, in fact, is Adam Smith's liking for agriculture (a preference he shares with Cicero) that he ranks it as the highest, the most productive of all economic pursuits.[17] But a small, crowded island like Britain can't possibly offer enough land for men to set up as landowners in any numbers. Unable to be "independent of all the world" in fact, men will have to console themselves with the memory or illusion of stoic independence.

In the sense that ideology involves "an idealizing appeal to the outdated values of an earlier system, in defense of a later system that in practice undermines the material basis of those values,"[18] Adam Smith's use of the resonant language of stoicism is ideological. The author imports an ideal of autonomy from the agrarian-military world of antiquity into an analysis of the commercial order, an order that he himself considers a more advanced stage of society. (Similarly, Smith continues to use the language of patriarchy even though, on his own showing, the commercial order emerged as the rich consumed their own patrimonies—the "material basis" of patriarchy—and thus cut the inheritance from father to son, and even though the pinnacle of patriarchy was reached ages ago, when shepherds of immense prestige and authority ruled their clans.) In defending a way of life in which men struggle blindly to achieve false goods, and which therefore subverts the very idea of self-command, Smith employs the language of self-command. He keeps stoicism alive beyond its date. In an analogous way, sublimity—which as we learn from Burke's treatise on the sublime more or less means majesty—keeps alive beyond their date the dread and reverence that attend kingship. And Burke himself praised the "sublime" account of stoicism in *The Theory of Moral Sentiments,*[19] as though this discussion of men's kingship over themselves possessed an air of majesty. Ciceronian values serve to ennoble Smith's moral theory, to cast a glow of greatness over it, and at the same time to obscure just how far the male of Smithian society falls short of rationality and conscious agency—obscurity being, as Burke says, the very element of the sublime. What kind of rationality and conscious agency does a man possess who is "led by an invisible hand to promote an end which was no part of his intention"?[20]

In the progress of capitalism the idea evolved that when men dedicate themselves to their own passion for "improvement," the results for society are better than they would be if the same men set out to advance the public good consciously, in the manner of intentional agents. The stoic serves the public good consciously; thus in Hume's essay on "The Stoic" that figure affirms, "Toils, dangers, death itself carry their charms, when we brave them for the public good."[21] (Similarly, the stoic insists on being an intentional agent, and considers that anyone not a stoic habitually crosses his or her intentions.)[22] The modern actor advances the public good by devoting himself to passions the stoic might well consider blind, such as the passion for private betterment. Traditionally thought to be unruly, passion yields such good results in this case because of its tractability and because its operation is regulated by society more closely than ever before; hence, for example, both Hume's and Smith's descriptions of the minute surveillance of social performances. Assuming that men yearn not just for wealth but for standing, or what Adam Smith calls "the admiration of mankind" (*TMS*, p. 159), then in order to stand well with others they will have to appreciate their dependence on the good opinion of society and conform their behavior to exact standards. As with women, so with men—their good name is their treasure. "The credit of a tradesman . . . is the same thing in its nature as the virtue of a lady."[23]

In theory, men's dependence on the good opinion of society improves them, teaching them propriety. Things work out when men submit to be regulated by such "invisible" agencies as society or the marketplace: while not Smith's alone, this idea is inscribed in his philosophy with notable clarity. Smith's doubts of the power of reason,[24] the reason once claimed as the privilege of men, led him to commend the regulation of things not to the deliberations of men but to that mysterious stage-manager, the Invisible Hand. If women were thought to possess a poor capacity for reason,[25] Smithian man is poor in reason himself. If traditionally reason was to govern the passions, Adam Smith finds reason itself unreliable.[26] "The weak eye of human reason," "the feeble efforts of human reason": these are characteristic Smithian locutions.[27] If passion is traditionally inferior to reason—if passion stands to reason as women to men—Adam Smith questions the potency of reason, with its "slow and uncertain determinations" (*TMS*, p. 77),[28] and sees men as driven by a craving for "approbation" that has all the effect and folly, although not necessarily the violence, of a passion.

Not only does Adam Smith put in doubt men's capacity for rationality and self-direction, even to the point of denying that men in commercial society act out of *rational* self-interest,[29] but he explicitly founds his moral theory on the principle of sympathy—a principle whose workings do not answer to reason, and probably not to volition either. Sympathy works like a Burkean tradition (also deeply binding and wiser than reason), thus preserving traditional relations in a belated or sentimental form.[30] Ideally, sympathy creates a community of the heart. I as spectator enter into your grief, while you are careful to keep your demonstrations of grief within bounds, for otherwise I would be put off and my sympathy would not flow. If it is to be distinguished from the misery of the ill-bred, grief had better be expressed decorously.

> When the original passions of the person principally concerned are in perfect concord with the sympathetic emotions of the spectator, they necessarily appear to this last just and proper, and suitable to their objects; and, on the contrary, when, upon bringing the case home to himself, he finds that they do not coincide with what he feels, they necessarily appear to him unjust and improper, and unsuitable to the causes which excite them. (*TMS*, p. 16)

Thus the actor gauges his performance to the spectator so that the spectator may take the part of the actor: such is the circuitous nature of sympathy. Delicately adjusted to others, Smithian man reduces his passions by habit. If that habit has left him without much feeling, he nevertheless behaves as if he belonged to the community of the heart. He is not rational, but he is reasonable, if by reasonableness is meant the tendency not to oppose others. In lieu of the traditional methods of discipline—the scepter, the sword, the miter—Smithian man is kept in line by the silken threads of conformity.

Indeed, Smith's moral theory celebrates conformity as a force for human improvement. "One of the principal reasons Smith favored the expansion of commerce was that by exposing men to the constant scrutiny of his [sic] neighbours, [the] habit of subordinating the impulse of passion to the sentiments of others would be enhanced."[31] In other words, the men of commercial society would learn to behave. And by carrying a habit of submission and subordination into a commercial age, these new men would assuage the corrosive effects of individualism.[32] In the case of the prudent man of *The Theory of Moral Sentiments,* the habit of submission is so settled that he submits even to his own equals, while the checking of passion has become so habitual that he is emotionally constricted, punctilious rather than feeling in his social relations, unconvivial. Not especially "disposed to general society" (*TMS*, p. 214), the prudent man is perhaps as little capable of real sympathy as of real stoicism. But the idiom of sympathy in *The Theory of Moral Sentiments* draws our attention away from the cold and unsympathetic nature of the very protagonist of commercial society, the prudent man. (Just so, the sympathy principle undoes the bind to which the philosophy of individualism condemns us—that of being unable to "really *know* what others experience."[33] By sympathy we know.) In any case, the prudent man attends to his own concerns and leaves the rest of the world to itself, superficially stoic traits. He does not challenge. The fact that the superior ranks do *not* deserve their favored position makes it the more necessary for men like him to submit humbly to the order of society as a wise dispensation of Nature.[34] Similarly, the rancor of politics makes it necessary for Adam Smith's "hero" to be at once too prudent and too modest to venture into public life. Once the man of trade does venture into public affairs, he is liable to become one of those vile merchants Smith curses in the *Wealth of Nations* for corrupting public policy with their "clamour and sophistry."[35] Having lost the modesty and inoffensiveness of the good woman, he takes on the impudence of the bad woman who corrupts the realm by making herself public.

Considering that Adam Smith wrote a theory of moral sentiments, and wrote during the vogue of Sympathy and Benevolence, it is not surprising that his analysis rests on a frankly sentimental model. In turn, sentimentality feeds a habit of consumption (consumption of emotions),[36] while Adam Smith depicts men as faintly voyeuristic spectators in the social theater—consumers in search of gratification. In his treatise on *The Sublime and the Beautiful,* which presents an analysis of sympathy that is close to Smith's, Edmund Burke goes so far as to argue that "there is no spectacle we so eagerly pursue, as that of some uncommon and grievous calamity," as though such scenes fed an appetite for misery.[37] In a strange sense, sentimentality mimics the conservatism of Burke— it hallows the society that produces such delicious scenes of woe. If sorrow is sacred, then perhaps we do best to leave a society so productive of sorrow just as it is. At least that is an unspoken message of the sentimental ethos, which itself likes to claim that woes speak deeper than words.

Sentimentalists, like the man of feeling, it is said, are "acutely sentient, expressive, and, above all, responsive through sympathy to the woes of their fellows."[38] We can discern the same qualities beneath the formality and abstraction of Adam Smith's language in the first sentences of *The Theory of Moral Sentiments:*

> How selfish soever man may be supposed, there are evidently some principles in his nature, which interest him in the fortunes of others, and render their happiness necessary to him, though he derives nothing from it except the pleasure of seeing it. Of this kind is pity or compassion, the emotion which we

feel for the misery of others, when we either see it, or are made to conceive it in a very lively manner. (*TMS*, p. 9)

Adam Smith's coolness, his skeptical reserve will not permit him to go all the way with sentimentalism, yet he has affinities with that literary school. Where it brings in the use of "half-conscious and almost subliminal means" to gain the sympathy of readers,[39] Adam Smith sees spectators as drawn into sympathy by some deeper-than-conscious process, some process almost of the body itself,[40] and as given to "waking dreams and idle reveries" (*TMS*, p. 52), while in their active capacity Smithian men go about their business not conscious either of the vacuity of the goods they seek or of the larger purposes their activity serves. As, in sentimentalism, man the conscious agent gives way to man the subject of "involuntary emotion,"[41] so in the moral theory of Adam Smith men are subject to involuntary responses[42] and "enchanted" states (*TMS*, p. 181).

If being part of a tradition means we can never fully stand outside it and be conscious of it, perhaps the sentimental ritual of swooning represents a return to the blessed unconsciousness of tradition. Certainly Adam Smith is concerned to heal breaks with the past, and sentimentalism enables him to portray commerce as a way of life that is traditional itself, in spite of the new methods of production, shifting styles of consumption, social dislocations, and generally rapid pacing of events that define that way of life. For in the moral theory of Adam Smith, all this activity is somehow governed by sympathy, a pull on the sentiments that binds like tradition. Even the stoicism of Smith's moral theory is purely sentimental, not only in the literary sense of being a late imitation of an earlier ethos,[43] but in that it doesn't issue in action. For as I will argue, the "stoic" modern doesn't act like a stoic at all. Like the sentimentalist who in the generosity of his heart keeps slaves,[44] the prudent man's stoicism is purely notional. The prudent modern acts the way other moderns do, if only because blending in is the prudent thing. As a child, Smithian man presumably learned the moral habits, like the love of "esteem" and the fear of shame, that would govern him later on; well primed for a life of emulation (copying and competition), he becomes in time a fully socialized and duly conforming adult, joined with others by the habits of imitation, affection, rivalry. He matches his conduct to others' and counts their good opinion his dearest pleasure.[45] To procure it, he dedicates himself to his own desire for "improvement," which is perhaps the most socially benign of all passions.

The idea that the public good is the unwilled outcome of economic behavior and private "improvement" (rather than the result, say, of citizens concerting their actions) has been traced to its sources by Albert Hirschman in *The Passions and the Interests*.[46] It seems that amid the passionate controversies of the early modern era, the theory arose that one passion in particular—the passion for gain, at one time stigmatized as cupidity—was comparatively innocent; and that this passion might actually civilize men and steady their relations better than repressive methods. On this view, superbly expressed in Hume's essay "Of Commerce," the well-being of society depends on the proper cultivation of our vices; or rather, one of our vices, properly cultivated, grows into a virtue. And with the notion that commerce civilizes men gently, improving their sentiments, the ground is broken for the eventual idealization of the Woman who personifies the civilizing influence of sentiment.

Before Adam Smith mused on the civility of commerce[47] and the calming of passions into sentiments, others did the same, among them Addison, whose *Spectator* essays underlie Smith's theory of spectatorship as a force for human betterment. Addison states explicitly that his intention in the *Spectator* is to divert minds from the furious passions of politics. The men of the Royal Society, founded so close upon the Civil War, "might have set their Country in a Flame" if they hadn't turned their energies to the air pump and the barometer.[48] The word "political" suggesting factional brawling and bitter emotions, Addison revises Aristotle and calls man a "sociable" rather than a political animal.[49] In theory, the sociable men of commercial society know their place, keep clear of the bad passions of politics—passions that Addison knew for himself, having been a determined Whig and sometime party hack—and dedicate themselves instead to the innocent desire for the love and esteem of their fellows, for respectability.[50] Addison likes men who are silent and invisible, modest and pure, as Smith likes the kind of virtue "attracting the attention of scarce any body but the most studious and careful observer" (*TMS*, p. 62). The public good is likeliest to emerge not when men venture into public life (all the more because few even know what the public good is or how it is promoted)[51] but when they attend strictly to their own "improvement." Because the ethic of stoicism calls for the calming of passion and acceptance of what is, it lends itself to those like Smith and Addison who believe that "improvement" comes about not through clashes of opinion but through such civil processes as trade and the gradual extension of sympathy.

Why does the drive to better one's condition have such good effects? Why was Macaulay, an inheritor of Adam Smith, able to say that "no ordinary misfortune, no ordinary misgovernment, will do so much to make a nation wretched, as the constant progress of physical knowledge and the constant effort of every man to better himself will do to make a nation prosperous."[52] The desire to better oneself seems to have recommended itself for this role as improver of society because it was so "constant," so little like a passion, in its operation—because it had nothing of the gusty nature of "enthusiasm." Adam Smith cites the "uniform, constant, and uninterrupted effort of every man to better his condition"[53] as the mainspring of well-being, both public and private, and indeed the desire for "improvement" as he describes it works with the regularity of a ticking watch. And if the accumulation of wealth proceeds irresistibly, improving men at the same time, the sweet influence of women was said to work in a similar way. Like the passion for gain, it is steadily exerted, it is hardly to be resisted, and it improves men. Thus James Fordyce writes in his highly popular *Sermons to Young Women,* "I can hardly conceive that any man would be able to withstand the soft persuasion of your words, but chiefly of your looks and actions, habitually exerted on the side of goodness."[54] Habitually exerting himself in little ways and so advancing the wealth of the nation, the prudent man is the counterpart of a dutiful woman. He shuns the glare of public life and yet is more than anyone responsible for promoting the public good; she is banished from public affairs and yet is the arbiter of "the fate of nations."[55] His efforts overcome the obstacles to progress imposed by folly and misgovernment; her influence melts the resistance of men.

Before Adam Smith, Vico theorized that the greater good is served when men devote themselves wholly to their own concerns. Through divine providence, he wrote, "the passions of men who are entirely occupied by the pursuit of their private utility are transformed into a civil order which permits men to live in society."[56] Women, of course, had traditionally been banned from the public realm; in Adam Smith's lifetime, moralists and pamphleteers still railed against public women, holding them responsible for the corruption of society.[57] Vico's line of argument implies that society is better off when *men* keep out of the public realm and devote their energies "entirely" to their own business, like Adam Smith's prudent man. When Addison beatifies the "silent Perfections" and invisible virtues of the good man who does not involve himself in public business, he makes over to men some of the traditional virtues of woman, without, of course, making any real sacrifice of male power and advantage.[58] When Adam Smith himself commends a becoming "modesty of behaviour" in a man of private station, when he applauds the effort "to be humble, assiduous, and complaisant," he holds up for men something like a model of feminine conduct (*TMS*, p. 41). Modesty, seemliness, pleasantness: these were the supposed graces of women.

Whatever other purposes stoicism serves for Adam Smith, it imparts an aura of autonomy to the men of his moral theory, who otherwise seem to expend their autonomy in the habit of minute conformity (sentimentalized as perfect concord between hearts that beat as one), the pursuit of worthless trifles, and the renunciation of interest in public affairs (for it is precisely every man's religious attention to his own business that bears society forward). Smithian man little knows what he is doing and fills his life with "frivolous nothings" (*TMS*, p. 41). Given to "waking dreams" (*TMS*, p. 52), responsive as if by social reflex when the right pitch of emotion is struck, he does not much seem like an autonomous agent. Such a man "cannot be . . . the dignified and rational captain of his own mental universe," as Marilyn Butler has written in a slightly different context.[59] The stoic is that captain exactly.

While commonplace has it that in the world of capitalism, men, unlike women, are "objective," the explicitly sentimental moral theory of Adam Smith proceeds, as we have seen, from an analysis of the "pity or compassion" of men (*TMS*, p. 9). Perhaps Smith agreed with those of his time who believed that the decisions of men, but not women, are "subject to individual consciousness and control."[60] All the same, his theory suggests provocatively that the *defect* of individual consciousness and control—habits of sympathy, unintended consequences, unreasoned responses, blind striving, sheer error—makes society go. The stoic idiom offers Smith a way of correcting that humbling impairment.

37

In his *critique* of Smith's moral theory, Thomas Reid (Smith's successor at the University of Glasgow) insisted that in order to be moral agents we must exercise consciousness and control, and he exalted the supremely conscious and controlled stoic, "secured from all accidents of time or fortune,"[61] as Smith himself would do in the sixth edition of *The Theory of Moral Sentiments*. There Smith observes, for example, that the stoic trait of self-command lends all the other virtues "their principal lustre" (*TMS*, p. 241). By building stoic values into the *Moral Sentiments*, and reinforcing them over time, the author may have been attempting to preempt the arguments of those like Reid that "the foundation of [the *Theory*] must fall."[62] The stoic is rational, conforming his actions to nature,[63] and lends some of that rationality to a social actor who otherwise seems so weak in reason and who conforms not to nature but to society. The stoic, guided consistently by a right intention,[64] lends dignity to a social actor who promotes the common good without ever intending to do so. The stoic manifests a "fixed determination" to do right,[65] imparting some definition to a social actor who cautiously abides by social usages. Not to be bowed by anything, the stoic strengthens a social male whose pliancy was a constant theme of theorists of human improvement.[66] Without stoicism, the pliant mind of the social male might look like "the ductile minds of the fair sex,"[67] for who can tell pliancy from ductility? So too, the stoic, secure in his ability to withstand Fortune's changes, offsets the "fundamental insecurity" of the man of trade as he seeks his fortune.[68] If "the delicate sensibility required in civilized nations sometimes destroys the masculine firmness of character" (*TMS*, p. 209), stoicism restores that firmness. In a moral universe so coded with gender that the sublime and the beautiful[69] are terms for the masculine and the feminine, stoic principles confer a certain air of sublimity—a saving pretense of male might—on the Smithian actor.

By dignifying "inferior" virtues like prudence and self-interest itself—even Smith was of the opinion that the prudential virtues were distinctly second best (*TMS*, pp. 216, 304)—commercial society in effect closed off traditional virtues like magnanimity that had long been closed off by male fiat to the "inferior" sex.[70] The commercial way of life revises traditional catalogs of the virtues.

The eighteenth/nineteenth century notion that "women were capable of greater sexual self-control and generosity than men"[71] can only have come in as the result of a profound revision, for traditionally women had been seen as sexually incontinent (a celebrated aspect of the image of woman that suffused medieval and Renaissance culture) and as incapable of generosity of soul, an ideal reserved for men (as it still is in *The Theory of Moral Sentiments* [pp. 190–91]). I would surmise that this change was at least partly owing to the displacement, not all at once, of the more illustrious and active virtues by the prudential virtues of capitalism, the unacknowledged theme of *The Theory of Moral Sentiments*. Magnanimity, or generosity of soul, belongs to the stoic,[72] not to the prudent man busily accumulating goods of doubtful worth, while woman is called upon to watch over and as it were secure the goods of a man in the commercial phase of civilization, in a distinct reversal of her proverbial role as waster of man's substance and sexual traitor.[73] As motives hitherto passionate, like avarice, took on the character of a rational interest, while the traditionally rational dictates of morality took on an emotional or sentimental coloring, there occurred "a revision of binary gender distinctions,"[74] one instance of which is the modest, proper, pitying (but also vain, luxurious, corrupt) males of *The Theory of Moral Sentiments*. And like the sentimental nostrum of a change of heart that leaves the injustices of the world untouched, this sweetening of men leaves the subordinate position of women much as it was.

As I say, the unavowed theme of *The Theory of Moral Sentiments* is the displacement of the militantly masculine virtues of the classical tradition by the lesser virtues of liberalism—lesser to Smith himself. Montesquieu would have us "indulge in lesser vices in order to avoid worse ones";[75] Smith would have us practice the lesser virtues and commemorate the great ones. This moderation, this shunning of the extremes of both virtue and vice, perhaps illustrates the tendency of sentiments toward "a certain mediocrity" that Adam Smith sees as a force for human improvement (*TMS*, p. 27). Indeed, "sentiment" itself, understood as something tamer than traditional passion and stronger than halting reason, has a middling nature. And I want to say that Smith invents a middling sort of stoicism, one that commemorates Roman virtue but can be practiced by men who possess no specially glorious qualities and indeed are as restricted by public opinion as women.

(Hence Smith's description of the prudent man's punctilious regard for social convention.)[76] When Nietzsche raves against prudent stoicism and a cautious mediocrity of affect, he might as well be raving against Adam Smith.[77] Middling stoicism was the prescription of Dr. Johnson, too; in a *Rambler* paper on stoicism, he writes that "though the boast of absolute independence is ridiculous and vain, yet a mean flexibility to every impulse . . . is below the dignity of that mind, which, however depraved or weakened, boasts its derivation from a celestial original."[78] Though we cannot aspire to the "absolute independence" of the stoic state, moderate stoicism is within our powers, and anything less is unbefitting our own nature.

Writing of Adam Ferguson, Smith's associate in the Scottish Enlightenment, David Kettler remarks on his "abandonment of the heroic ideal" and particularly of the stoic ideal of the man who maintains an austere independence under all conditions.[79] ("Whip me such stoics, great governor of nature!" says Sterne's sentimental traveler.)[80] In the *Moral Sentiments* we witness not so much the abandonment of ideals like magnanimous action and stoic dispassion as the going-down of those ideals in a sort of sentimental twilight or last-light. Stoicism indeed casts its glow over Adam Smith's argument, but it is a glow soon to dim. The last edition of *The Theory of Moral Sentiments* was published in 1790, the year of Smith's death, and as Robert Adams has observed, the literary career of stoicism ends just about then, its last exponent being the illiberal Dr. Johnson. "When we look through the nineteenth century for another work informed with stoicism, defined by stoicism, we look in vain. What happened to stoicism? Without undergoing refutation or criticism, without being so much as remarked in its stealthy departure, stoicism faded away and became obsolete. We do not hear of it in the nineteenth century."[81] What did happen to stoicism? Adams offers one cogent explanation for its death: involving as it does a chastened acceptance of things and a quieting of the claims of the self, stoicism could not very well survive the romantic cult of the self. The disillusionment left by the French Revolution, we might add, recast the doctrine that the really free man can't be enslaved into the belief that a really enslaved people can't be (politically) freed: in a sense, stoicism was displaced by romanticism.[82] To these explanations, however, another might be coupled—that despite Adam Smith's skillful work, there is really no way to root the stoic values of resignation and indifference in a way of life where men anxiously struggle to better their lot and chase after a vision of happiness. In theory, moreover, it is advantageous that Smithian man seek to satisfy what were called imaginary wants, for it keeps his imagination safely occupied—immunizes him against the dangerous political imaginings of those who would do things like "new-model the constitution" (*TMS*, p. 232). The variety of stoicism that Adam Smith espouses, therefore, rules out revolution but allows for the pursuit of imaginary happiness, even as it allows for the ironic contemplation of that very quest.

Not only wealth but status, or what Adam Smith calls by more august names like "approbation" and "esteem," is sought by the man anxious to improve his condition. In his more sardonic moods Adam Smith tends to despise both wealth and status, the first because it conduces so little to real happiness, the second because it is so much a matter of vanity and show (proverbially feminine vices) and depends on the rabble. It is as though when the full meaning of the "prudent" pursuit of happiness appeared to him, the author drew back in disgust. I believe the vision of a society whose moving force is the vanity of men like "the wives of aldermen" (*TMS*, p. 57) no more pleased Adam Smith than the thought of the British economy resting on the bubble of credit pleased the critics of the public debt—vanity itself being in Smith's opinion a bubble. (It seems Smith had a point when he likened socially ambitious men to the wives of aldermen. "Not just a few burgesses' wives desirous of following fashion but virtually all the middle class" and many others were caught up in the rage for showy consumption at the time.)[83] By writing stoicism into *The Theory of Moral Sentiments,* he installs something more solid than the imagistic quality of vanity, a kind of social credit, at the basis of the commercial order.[84] He gives his argument the solidity that makes it so impressive.[85] He endows it with that "awful gravity" which Burke says belongs to noble male ancestors. He settles it on "manly" principles after all.[86]

But that foundation is itself illusory. If Smith's men manifest the reputedly feminine vice of vanity—behave like aldermen's wives competing for social advantage—in their better moments they manifest the propriety, the submission to social rules, of a conventionally good woman. Indeed, if in *The Theory of Moral Sentiments* propriety more or less comes down to the careful regulation and seemly presentation of the passions, it was women who were thought to be the masters of the art of composure; the preceptor of women, Dr. Gregory, says that women "are thought to possess in a degree far beyond us" the ability to compose their features.[87] Such in fact is the composure of the Smithian woman that she performs her wifely duties faultlessly even if she feels no love for her husband (*TMS*, p. 162). Her counterimage, the Smithian man, abides faultlessly by the rules and customs of society (*TMS*, p. 214) even if his social affections have been more or less extinguished, or composed out of existence. Again, we might say that the man of prudence composes himself as a woman would compose a letter with "stylistic propriety and moral exactitude";[88] Smith calls attention to the exactness of his observances and the vestal propriety of his social dealings. Significantly implied in Smith's model of the composing of the passions is the quieting of political passions, passions highly threatening in a political order where the grounds of deference are slipping. Smith himself would have subjects defer not because it is their sacred duty or because the powerful really merit deference, but because the alternatives are bad.

Implicitly, Adam Smith figures man as woman (hence "the weakness of his powers" and "the narrowness of his comprehension" [*TMS*, p. 237]), for he would much prefer that men live in quiet submission than upset the established order, possessing as they do such dubious power to change things for the better and such proved ability for mischief. Thus, much as good women are defined as those who keep within narrow bounds and bad women as those who wander, publicize themselves, and thereby corrupt the realm, so Smithian man is good as long as he confines his attention to his own affairs and sees to them with diligence; when he steps into public affairs, he is apt to become one of those merchants who are the demons of the *Wealth of Nations,* perverting the policy of the nation and deceiving Parliament with the fallacious charms and shameless appeals of their rhetoric.

In spite of his generally republican ideals, then, Adam Smith would have almost all men keep out of public life. He would have them quietly perform the duties of their station. In other words, Smith would keep alive a spirit of deference, a habit of submission in a society whose theme is individual effort. The male actors of Smithian society even bow to the opinions of one another. For men of the middle class, says Adam Smith, success "almost always depends upon the favour and good opinion of their neighbours and equals" (*TMS,* p. 63), a boon that cannot be won by clashing with their own judges. Paradoxically dependent upon his equals, the prudent man most likely has no sympathy with republicans who mourn the loss of independence or decry the corrupting effects of inequality. So little does he insist on his own equality that, as Adam Smith says, he humbly places himself "below . . . his equals" (*TMS,* p. 214).

We may think of Smithian man, the dependent of his equals, as suing for the title of gentleman. The possession of land in and of itself no longer qualifying a man for that honorific, it was for society to say whose manners and virtue were fine enough to be considered those of a gentleman; in this shift of meaning, gentler qualities came to the fore, just as the squire's sword yielded to the gentleman's cane.[89] (Among others, Adam Ferguson, Adam Smith, Tocqueville, J. S. Mill, and in our own day Norbert Elias have remarked on the mildness of bourgeois manners as compared to some earlier epoch when emotions were less closely and evenly policed. The mildness of manners contrasts curiously, however, with the ferocity of the laws protecting property in the eighteenth century.) Unimpressed by hereditary distinctions, convinced of the need for a fine sense of audience, imputing delicacy of sentiment to men, Adam Smith marks an episode in the changing meaning of the gentleman. If you are a man and you mean to pursue happiness, you will perhaps aspire to the title of gentleman even if this should mean styling your behavior by rules as narrowly binding as all the images of constriction, such as "a Chinese lady's foot," later used by J. S. Mill.[90]

In principle, the improved society relies less on the visible hand of authority than on such invisible mechanisms as social rules; thus, for example, Adam Smith's analysis in *The Theory of Moral Sentiments* of those subtle mechanisms that tune our conduct, even our emotions to one another.[91] Improved society is held together by processes quite unlike deliberate political choices. Provided that the state secures property rights and sees to the other minimum requisites of justice, society will work like a "spontaneous and self-adjusting order." It will also adjust persons as they go about their spontaneous activities.[92] "Is there even any need," asks Terry Eagleton, "for some cumbersome apparatus of law and the state, yoking us inorganically together, when in the genial glow of benevolence we can experience our kinship with others as immediately as a delectable taste?"[93] Here Eagleton derides the bourgeois dream of replacing the old instruments of authority, which confront us with hostile intent, with a community of sentiment, a blissful communion of actor and spectator "in perfect concord" (*TMS*, p. 16), a consensus. In order for the community of feeling to be realized, "ethical ideology must lose its coercive force and reappear as a principle of spontaneous consensus within social life,"[94] a principle as mysteriously irresistible and binding as that force of sympathy which provides the starting point of Adam Smith's analysis in *The Theory of Moral Sentiments*.[95] When the sympathy binding person to person loses its mystery, efficacy and charm, it takes on ugly names like conformity. But in its ideal version, the regime of sympathy would (we may imagine) dispel the idea that either men or women ever possessed the will or the power to resist others; contradicting one's neighbor might kindle those causes of public strife that theorists of civil society from Locke forward seek to defuse by concentrating men's efforts on their own "improvement." People being bound by a deep inarguable force, their disputes would cease. They would be so closely attuned to one another in a community of the heart that the idea of opposition would wither away.

Wary of political passions, Adam Smith does not want to rouse the spirit of opposition, even though he finds the political order unjust.[96] He would rather that we emulate the rich than dispossess the rich, as corrupting as emulation is (*TMS*, p. 61). In a modern commercial society where traditional precepts of poverty and passivity make less and less sense, and where revolution is therefore a danger, it is expedient that people direct their energy toward private acquisition and away from political endeavor, the more so in that the rich in their blank idiocy pose such a tempting political target. Not in any political sense are we to be the masters of ourselves. We are, however, to conduct our affairs with a measure of stoic self-mastery, enough to make up for the deluded envy, the fallacies of imagination, and the constant anxiety that keep us in motion as economic beings.

Tocqueville warned particularly against dependence on government, but the organism we may call bourgeois man was subject to other forms of dependence as well. Precisely to the degree that it enmeshed men in mutual dependence, society could be considered improved. At the near end of the scale, perhaps, would be Rousseau's vision of an agrarian republic—a political community with virtually no division of labor, no foreign trade, none of the elaboration of dependence that both he and Adam Smith believed impair the virtue of men.[97] Close by on the scale would be "primitive" peoples who didn't much practice division of labor but who, like the Indians of North America as described by Adam Smith, seemed capable of a heroic autonomy, a defiant indifference to fate (as well as a contempt for patient labor) quite beyond the reach of Europeans. In clearing natives from the land, Americans were getting rid of people who to the white imagination represented a heroic ideal of magnanimity[98]—the very word that sounds throughout *The Theory of Moral Sentiments;* they were clearing space for the values of civil society, such as trade and "improvement."

On the far end of the scale would be Europeans with a highly elaborated division of labor that served needs and awakened wants and caught the individual in "a strong *web*"[99] of dependence running in all directions, like the strong invisible filaments of sympathy binding Adam Smith's moral universe. In principle, that web restrains men's dangerous passions and stabilizes their dealings with one another better than the rough engines of repression. It improves men themselves, endowing them with what Adam Smith likes to portray as a kind of Ciceronian civility. In the improved state of society, men channel their energies narrowly and worry about their standing with their fellows almost as though their fate depended on it. Thus Defoe warns tradesmen they had better behave sweetly, because their reputation and credit depend utterly on the opinions held of them.

Ideally, the commercial way of life improves men by polishing their manners and winning them away from uncivil passions. Trade smooths away the roughness of men as pebbles shaken in a bag lose their "sharp angles"—the erasure of outline that Mill complains of in *On Liberty.*[100] Such are the benign effects of mutual dependence. Hence the discourse of the douceur (gentleness) of commerce, dating from the late seventeenth century. Providence has

not willed for everything that is needed for life to be found in the same spot. It has dispersed its gifts so that men would trade together and so that the mutual need which they have to help one another would establish ties of friendship among them. *This continuous exchange of all the comforts of life constitutes commerce and this commerce makes for all the gentleness* (douceur) *of life.* [101]

Classic expression of the notion of the gentleness of commerce is found in Joseph Addison's *Spectator* No. 69 (1711), where the author envisions a charming international division of labor that works out for the good of all, thanks to merchants.

> . . . There are not more useful Members in a Commonwealth than Merchants. They knit Mankind together in a mutual Intercourse of good Offices, distribute the Gifts of Nature, find Work for the Poor, add Wealth to the Rich, and Magnificence to the Great. Our *English* Merchant converts Tin of his own Country into Gold, and exchanges his Wooll for Rubies. The *Mahometans* are cloathed in our *British* Manufacture, and the Inhabitants of the Frozen Zone warmed with the Fleeces of our Sheep. [102]

When in his discussion of propriety Adam Smith speaks of the "acute and delicate discernment of the man of taste" (*TMS*, p. 20), he could practically be referring to Addison. Addison's *Spectator* metamorphoses into the "spectator" of the *Moral Sentiments*.

At once sympathetic and impartial, a fellow in feeling and a censor of manners, the Smithian spectator possesses a duality befitting those like Smith himself who belong to a small intelligentsia, bound by ties of intellectual sympathy and friendly feeling, that nevertheless speaks in the name of universal values, even of Nature. The prototype of such clubs is the Spectator club of Addison and Steele. In a sense, indeed, the highest expression of the morality of "improvement"—the gentle morality of commerce—is Addison himself, a man so sweet (in one of his aspects) that in an homage to Addison, Macaulay makes a woman of him, citing his "delicacy," his "modesty," his virtue "without stain." [103] (A contemporary commentator ironizes this portrayal of Addison by casting him as a siren who "seduce[s]" readers with his potent ideological charms.) [104] In his reliance on the approbation of society, the favor of his readers (many of them women), the services of merchants, the good offices of political patrons, Addison seems to be recognizing dependence as his condition.

And generally speaking, while still taking pride in his ancestral superiority to the female sex, bourgeois man was himself undergoing new forms of dependence. For as we have seen, it was an article of the ideology of commerce that trade has the benign effect of making men dependent. The exquisite dependence of men led Defoe to remark that a tradesman's credit "is the same thing in its nature as the virtue of a lady"[105] (both tradesman and lady depending on their reputation) and led Adam Smith to build his moral theory on the "delicate sensibility" of men in advanced societies (*TMS,* p. 209), Tocqueville to remark men's gentle manners, and Mill men's moral chastity and miserable lack of nerve.

In his study of "the civilizing process," Norbert Elias observes that as the individual comes to be "more tightly bound by his functional dependence on the activities of an ever-larger number of people,"[106] it becomes necessary to take long views and keep the passions under close and even, though not in truth stoic, regulation. Another theorist of the civilizing process, Adam Smith, finds that in societies with the most minute division of labor, the release of passion is not as severely checked as among "barbarians" (*TMS,* p. 208), but nevertheless closely judged; well-behaved people internalize the spectator who surveys their emotional performances with a censor's eye. Where Elias finds that the rules of bourgeois life "tend toward a more even moderation, a more continuous restraint, a more exact control of drives and affects"[107]— in short, a regulation of the emotions that misleadingly resembles the self-mastery of the stoic ideal—Adam Smith discourses on the workings of this very process, justifying as seemly what later voices would lament as the flatness and constriction of bourgeois life.

Smith shows us agents carefully moderating their emotions, setting them at the exact pitch that makes them suitable for public presentation. He becomes the Newton of the moral universe, disclosing mechanisms as marvelous and minute in their operation as the principles of the physical world. I may easily be too angry or not angry enough, too grief-stricken or too unfeeling, and in all these cases I lose the sympathy of the spectator, which I covet, perhaps, more than anything else. In order to win sympathy, then, I must possess a kind of social perfect pitch—an exact sense of social nicety, a knowledge of how to please.

If my animosity goes beyond what the indignation of my friend can correspond to; if my grief exceeds what his most tender compassion can go along with; if my admiration is either too high or too low to tally with his own; if I laugh loud and heartily while he only smiles, or, on the contrary, only smile while he laughs loud and heartily; in all these cases, as soon as he comes from considering the object, to observe how I am affected by it, according as there is more or less disproportion between his sentiments and mine, I must incur a greater or less degree of his disapprobation: and upon all occasions his own sentiments are the standards and measures by which he judges of mine. (*TMS*, pp. 16–17)

This, then, is what Norbert Elias's "more even moderation" comes to. This is what is meant by the polishing of manners, the rubbing off of rough edges. Thanks to the gentleness of human commerce, manners become sweetly pleasing.

Some would have said, thanks to *women* manners sweeten. Thus the influential moralist James Fordyce contends that associating with good women, "beyond everything else, rubs off the corners that give many of our sex an ungracious roughness. It produces a polish more perfect, and more pleasing, than that which is received from a general commerce with the world. . . . A certain flowing urbanity is acquired; violent passions, rash oaths, coarse jests, indelicate language of every kind, are precluded and disrelished."[108] In all this rubbing off of roughness, will the effeminacy of women rub off on men? Sensing that his own language points at that conclusion, Fordyce denies it: "I do not mean that the men I speak of will become feminine; but their sentiments and deportment will contract a grace."[109] Fordyce can count on established religion to keep gender distinctions in force even as men become decorous and proper under the influence of women. Less orthodox than Fordyce, Adam Smith relies on the language of fortitude and self-command, the language of stoicism, to keep men men even while they behave with the "grace" and propriety of women and, like women, faithfully perform their small offices. (Moreover, stoicism itself looks enough like Christianity—what with the resemblances between Epictetus and the New Testament, between Boethius and medieval Church doctrine—that Adam Smith passes for more of an orthodox Christian than he perhaps really is.)[110]

Rousseau considers that in the natural order of things women—not men—live subject to the rule of public opinion. Emile is warned of the trap of a social existence that will put him in a "dependent state, and force him to adjust his morals, his sentiments, and his conduct to the example and prejudices of others," the very adjustment of persons to one another that is at the heart of Adam Smith's moral theory.[111] In the Smithian model, men are under such strict rules of propriety, and such an obligation to please, that even in the expression of grief they had better gratify society in the form of the vigilant spectator. Society is always there watching, like a censor. And this "constant scrutiny" of one's performances,[112] this close policing by behavior-wardens on the lookout for the least infraction of propriety—this Adam Smith thought the very mechanism of improvement. More realistically, the Smithian model would make for the kind of insipid conformity that was taught to women. In particular, as I have said, the composing of the passions implies a subduing of political passions, which I think is the deeper reason Adam Smith lays such stress on the process. In theory, by submitting, by accepting the "dependent state," we allow the process of improvement to take its own course, wiser than we ourselves could design. Similarly, our imagination is not to assume the political shape that Burke finds so pernicious, but to be channeled into the satisfaction of what were called imaginary wants, wants that Smith himself views with high irony.

What is it men hope to gain when they strive to get on in the world? "What," Smith asks in a tone of stoic disengagement, "are the advantages which we propose by that great purpose of human life which we call bettering our condition? To be observed, to be attended to, to be taken notice of with sympathy, complacency, and approbation, are all the advantages which we can propose to derive from it. It is the vanity, not the ease, or the pleasure, which interests us" (*TMS*, p. 50). By Adam Smith's time there had sprung up in England a culture of consumption for show—conspicuous consumption, as the economists say.[113] With display in mind, good numbers of people bought pottery and cutlery, wigs and buckles, all that Adam Smith comprehends in the phrase, "mere trinkets of frivolous utility" (*TMS*, p. 181). If, as Smith contends in his case for noninterference, every man's wish to better his condition is enough to carry society to prosperity provided only that this motive is allowed to operate, we now see how worthless, in the author's opinion, is the motive behind the motive—sheer vanity, that proverbial woman's vice.

To be sure, the word "vain" was applied to men as well, as in Dr. Johnson's "Vanity of Human Wishes," where the term denotes the blind ambition of men, their desire to figure in the world, and the final nothingness of their efforts. But tradition had specially assigned vanity to women,[114] such as Pope's Belinda, a queen of consumption. The vanity of women is a constant theme of antifeminist satire. "Above all else . . . women's 'prevailing passions' were reputed to be 'vanity, and the love of admiration.'"[115] Both Mary Wollstonecraft and more orthodox moralists such as James Fordyce and Sarah Ellis censured female vanity, the last sermonizing upon "that great root of more than half the folly and the misery existing among women—*the love of admiration.*"[116] The twin of vanity, luxury, was habitually personified in art and literature as a woman.[117] In women were concentrated as it were the power of delusion, the craving to show, the corrupt love of luxury—an ancient prejudice that found seeming confirmation in a society where women were constrained to play the marriage market and display themselves like wares in order to play it. Such is the identification of women with vanity and luxury that Werner Sombart contends women were "the guiding spirit" behind the making and marketing of luxury goods as the European economy shifted from what Adam Smith considered unproductive modes of luxury, such as feasts, to productive ones.[118] Milton's Dalila, perhaps the very apogee of the antifeminist tradition, is herself a sort of visual feast, a human image of the banquet used to tempt Christ in *Paradise Regained,* a spectacle. In imputing to men the "essentially" and notoriously female quality of spectacle, and indeed in building his theory of commercial society on such dubious traits, Adam Smith risked making a mockery of men and their virtue, like the irreverent Mandeville (who was in many ways Smith's denied "other"). As it is, Smith made out the ruling passion of commercial society to be the vanity of "weak men," which presumably means men like women.[119]

Although Smith went beyond the thinking of earlier economic theorists who preached against high consumption, although the more scandalous connotations of "luxury" and "consumption" were questioned in Smith's time, the old association of luxury with vice and effeminacy survived. In his jeremiad against commercial society, John Brown dwells constantly on the vanity and effeminacy of the rich. Smith himself alleged in his lectures that luxury saps the valor of men and leaves them effeminate. What protects Smith's social actor against the accusations of effeminacy that were commonly brought against the lovers of luxury?[120] Sto-

icism. "A 'masculine,' antiexhibitionist ideal of self-mastery"—
in a word, stoicism—shores up Smith's own theory of men as vain
exhibitionists.[121] One difference between Mandeville and Smith,
both ironic theorists of commercial society, is that the former
scoffs at classical values in a way the latter would resent. That
Mandeville debunked stoicism while writing as a woman in the
Female Tatler suggests the very confusion of gender that Smith
risked when he pictured men as vain and corrupt or else as proper
and delicate.[122]

Montesquieu censures the luxury and vanity of women who
crave to show; he sees them as symbols of corruption. (At the
same time, though, he distances himself from the Persian who
makes sure his wives are locked up and veiled.)[123] Adam Smith
bemoans the corruption of our moral sentiments while knowing
that luxury and vanity keep commercial society in business. The
rich set fashions, stage displays of grandeur, ornament themselves
with gold;[124] others devotedly imitate the vanity—the effeminacy—
of the rich.[125] This is what the "historic alliance" of the bour-
geoisie and its social betters comes to.[126] On Adam Smith's own
terms, the social actor of capitalism lacks male virtue, a defect cured
by the rhetoric of manliness in *The Theory of Moral Sentiments*.

That Adam Smith rebelled at the thought of men lacking republican manhood becomes clear in a widely different context. Deep in
the *Wealth of Nations* Smith inserts a commentary on the hideous
corruption of body and mind of the great majority of men in
commercial society. Restricted by the division of labor to the performance of a few simple tasks, the laboring man

> generally becomes as stupid and ignorant as it is possible for a human crea-
> ture to become. The torpor of his mind renders him, not only incapable of
> relishing or bearing a part in any rational conversation, but of conceiving any
> generous, noble, or tender sentiment, and consequently of forming any just
> judgment concerning many even of the ordinary duties of private life. Of the
> great and extensive interests of his country he is altogether incapable of judg-
> ing; and unless very particular pains have been taken to render him other-
> wise, he is equally incapable of defending his country in war.[127]

As we have seen, the prudent middle-class man is also deficient in
public spirit; a natural shirker, he wants "the public business [to

be] well managed by some other person" rather than having to act in his own person (*TMS*, p. 216). But Adam Smith doesn't judge this figure as ruthlessly as he does the laborer. Much as though there were a class double standard on the order of the sexual,[128] he seems willing to palliate the failings of one man but not the other. Viewed more impartially, the prudent man averse to acting politically in his own person bears a family resemblance to the woman who was barred from acting in that way but whose power "to act indirectly" on society was constantly eulogized in prescriptive literature of the late eighteenth and nineteenth centuries.[129]

While Adam Smith's language surely points to the effeminacy of the vestal man of prudence, he may or may not have intended this meaning. In the case of the laborer there is less doubt. His very manhood has been lost. As Smith once claimed that in commercial society "the minds of men are contracted and rendered incapable of elevation" and their courage fails[130]—in other words, that men are unmanned—so in the *Wealth of Nations* he judges that

> even though the martial spirit of the people were of no use toward the defence of society, yet to prevent that sort of mental mutilation, deformity, and wretchedness, which cowardice necessarily involves in it, from spreading themselves through the great body of the people, would still deserve the most serious attention of government; in the same manner as it would deserve the most serious attention to prevent a leprosy or any other loathsome and offensive disease, though neither mortal nor dangerous, from spreading itself among them; though, perhaps, no other public good might result from such attention besides the prevention of so great a public evil.[131]

Just how government is to make men men again, Smith does not say. But he is sure something must be done. And this worry over public degeneracy is central, not parenthetical, to the liberty tradition. From the language of Adam Smith to the imagery of mutilation and deformity in John Stuart Mill's *On Liberty* is a straight line, although the latter argument is directed against the middle class. So persuaded was Mill of the decay of public spirit that he strongly favored a citizen militia as a way of instilling valor in the prudent man and getting him into the habit of acting in his own person—a worthy end in Mill's eyes even if no utilitarian purpose were served ("even though the martial spirit of the people were of no use"), even if compulsory military service is patently a grave violation of negative liberty, even if, as Adam Smith says, military service runs against "the whole bent of the interest, genius and inclinations of the people."[132] But Smith himself, concerned as he is to keep the powers of government to a sensible minimum, calls on the state to somehow check the spirit of cowardice. Both of the most celebrated theorists of negative liberty imbue their arguments with the language of republican virtue.

What is it that, in the opinion of Adam Smith, reduces the modern laborer to such degradation? Nothing but the division of labor, a principle so fundamental to Smith that he begins his analysis of it on the first page of the *Wealth of Nations.* In the more advanced societies the division of labor has progressed the furthest, which means that most men are condemned to perform some few operations over and over again. "But the understandings of the greater part of men are necessarily formed by their ordinary employments. The man whose whole life is spent in performing a few simple operations . . . has no occasion to exert his understanding. . . . He naturally loses, therefore, the habit of such exertion, and generally becomes as stupid and ignorant as it is possible for a human creature to become."[133] Thus the same division of labor that powers the advance of society to the highest phase of civilization—the division of labor that allows for the multiplication of wants—also, and "necessarily," cripples men.[134] And as the division of labor essential to prosperity saps the valor of the laborer and confines his views, so the middle-class pursuit of status—equally necessary to the activity of a commercial society—corrupts men, making them behave like "the wives of aldermen": "And thus, place [that is, precedence or privilege], that great object which divides the wives of aldermen, is the end of half the labours of human life; and is the cause of all the tumult and bustle, all the rapine and injustice, which avarice and ambition have introduced into this world" (*TMS,* p. 57). Invoked here is the commonplace of the competitive woman, which goes back at least as far as the status-hungry citizens' wives of the General Prologue of the *Canterbury Tales,* and was sensationally realized in Swift's image, in "A Modest Proposal," of wives vying with one another to bring the plumpest child to market.

In a sense, all Adam Smith is doing in the passages just cited is playing out the old language of gender, which makes courage male and vanity female. Without doubt he is stuck in traditional gender categories. All the same, he does well to bring up for discussion the punishing effects of the division of labor, rather than censoring the issue, and he does well to acknowledge the pettiness and vacuity of the desire for status, and the debased motives that lie behind so much respectable activity. But aside from calling on government to somehow stop the spread of cowardice, what remedy does he advise for ills like these, at once so serious and so deeply a part of commercial society? Before answering this, it might be instructive to review his colleague Adam Ferguson's response to what is really the same set of problems: the forces that "crush [man's] spirit, that debase his sentiments, and disqualify his mind for affairs" (again, the very substance of Mill's complaint in *On Liberty*);[135] the specialization of labor; the confinement of men's capacities and views; the "dismember-[ing]"[136] of male character, so suggestive of Adam Smith's language of deformity and emasculation. For these problems Ferguson proposes a curiously ritualistic remedy: the citizen militia.

In theory militia service will revive that sense of oneself as a citizen which modern society does so much to vitiate. What makes the militia a theoretically ideal cure for the woes of commercial society is not only that it invigorates men but that the entire exercise leaves society just as it was; indeed, military discipline teaches men to keep their places. The division of society into orders remains. The division of labor remains. The life of petty vanity and envious emulation, what Rousseau calls "amour-propre," remains. In practice, introducing the archaic ritual of a Roman militia into commercial society would serve a purely ceremonial function like the Latin on diplomas, or, again, like the mottoes on public buildings.

While Smith rejects the citizen militia (unlike his teacher Francis Hutcheson), I want to say that stoicism performs the same ennobling function in *The Theory of Moral Sentiments* as the citizen militia in republican thought. Stoicism is Adam Smith's citizen militia. And just as archaic military exercises do not really alter the order of society—in theory tending rather to confirm men's habits of discipline and deepen their attachment to the existing order—so the antique cast of the language of *The Theory of Moral Sentiments* does not obstruct the activity of a commercial society: the feverish pursuit of an image of happiness.[137] The stoic governs himself rather than turning himself over to "the blind guidance of appetite and instinct,"[138] but on Adam Smith's showing, blind cravings are exactly what govern the behavior of men in commercial society. If the threat of effeminacy is built into the very structure of commercial society (built into the division of labor and the drive to better one's condition and show up the others), Adam Smith looks to the stoic as a saving exception to the rule of unmanly men.[139] Unresolved are deeper questions such as: How can the division of labor promote the happiness of society if it does such violence to so many? How can moderns gain a sense of themselves as citizens? Can people live with their eyes open, or do they require to be deceived by a cunning Providence into pursuing false goods? Must human beings lack the dignity of conscious agents—must they act blind?[140] If men need to be deceived by Providence in order for society to prosper, what makes them better than their own image of woman as a creature whose tender sensibilities must be protected from harsh truths?[141] Are the distinctions of gender really inscribed in nature?

A reader who knew Adam Smith only as a philosophical founder of capitalism might well be shocked to discover his contempt for the quest for wealth. In book 4 of the *Moral Sentiments,* Smith illustrates his views with a mordant parable of a "poor man's son, whom heaven in its anger has visited with ambition" (p. 181). So dazzled is this youth with the splendor of the rich that he dedicates himself body and soul to the pursuit of wealth: "To obtain the conveniencies [of wealth], he submits in the first year, nay in the first month of his application, to more fatigue of body and more uneasiness of mind than he could have suffered through the whole of his life from the want of them. . . . With the most unrelenting industry he labours day and night to acquire talents superior to all his competitors."

Thus Adam Smith disenchants the fairy tale of commoner-turned-prince. He instructs us that dreams of wealth are vanity and that real wealth is to be found in patient endurance—the stoic state in which we depend on nothing external to ourselves. In contrast to the unquiet mind of the poor man's son, he recommends mental tranquillity and self-possession. Rather than endorsing the capitalist dream of rising in the world by hard work, Adam Smith seems to view that dream as a mere bubble and offers counsels of quietude Boethius could have spoken a thousand years before. The poor man's son—the man who would be rich—

makes his court to all mankind; he serves those whom he hates, and is obsequious to those whom he despises. Through the whole of his life he pursues the idea of a certain artificial and elegant repose which he may never arrive at, for which he sacrifices a real tranquillity that is at all times in his power, and which, if in the extremity of old age he should at last attain to it, he will find to be in no respect preferable to that humble security and contentment which he had abandoned for it. (*TMS,* p. 181)

Adam Smith, charterer of capitalism, views the pursuit of happiness in the spirit of Epictetus himself (quoted in *The Theory of Moral Sentiments*). For the stoic claims "that the things that are eagerly followed and admired are of no use to those who have gained them; while they who have not yet gained them imagine that, if they are acquired, every good will come along with them; and then, when they are acquired, there is the same feverishness, the same agitation, the same nauseating, and the same desire of what is absent."[142] Of vain seekers like the poor man's son, "always seeking prosperity without, and never able to find it," Epictetus says that they are enthralled to their own "effeminacy."[143]

The first thing to note about the case of the poor man's son is that it isn't special. It is the very story of capitalism. Every man who works hard to rise above the conditions of his birth and get hold of the grail of happiness is the poor man's son. J. Ralph Lindgren takes the other side of this question, contending that the young quester belongs to that small category of men foolish enough to want to change rank. "Most of the men of the middle ranks of society do not intend to improve their condition so much that they achieve a place among the rich." Another able reader of Smith, David McNally, affirms that most men *do* emulate the rich.[144] The reason for the confusion on this point may be that Adam Smith was reluctant to state with full clarity that his theory of society rests squarely on a love of status as blind, envious, and corrupt as the motivation of the poor man's son. In the *Wealth of Nations,* however, Smith does remark that in the commercial phase of civilization "*all* the different orders of people are growing every day more expensive in their houses, in their furniture, in their tables, in their dress, and in their equipage,"[145] like the poor man's son who contracts expensive tastes.

In fact Smith states that the case of the poor man's son is not rare but common; what actuates him is "often" (*TMS,* p. 181), not rarely, the secret motive of human pursuits. Going further, the author identifies the worship of the rich—exactly the error of the poor man's son—as "the great and most universal cause" of moral corruption (*TMS,* p. 61), which makes the case of the young striver sound like anything but an isolated instance. The story of the poor man's son is simply a heightened version of the ordinary condition of striving in Smithian society, where people work with "the most unrelenting industry" to achieve imaginary goals.[146] Moreover, the pursuit of a false image of happiness is in no way incidental to the business of commercial society, according to Smith, but the very axis of that society, what its activity turns upon. Indeed it was argued at the time that unless the men of advanced societies exerted themselves in the quest for false goods, there wouldn't be enough activity to keep people employed, and society would sink.[147] A kind of class double standard spares the middle-class man the philosophic irony Smith heaps on the poor man's son, but the cases are much the same. The poor man's son is the Everyman of capitalism, and whatever impairs his dignity as a conscious agent or vitiates his efforts, acts with theoretically similar effect in all other cases of a man working hard "to better his own condition."[148] And we cannot mistake that Adam Smith takes a most coolly ironic view of the efforts of the poor man's son. The poor man's son should have stayed poor.

Although Smith counted it one of the great merits of commercial society that it raised the living standard of the poor (for he was not one of those who believed that comfort would make workers lazy and unruly), he nevertheless thought little of the poor man's son who goes after the fruits of prosperity rather than waiting for prosperity to come to him in its own time. Perhaps the primary object of Adam Smith's disdain in this parable of social striving isn't hard work and self-denial as such, so much as the beau monde, false in itself, that has blinded the young man with its splendor. "He is enchanted with the distant idea of this felicity" (*TMS,* p. 181). Like the Parisian commoner who dresses up pretending to be employed at court,[149] the poor man's son has chosen a corrupt scene to admire, and now *his* sentiments are corrupted. For as we have seen, Adam Smith holds that the adulation of the rich is the principal source of "the corruption of our moral sentiments" (*TMS,* p. 61).

Possibly Smith even regards the aristocracy as effeminate, like those "Commonwealthmen" at the time who combine a powerful critique of class privilege with a ritualistic language of manliness.[150] If he does not see the upper class as effeminate, he nevertheless sees it as vain, trivial, idle. Mary Wollstonecraft deems the aristocracy effeminate. Repeatedly she likens pampered women to aristocrats in order to illustrate their worthlessness; indeed, in prosecuting the aristocracy in the *Vindication of the Rights of Woman*, she cites *The Theory of Moral Sentiments*. If the corruption of the rich themselves spreads to those who blindly admire and ape them (and it is supposed to be in the nature of corruption to spread), perhaps the effeminacy of the rich can extend to people like the poor man's son. When the author adverts to the corruption of our moral sentiments, he uses a technical term that connotes not only a spoilage and a loss of simplicity, but a loss of virility as well.[151]

In the *Vindication of the Rights of Woman* Mary Wollstonecraft takes issue with James Fordyce, the popular homilist whose *Sermons to Young Women* (first edition, 1765) prescribed sweet submission. Fordyce's pet complaint is the vanity of women—their love of show. He censures the woman who gapes at the pageantry of the rich, yearning to make a brilliant figure like theirs. The light-headed woman is dazzled at the sight of "shining equipages" and other "enchanting visions." "Intoxicated" with the seeming beauty of the gay world, she loses her reason. "All is romance and distractions, the extravagance of vanity." Nothing "rational" can hold her mind. She is "addicted to external show," totally given over to vanity and illusion.[152] And so it is with the poor man's son. He too is given up to star-worship. He too gapes at the sight of equipages. ("He sees his superiors carried about in machines, and imagines that in one of these he could travel with less inconveniency" [*TMS*, p. 181].) His mind "enchanted" (*TMS*, p. 181), he begins to do things contrary to reason. In fact, he too becomes a slave of vanity, at once enviously adoring the rich and driven, against all reason, by the desire to show as beautifully as they. If vanity is a feminine vice—and it is to the conventional Fordyce— the poor man's son is effeminate. He succumbs to the enchanting spectacle of power as women were thought liable, by reason of their fancy, to succumb to the powerful enchantments of romance reading.[153] Going further, we might say that in his dream state and his aroused desire, the poor man's son resembles women in erotic novels of the eighteenth century who are allowed to feel sexual desire provided that they are in something less than a waking state and "don't know what they're doing."[154] Smithian man, busy chasing illusions of delight, deceived for his own good by a wise Providence,[155] simply doesn't know what he is doing.

So suggestively does the characteristic figure of the poor man's son correspond to the young woman who desires too much and abandons the duties of her own sphere for the love of glitter; so curiously does his appetite for luxury and show suggest the appetites that are illicit in her, that what Mary Wollstonecraft says of the woman of overheated imagination holds true of the poor man's son. In both, a racing imagination "prevents intellect from attaining that sovereignty which it ought to attain to render a rational creature useful to others, and content with its own station."[156] The poor man's son, weak in rationality, unmindful of his station, enthralled to the imagination, is like a straying woman. Even Fordyce finds the age "effeminate"; even Mary Wollstonecraft concedes that Fordyce presents "many sensible observations."[157]

So firm is the association of women with luxury and show that on this point Mary Wollstonecraft agrees with her bane, Rousseau. In Rousseau's *Discourse on Inequality,* Adam Smith would have read, "Let those who set themselves up as men of taste admire in other places the magnificence of palaces, the beauty of carriages, splendid furnishings, the pomp of ceremonial and all the refinements of effeminacy and luxury. In Geneva there will be only men."[158] The gorgeous trappings, the sensual lure of power: just this has enthralled the poor man's son. But although Adam Smith shares Rousseau's contempt for display, his theory turns upon the love of elegance, for that is what keeps commercial society going and, what is more, diverts us from the rude republicanism of Rousseau. The worship of power (the love of beautiful equipages comes to that) preserves the deference-habits of the old regime; the very rottenness of the old regime makes it too dangerous to attack it like Rousseau.

The poor man's son is such a stranger to habits of equality that he grovels. Hard work is not in itself enough to win the prize our young fantasist seeks. In order to do that, he must also make himself pleasing. Approval brings wealth as wealth brings approval. Therefore the poor man's son "makes his court to all mankind," "is obsequious to those whom he despises," the phrasing itself suggesting that there is something servile and unmanly in the expenditure of moral autonomy that could have been conserved if only the young man had not made himself so dependent on society. Here again a comparison with Rousseau's *Discourse on Inequality* is revealing. In an article in the *Edinburgh Review* of 1755, Smith himself translated passages from this work, one of which clearly prefigures his own description of the servility of the poor man's son. Civilized man, he quotes Rousseau as saying, "toils, bestirs and torments himself without end, to obtain employments which are still more laborious. . . . He makes his court to the great whom he hates." In contrast to this wasting frenzy of activity, the savage feels a calm so deep that it exceeds even "the *ataraxia* [indifference] of the Stoic."[159] For Adam Smith, less given to hyperbole than Rousseau, the stoic himself is a sufficiently noble example of moral autonomy and sufficiently weighty exception to the anxieties of class society.

Remarkably, for all of his reliance on theater metaphors, Adam Smith shares something of Rousseau's understanding of the corrupting power of "the play of the imagination that lies at the heart of all drama."[160] (The rich are so corrupting because their lives are so theatrical; "to figure at a ball is [their] great triumph" [*TMS,* p. 55].) At the heart of the drama, according to Rousseau, is imagination, the same imagination that vitiates men by turning "natural and tractable needs into complex, insatiable wants."[161] The evolution of natural needs into false wants is the very history of the poor man's son, as it is in the nature of commercial society, according to its early theorists, to multiply human wishes. One of those theorists, the anonymous author of "A Vindication of Commerce and the Arts" (1758),[162] contended that if it weren't for men's "imaginary wants," there wouldn't be enough for the workers of advanced societies to do; on this showing, men become creatures of error and desire, but whereas the cravings and wayward imaginations of women are said to threaten the social order, those of men actually secure it, by keeping the poor employed. Another theorist, the scandalous Mandeville, argued that "the wants of men are innumerable," and accordingly "what ought to supply them has no bounds."[163] If women were for centuries condemned for their reputedly insatiable desires (the "luxury" of women connoting indiscipline, overconsumption, raging appetites), Mandeville finds the men of commercial society with boundless desires. In the *Wealth of Nations* Smith himself claims that rich men's appetite for luxury adornments "has no bounds," and while he does not call their self-infatuation womanish, he does call it "most childish"—the next thing to womanish—and does assign it the same effect as the costly habits of woman in antifeminist lore, that of devouring a patrimony.[164] Thanks to luxury, and by a providential irony, the barons of England lost their power. Blindly imitating the rich dedicated to their own ruin, the poor man's son loses his own patrimony. He loses it when he abandons "the cottage of his father" in his quest for bigger things (*TMS*, p. 181).

Mandeville could be, and was, dismissed as an immoralist—for example, by Smith, whose own wants were "strictly limited"[165]— but the fact is that as consumer values took hold in eighteenth-century Britain, his thesis became common doctrine, and not only were men talked of as possessing the limitless desires long said to be women's worst vice, but those desires were given a role of honor: they fueled the entire economic system. "Consumption is the sole end and purpose of all production,"[166] in the words of Adam Smith. The emergence of consumer society was indeed a revolution in the sense that it turned traditional concepts perfectly upside down. With its constant creation of "imaginary wants," consumer society inverts the traditional ordering of things—change dethrones stasis, illusion claims parity with the real, appetite challenges reason. (Notoriously changeful and deceptive, given to desire and arousing desire, the traditional image of woman is indissolubly associated with everything philosophically bad.) As I observed before, it is in part his commitment to something as novel as consumer society in spite of his own distinctly conservative temperament that makes the thought of Smith so interesting. That temperament reveals itself in his cool, dubious view of the poor man's son who didn't know his place in a stratified society, in his deflationary appraisal of luxury (in point of real utility, he might rank a retinue of servants below a toothpick), and in his feeling for the "manhood" of ancient philosophy (*TMS*, p. 283).

In the case of the poor man's son, as a result of an imagination teased into play by the theatrical glories of the rich, peace of mind and body is lost, independence is sacrificed, life is sophisticated in the old sense of both complicated and ruined, and in all the seeker just about loses the dignity of a man. Recall in this connection that the craving to be admired (the motive of the poor man's son) was conventionally associated with women: "The unbounded and undistinguishing love of admiration, has been thought the most common, the rankest, and the most noxious weed, that grows in the female heart."[167] Yearning to be admired, filled with the "contemptible vanity" of the weak (*TMS*, p. 117), overstepping bounds, the poor man's son has turned into an image of the proverbially vain woman. And this is a representative case. Heavy costs like the loss of reason and the corruption of the moral personality are exacted whenever men struggle to get hold of the faux pearls of happiness. Notwithstanding Adam Smith's language of self-command, it seems that the men of commercial society are not in command of themselves at all (at least if they resemble the poor man's son) and perhaps even fall under "the despotism of speculative fantasy." Or as we might say, the brave rhetoric of self-command keeps us from perceiving how much commercial conduct is driven by sheer "hysteria."[168] And unless men are seen as possessing self-command, their pretense of superiority over women crumbles, for it is just because women allegedly cannot govern themselves that men claim the right to govern them.

In his somehow libidinous quest for happiness, the poor man's son morally bankrupts himself. And the manhood that he dissipates, the stoic conserves. Stoic principles lend moral weight or gravitas to the ideology of commerce, at the same time that the mystique of the author's language blocks out the question of whether the sheer loss of one's mind, as in the case of the poor man's son, is really "necessary" (*TMS*, p. 61) to maintain the peace of society, and whether an order that actually depends and thrives on "the corruption of our moral sentiments" (*TMS*, p. 61) can be defended. Stoicism makes a virtue of necessity, and Adam Smith, as economist and moral philosopher, makes a virtue of a class system that is decadent in his own eyes, and of the life of anxious emulation that is, in his own judgment, corrupt and mistaken. He leaves the class system and the life of anxious emulation exactly as they are. It is ironically fitting that Smith is remembered as one who accredited the commercial way of life, but not as one who despised the dream of getting rich; as one who immortalized the manufacture of pins, but not as one who viewed with Olympian disdain the buttons, buckles, toothpick cases, sauceboats, and miscellaneous fripperies the production and consumption of which accelerated commerce to a pace never reached before.

From ancient stoicism Adam Smith derived a number of principles congenial to his thought and temperament. That the universe is a well-ordered whole of which the individual is a minute part; that we are called upon to bear well and virtuously what we cannot change; that we are called to the performance of the duties of our station (like the poor man's son, who should have known his place); that "every man . . . is first and principally recommended to his own care" (*TMS*, p. 219), which in Adam Smith sounds less, perhaps, like a counsel of quietude and more like a justification of enterprise—such stoic principles as these leave their stamp on *The Theory of Moral Sentiments*. Yet stoic doctrines do not in the end pertain to the commercial way of life; I believe it is their absence from it that calls for their stabilizing presence in Smith's moral theory. Men driven to constant activity—men so little the masters of themselves that they devote their days to acquiring things on the order of "mere trinkets of frivolous utility" (*TMS*, p. 181)—are just not given to stoic quietude. Good theories, according to Adam Smith, yield aesthetic satisfaction by revealing uniformity where there was disparity before.[169] His own moral theory is framed to this standard, and in smoothing the differences between ancient and modern—in making the man of trade a minor stoic—it affords an aesthetic pleasure that we don't want to ruin by skeptical questioning, even if the author's own thought arises, like Hume's, out of skepticism itself.

The poor man's son, "enchanted" (*TMS*, p. 181), goes through life as though in a state of hallucination. The stoic suffers from no such defect of consciousness. He wills virtue consciously. For in stoic doctrine, it is of the essence that a man "consciously wills to bring his own desire into harmony with" the order of things.[170] "To all other pleasures oppose that of being conscious that you are obeying God, and performing, not in word, but in deed, the duty of a wise and good man."[171] In his critique of Adam Smith's theory of sympathy, Thomas Reid revives the old equivalence of consciousness and conscience, again and again speaks of the "consciousness of Integrity," and, as we have seen, celebrates the magnificently aware stoic, "secured from all accidents of time or fortune,"[172] much as Smith himself would do in the last revision of *The Theory of Moral Sentiments*. The high premium on consciousness is evident as well in Adam Ferguson's opinion that "it is surely happy for anyone to be conscious that the best things are in his own power";[173] he too wrote under stoic influence. Less abstractly, Smith himself was deeply moved by the perfectly conscious and composed way in which his friend Hume died. (In our own time, Freud, an heir of the Enlightenment, displayed stoicism in the face of death.) But by Smith's account, the actors of commercial society are not conscious but blind, as blind as the poor man's son. Not only do they not have in view the larger public ends served by their actions, but the ends they do seek are totally meretricious. What are those ends?

> From whence, then, arises that emulation which runs through all the different ranks of men, and what are the advantages which we propose by that great purpose of human life which we call bettering our condition? To be observed, to be attended to, to be taken notice of with sympathy, complacency, and approbation, are all the advantages which we can propose to derive from it. It is the vanity, not the ease, or the pleasure, which interests us.[174] (*TMS*, p. 50)

How little like philosophic composure is the mindless striving "to be observed." The tone of the statement is enough to convey Smith's low opinion of the craving for admiration, but just so there is no doubt, he later tells us, "To a real wise man [such as a stoic] the judicious and well-weighed approbation of a single wise man, gives more heartfelt satisfaction than all the noisy applauses of ten thousand ignorant though enthusiastic admirers" (*TMS*, p. 253). According to Adam Smith, then, the driving force of the commercial order is the hunger to be noted, to be admired, to be applauded by large numbers of people who probably in no way merit our applause in turn.[175]

The conclusion is inescapable that in Adam Smith's opinion, people in commercial society busily go through life not knowing what they are doing.[176] The stoic knows just what he is doing. And so stoic values disengage Adam Smith from the follies of emulation and social striving, at the same time that they cast an august glow over *The Theory of Moral Sentiments* and by some kind of association of ideas confer standing and legitimacy on the commercial way of life. To phrase this dialectic another way: while Smith abundantly shares the contempt for the pursuit of "airy good" expressed in Dr. Johnson's "Vanity of Human Wishes" (a poem inspired by the stoic, and virulently antifeminist Juvenal), he knows that the commercial way of life hinges on the love of false goods and he defends that way of life even so.[177] The pursuit of imaginary wants is a benign form of those distractions of the imagination that Imlac discourses on in *Rasselas,* benign because it secures the commercial order and, as Mandeville would have said, makes for a busy and prosperous "hive." It turns risk into gain. In theory, social men who crave what others crave, even if trinkets and baubles, will have no use or occasion for those flights of the political imagination which excite solitary minds.[178] Such a solitary is the political speculator of *The Theory of Moral Sentiments,* who likes "to imagine," "to fancy," that he is the only wise man in the polity (*TMS,* p. 234). Though enthralled to imagination himself, the poor man's son poses no such danger to the existing order. Smithian theory, then, commits men to the quest for the imaginary that is illustrated in the parable of the poor man's son, while it consoles them with the language of ancient virtue for the loss of their reason. And this strategy is consistent with the aim of diverting men from public strife and political imaginings into the pursuit of private betterment.

A commercial society "depends on a spirit of enterprise, ambition, and astute pursuit of personal interest," none of which, it is said, is "readily assimilable" to stoicism.[179] If despite everything, moreover, people really became stoics, commercial society would come to a stop, or rather devolve: "Were the majority of human beings capable of Stoic *ataraxia,* were they capable of seeing through the baubles and trinkets, and were they to act upon their occasional flights of nostalgia for a life of detached and Stoic simplicity, the species would have been condemned to an eternity of egalitarian barbarism."[180] People must blind themselves and must dissipate their powers of action because otherwise they would wreck everything: note how decisively this proposition rules out the conscious action of political beings. (Analogous is the thesis that unless women were kept busy doing make-work—occupied with trinkets—their sharp understanding would wreak havoc on the world.)[181] With too little stoicism men might lose the habit of submission and resignation; with too much they would see through the deceits that keep commercial society going. With too little they might become politically restive, and with too much, economically quiet.[182] Hence the middling, Smithian stoicism that somehow allows for the "bustle" (*TMS,* p. 57) of an orderly society where the guiding motives, such as the pursuit of a fantasy of happiness, seem anything but stoic. Just as we are to cultivate apathy, or at least subdue our passions, precisely to gain sympathy, so we are to use "stoic" principles in unstoic pursuits.

Thus arises the paradox that the chief influence on Adam Smith's ethical thought was the same stoicism of which he wrote in *The Theory of Moral Sentiments* that it is "altogether" at odds with the "plan and system which Nature has sketched out for our conduct" (*TMS*, p. 292). In Sheldon Wolin's description of the economic actor, we glimpse a man who is indeed altogether a stranger to stoicism: "It was anxiety which drove liberal man to unrelenting activity—anxiety from struggling to eke out existence in the face of a hostile nature, anxiety from the precarious state of possessions in a society where the masses were often desperately hungry, and, equally strong, anxiety stemming from the appetites instilled by society."[183] By "anxiety" we may understand the desperate absence of stoicism.

A comment by Robert Adams on Samuel Johnson's "Vanity of Human Wishes," seen by Adams as "authentically stoic," hints at the anomaly of the stoic ideal in a commercial age. Of the stoic Adams says, "The more he sees, the more he's confirmed that the only place to live securely is a cellar. This readiness to see more and more widely at the cost, and perhaps with the end, of defining one's own existence more narrowly but more securely, is the root of the stoic mood."[184] This picture of a virtual cave-dwelling serves as a sort of antithetical reminder that for all of his irony Adam Smith saw the increased wealth and improved manners of a commercial society as the fruit and proof of a high stage of civilization. Stoicism, which dwells constantly on the man who depends on nothing but himself, is the poorest kind of soil for a way of life wherein people depend on one another to a high degree, as in commercial society with its elaborate division of labor. Epictetus writes with the air of someone who has gotten down to bedrock, but by the same token nothing can grow on rock; the barren simplicity of stoic doctrine cannot sustain the flourishing way of life that is Adam Smith's ideal. If all roads lead to Rome, the roads of stoic thinking lead to the fixed idea of heroic death. And from that end point there is nowhere to go. The madman of Chekhov's "Ward Number Six" is correct in asserting that stoic thinking hasn't advanced an inch in two thousand years. Thus stoicism is logically unsuited to Smith's own understanding of the progressive phases of civilization. At the same time, if Adams is right and stoicism reflects a wish for security—"more narrowly but more securely"—this makes it a good device to dignify the narrow regimens and prudent calculations of the bourgeois way of life, itself dedicated to the security of property.[185] For liberal man, "everything hinged on having secure expectations,"[186] which the stoic has rather perversely attained.

I have suggested that Adam Smith uses the exaggeratedly manly language of stoicism to mask the weak autonomy of men that is written into his analysis of society. A certain diminution of autonomy, in the primary sense of self-rule, is already suggested in Vico's intriguing idea, earlier cited, that men act blindfolded, without an image of the larger design their actions serve. Unlike a stoic who consciously wills virtue, the social actor, "entirely occupied" with the pursuit of private advantage,[187] has no consciousness at all of the ends that his actions advance in the larger scheme of things. This Viconian figure becomes the private man of *The Theory of Moral Sentiments,* "humble, assiduous, and complaisant" (p. 41)— the attributes of a good woman, whose presumed lack of autonomy, however, bars her from participation in public life.[188]

The notion that men act without an understanding of the script they are acting, was elaborated by Kant, said to have been "directly influenced" by Adam Smith.[189] Particularly in his "Idea for a Universal History with a Cosmopolitan Purpose" (1784), Kant theorizes that it is the design of Nature to develop the moral capacities of man in spite of himself—to bring him up from moral nonage and gradually induct him into freedom. This theory is not flattering to men's autonomy; it envisages them virtually as puppets playing out a script beyond their ken. But puppets who will one day come into their own, and into a comprehension of Nature's wisdom in preparing them for that happy occasion. The autonomy of men awaits them on their day of majority. And that far-off prospect of autonomy serves to divert our eyes from the indignity of men's present situation as they blindly act out Nature's plan for enlightening the human race.

We may hope, writes Kant,

that what strikes us in the actions of individuals as confused and fortuitous may be recognised, in the history of the entire species, as a steadily advancing but slow development of man's original capacities. . . . Individual men and even entire nations little imagine that, while they are pursuing their own ends, each in his own way and often in opposition to others, they are unwittingly guided in their advance along a course intended by nature. They are unconsciously promoting an end which, even if they knew what it was, would scarcely arouse their interest.[190]

That end is the achievement of their own moral nature. An Invisible Hand, then, brings out the moral nature of men little by little, in ways unknown to the actors themselves. Blinded by their passions, imprisoned in their small conceptions, men are nevertheless enough stimulated by all the strife they create and enough impressed with the necessity of inventing a way out of their own turmoil that their capacity for good is awakened. "Nature should thus be thanked for fostering social incompatibility, enviously competitive vanity, and insatiable desires for possession or even power. Without these desires, all man's excellent natural capacities would never be roused to develop."[191]

A disreputable version of this argument is Mandeville's thesis that "man never exerts himself but when he is roused by his desires" and that the "envy and emulation" of men make for a rich and powerful society.[192] Kant sees moral gains. Much as the public good is thought to emerge from the play of private interests, so, on Kant's showing, the moral good comes into being through the playing out of men's passions and vices. Adam Smith subscribes to more or less the same argument. When women act like aldermen's wives, with their "enviously competitive vanity," men laugh at their pettiness; when men act in the same way (*TMS*, p. 57), they are keeping commercial society going and thus promoting their own moral improvement even if they don't know it. When women ape fashions, men rail against them or mock them or humor them; when men ape fashions, they are unknowingly strengthening "the peace and order of society."[193] The "insatiable desires" of women are the constant theme of moralists who condemn the sex for lewdness and license; when men exhibit "insatiable desires," their own capacity for good is awakened without their knowing it. Men promote the greater good most effectively when they give it no thought. Indeed, if they once became conscious, if they once perceived the nothingness of their pursuits,[194] society would fall. So carefully does Adam Smith prop up the dignity of men that their most "feminine" failing—the utter frivolity of their pursuits—saves them.

Similarly in Kant: thanks to Nature, the very traits that would seem to disqualify men for citizenship in Kant's republic—their deficit of reason, their appetitive ways—serve to ready men to take their place eventually in that republic. On this view, men aren't men so much as unruly children who require time and education to grow into the full possession of their abilities—wards of history. Or perhaps they are like women, whom we have come to associate with children ("women and children") and who had long been assigned a lack of reason and inferior moral status. But if women's vices, like "enviously competitive vanity," were thought to disqualify them for the public realm, men's vices seem rather to qualify them to act out the ingenious comedy scripted by Nature for the world's stage. ("In descanting on the folly of the [female] sex," writes Mary Wollstonecraft, "let [man] not overlook his own.")[195] In Adam Smith, as we have seen, fools and fops play out their parts daily in the social theater, competing "to be observed, to be attended to" (*TMS*, p. 50). All this vanity works out for the best, however. Men are corrupted for their own good. The same worship of the rich that corrupts moral sentiments secures "the order of society" (*TMS*, p. 61).

By a sort of twist in the plot, then, Nature in both Kant and Adam Smith has made the vanity and blindness of men work for them and not against them. Prompted by Nature, men contrive (says Kant) to "arrange [things] in such a way that their self-seeking energies are opposed to one another, each thereby neutralising or eliminating the destructive effects of the rest. And as far as reason is concerned, the result is the same as if man's selfish tendencies were non-existent, so that man, even if he is not morally good in himself, is nevertheless compelled to be a good citizen."[196] In America, Madison proposed to play interest against interest in order to secure the polity against the dangers of faction itself, as Adam Smith envisioned religious sects canceling one another out.[197] Kant theorizes similarly, but without much close argument, that a well-wrought constitution will turn men's moral blindness to the service of good. As one might support a toddler learning to walk, so Nature has provided for man to act as though he were virtuous even when he is not morally freestanding. Nature "guarantee[s] that what man *ought* to do by the laws of his freedom (but does not) will in fact be done . . . *without* the free agency of man."[198] Lacking as yet the capacity to direct their actions to moral ends, men resemble women, who were also seen as not being their own masters, hence as needing a master. In his essay "What Is Enlightenment?" Kant forcefully makes the point that as yet men are lifelong children, unable to exercise their reason for themselves, much as though they shared the famous incompetence of women. His vision of gradual progress implies, however, that a republican constitution will accustom men to virtue, until by long habituation they really become citizens and grow into the moral agency they don't at present possess.

Kant holds that man is a progressive being, which implies that in time he can learn to act autonomously (or more nearly so), that is, in accordance with the sacred dictates of duty.

> . . . No idea can so greatly elevate the human mind and inspire it with such enthusiasm as that of a pure moral conviction, respecting duty above all else, struggling with countless evils of existence and even with the most seductive temptations, and yet overcoming them—for we may rightly assume that man can do so. That man is aware that he can do this just because he ought to discloses within him an ample store of divine capabilities and inspires him, so to speak, with a holy awe at the greatness and sublimity of his true vocation.[199]

So autonomy is ours in prospect. We struggle toward that condition in which the moral will is self-determining, subject to nothing but rationality itself.[200] For the present, the heroic image of male self-command—Miltonic resistance to "the most seductive temptations"—not only inspires us but draws our eyes away from the sorry spectacle of men as they are, paltry beings not the masters of themselves. As we have seen, Adam Smith, similarly, employs an idiom of self-command from the august tradition of positive liberty to make up for the actual deficit of autonomy and reason in a social universe where men expend themselves in the pursuit of false goods.

If Kant contends that men are capable of outgrowing their lack of self-determination and assuming the stature of moral agents, Mary Wollstonecraft claims the same of women, with this difference, that women's capacity for growth is being forcibly held back. One argument was open to Mary Wollstonecraft that she did not use in the *Vindication of the Rights of Woman:* men's pretended superiority to women is simply a lie, men being, as Kant says, mired in "immaturity," unable "to use [their] own understanding without the guidance of another"[201]—men being their own image of women. Says Kant, immaturity "has become almost second nature to [man]. He has even grown fond of it and is really incapable for the time being of using his own understanding, because he was never allowed to make the attempt."[202] "For the time being": that qualification saves the dignity of men, who otherwise would appear, like women, to be condemned to perpetual immaturity. There is no mistaking the correspondence between Kant's picture of men in leading-strings and the picture of women in leading-strings in Mary Wollstonecraft's *Vindication of the Rights of Woman,* a work written in that spirit of audacity and duty— contempt for hereditary prejudice and loyalty to the project of human freedom—that Kant identifies with the Enlightenment. Not yet having grown into their rationality, not yet able to stand on their own in a republic, not yet able to get rid of privilege and prejudice, still dependent on the hidden hand of Nature to guide them—men are in leading-strings themselves: so Mary Wollstonecraft might have argued. Indeed *The Theory of Moral Sentiments,* which she read, makes a point of men's weak reason and prejudice in favor of the mighty. In the *Moral Sentiments,* the new ideology of commerce is supported as it toddles by the ancient language of stoicism.

If an Invisible Hand keeps things in order as men seek their own advantage, sympathy serves in *The Theory of Moral Sentiments* as an Invisible Band linking men at an emotional level and relieving some of the destructive effects of individualism. And I want to say that the passive response of sympathy on which Adam Smith's moral theory is based likens men to women, who were long idealized as perfectly passive and are thought by some to this day to possess a special sense of sympathy, in contrast to men.[203] Without intending to derogate from the dignity of men, and certainly without intending to loosen traditional gender distinctions, Adam Smith used a model of sympathy that hints at men's lack of inner direction. Ironically, cultists of stoicism might even have found the sympathy model effeminating, for it was a stoic teaching that we need not feel the misery of others in order to remedy it, that indeed to bathe in the afflictions of others is a kind of effeminacy: "Must we be guilty of effeminacy, to perform Acts of Generosity? Can we not be charitable without being afflicted? And can we not relieve those that are in misery, unless we mingle our Sighs with their Sobs and Groans, and our Cries with their Tears?"[204]

Adam Smith's model of mingled sobs, of a sympathetic spectator who "derive[s] sorrow from the sorrow of others" (*TMS*, p. 9), so nearly feminizes men that the author at once balances it with stoicism. He claims the spectator's tendency to enter into the actor's passions is met on the other side by the actor's manly efforts to keep his passions down to a decent level—by self-command.[205] The mingled-sob model hints at the small role of reason in human affairs and in turn perhaps at men's doubtful qualifications for the tasks of government, as though they secretly partook of some of the loudly proclaimed debilities of women. In *The Theory of Moral Sentiments* "self-government" (*TMS*, p. 23) simply refers to composing one's passions for presentation to society. It means proper behavior. It has nothing to do with self-government in any political sense. It does not refer to citizens who both rule and are ruled. Such is the author's distrust of political strife that in spite of his generally republican sentiments, "self-government" is perfectly without political meaning in the *Moral Sentiments*.

If "self-government" in Smithian theory is nonpolitical, sympathy is a kind of natural, nonpolitical force as basic as gravity or, in the human realm, mother-love. *The Theory of Moral Sentiments* begins, as though at the level of first principles, with an analysis of a sympathy swifter than the workings of reason, wiser than our conscious decisions, and infinitely more healing than argument. The sympathetic spectator is something like the good wife who sorrows when her husband sorrows and delights when he delights: "How amiable does he appear to be, whose sympathetic heart seems to re-echo all the sentiments of those with whom he converses, who grieves for their calamities, who resents their injuries, and who rejoices at their good fortune!" (*TMS*, p. 24).

As Terry Eagleton observes, bourgeois society gives rise to the ideal of a precious "community of feeling," presumably to powder over the blots of "class division and market competition."[206] The sphere of "higher" feelings and spectatorship Eagleton calls the aesthetic. We might also call it the domestic. In theory the domestic sphere shelters all the finer feelings that have no place out of doors, in the strife of a competitive world. (The fullest expression of this ideal would of course be the Victorian cult of the home.) And though inside the domestic sphere, the wife accompanies her husband in spirit, radiating a healing sympathy: she is the sympathetic spectator. Repeatedly Adam Smith speaks of the sympathetic spectator "bringing the case home" (e.g., *TMS*, p. 10), his very choice of words setting up a connection between a beneficent sympathy and the domestic sphere. If as sympathetic spectators we involuntarily imitate (so that when we gaze "at a dancer on the slack rope, [we] naturally writhe and twist" [*TMS*, p. 10]), the Victorian mother was said to elicit the "unconscious imitation" of the child it was her sacred trust to educate; the moral level of society depended on her performing her educative work, which in turn depended on her ability to train the imitative habits of the child. Thus the unreflecting responses and habitual sympathies of the Smithian moral universe become the "unconscious imitation" and habits of sentiment of the Victorian domestic ideal.[207] Indeed, in Smith's own time, the influential James Fordyce preached that the good mother will teach by example rather than precept, "insinuate" rather than lecture. Skillful "in moulding the behaviour [of her children] without constraint,"[208] she is like an invisible hand.

The idealization of "influence" and "sympathy" implies that these deeper-than-rational forces are somehow wiser than our conscious deliberations and certainly to be preferred to the discords of politics; the sweet constraints of influence are better than those clashes of opinion which theorists of improvement, from Locke on, hoped to defuse. We can't be argued out of our opinions, but we can be conquered by sweetness. The literary equivalent of this principle is the maxim, current during the life of Adam Smith, that readers respond to lovely examples, not harsh precepts; hence the best novels are said to work "insensibly" on the minds of readers,[209] much as the accumulation of capital, also proceeding insensibly (or irresistibly, like gravity), improves society more profoundly than any model or design of human contrivance. The Smithian theory of social relations projects men who are much better at yielding to customary responses and binding influences than at making conscious political decisions—men with something like the supposed civic disqualifications of women. In the theory of Adam Smith, "improvement" comes about far less as a result of conscious political decisions than of the steady accumulation of capital, the advance of manners, and the deepening of sympathy. Perhaps the first two will do; though unsocial, the prudent man advances society by his industrious habits and correct manners.

If "improvement" is the name for the quieting, the even-ing out of men's passions, it was women who came to be understood as the improvers and soothers of men. Before Adam Smith's time, Addison had written that "Women were formed to temper Mankind, and sooth them into Tenderness and Compassion."[210] Yet that is the very task Addison sets himself in his *Spectator* papers, to temper and soothe, to "asswage private Inflamations, [and] allay publick Ferments."[211] I bring up Addison because his *Spectator* stands behind that Smithian construct, the spectator,[212] but also because Addison's role of calming the passions excited by politics, and shedding grace and healing influence onto the world, prepares us for Adam Smith's dislike of ill-composed passions and depreciation of the public sphere and almost all men's fitness for it. According to Marilyn Butler, the most characteristic figure of the age of sensibility was "the sensitive observer"—a man "helpless" to shape the course of events.[213] Adam Smith's sympathetic spectator belongs to this line (sympathy being a helpless response in the final analysis), as the stoic principle of bearing well what you can't change offers, perhaps, philosophical solace in the face of man's small power to change things, his dubious abilities as an intentional political agent.

The sympathetic spectator looks forward to one of those women beatified by the Victorians—women who feel with others and radiate blessed influences into the world. Where the sympathetic spectator in *The Theory of Moral Sentiments* prompts us to subdue our unruly passions to the level required by civility, the sympathetic woman of Victorian lore performs a civilizing function too, shedding her sweet influence over a rough and ill-civilized world. Where the sympathetic spectator calms and improves us, the domestic woman heals "hard and rancorous feelings, engendered by political strife."[214] Where the sympathetic spectator personifies "the soft, the gentle, the amiable virtues" (*TMS*, p. 23), the Victorian Angel was celebrated for the same graces. Where

Adam Smith concludes that "to feel much for others and little for ourselves, that to restrain our selfish, and indulge our benevolent affections, constitutes the perfection of human nature" (*TMS,* p. 25), many a Victorian woman was taught not merely to feel but to live for others. Where Adam Smith's spectator serves as a kind of external conscience, the virtuous Victorian wife was idealized as a "humble monitress" whose good influence accompanied her man "like a kind of second conscience."[215] Where it was said to be the high privilege of the Victorian woman to enjoy "the honors of office, without feeling its cares, and the glory of victory, without suffering the dangers of the battle,"[216] the effect of the moral theory of Adam Smith is to transfer some of the prestige of the classical virtues to conduct that takes place not in the forum or the field of war but in the social theater.

When Smith remarks that "the delicate sensibility required in civilized nations sometimes destroys the masculine firmness of the character" (*TMS,* p. 209), he could almost be commenting on the tendency of his own moral theory model to make men over in the image of a conventionally virtuous woman—a figure who keeps strictly within the bounds of propriety, prefers sweetness to strife, and especially avoids public contention. If, as Joseph Addison says, "Women were formed to temper Mankind," Smith's model of the tempering of the passions feminizes mankind. In order to impart masculine firmness to his doctrine, he resorts, as we have seen, to a sentimental stoicism whose counsels of resignation idealize the withdrawal from political life and encourage the practice of keeping in your own sphere (minding your business). While Adam Smith's stoic principles ridicule the efforts of the poor man's son to better his station, they nevertheless commend the life of patient labor. While they celebrate deeds of magnanimity, they nevertheless vindicate a quiet life concerned with little things. Stoicism enables the author both to criticize and to justify the commercial way of life. For he did both. He indicted the present distribution of wealth as grossly unfair,[217] for example, but defended the distinction of ranks as a wise and natural arrangement.

Smith was alive to issues of fair play, and maybe if he had founded *The Theory of Moral Sentiments* on the principle of reciprocity, rather than on the principle of reciprocal sentiments (heart beating to heart), he would have done away with the traditional double standard as simply unfair. The change I am hypothesizing—fair play as between men and women—is not so historically farfetched as it appears. It was proposed by Mary Wollstonecraft, whose *Vindication of the Rights of Woman,* appearing two years after the last edition of *The Theory of Moral Sentiments,* cites that "acute observer," that "grave philosophical reasoner," Adam Smith.[218] For the purposes of Mary Wollstonecraft, Adam Smith's steady views made him a good choice to offset the febrile Rousseau. And she thought she saw in Adam Smith an indictment of an effeminate aristocracy which she could turn to use in her own argument that women were being corrupted like the rich.

Mary Wollstonecraft claims that when Adam Smith wrote, "To be observed, to be attended to, to be taken notice of with sympathy, complacency, and approbation, are all the advantages which we can propose to derive from [bettering our condition]" (*TMS,* p. 50), he was referring to the vanity of the rich. (Indeed she misquotes Smith as writing "they," not "we" propose to derive advantages.) She is wrong. The passage in question, where Smith names vanity—a vice indelibly associated with women—as the master motive of human striving, plainly refers to "all the different ranks of men." (Evidently Mary Wollstonecraft did not want to consider that the values of the class "in the most natural state" were just as trifling and inauthentic, just as theatrical as those of the rich.[219] Nor did Smith himself relish the thought.) The passage does not refer to an effeminate aristocracy, although it does implicitly cast the would-be aristocrats of the middle class as effeminate. The rhetoric of stoicism serves to dispel the suggestions of effeminacy raised by the highly polarized language of gender still informing *The Theory of Moral Sentiments.*

The author of a magisterial study of civic humanism, J. G. A. Pocock, has argued that the image of the classical citizen suffered with the rise of commercial society. The classical citizen comes to seem rude and harsh as against the man of polished taste; comes to seem wedded to a backward ideal of autonomy as against the modern who benefits from the minute division of labor. From the point of view of a modern who knows his dependence on others for goods and services, the ancient citizen ("master of his land, family and arms")[220] has carried independence to the point of obsession. If the classical citizen acts in his own person, the modern is perhaps little inclined either to take part in public business or to take up arms. (Thus Adam Ferguson's insistence on the need for a militia to restore public spirit.)

This is a highly schematic diagram, of course, and we may expect a figure as richly interesting as Adam Smith to have double loyalties in the debate. Certainly Smith is the great exponent of the division of labor, and yet we detect a note of distaste in his description of the prudent man who accepts a political division of labor and leaves it to others to fulfill his public responsibilities rather than acting in his own person. This characteristic modern is a shirker:

> [He] would be much better pleased that the public business were well managed by some other person, than that he himself should have the trouble, and incur the responsibility, of managing it. In the bottom of his heart he would prefer the undisturbed enjoyment of secure tranquillity, not only to all the vain splendour of successful ambition, but to the real and solid glory of performing the greatest and most magnanimous actions. (*TMS*, p. 216)

The antique tenor of these last words suggests that Adam Smith is not ready to bury the ideal of the man who acts in his own person, not ready to proclaim the pusillanimous man. The same antique tone suggests that the author has not really found a basis for male autonomy beyond the rude old model of the master of land and family.

According to Pocock, liberal ideology rises in response to civic humanism and its harsh ideal of the armed freeholder. On this reading, liberalism speaks for politeness and civility in contrast to an uncouth "virtue," modern ease in contrast to ancient discipline and deprivation. "With the growth of trade and more complex exchange relationships," the story goes, "manners began to be softened and passions refined, [and] *le doux commerce* made its appearance."[221] With his searching analysis of the division of labor, his pronouncements on taste, his description of the sweetening of manners as men are fashioned in the image of gentle commerce, Adam Smith clearly answers to what Pocock calls the liberal paradigm. And yet that is only about half the truth, for if stoic principles belong, as Pocock says, to the civic-humanist paradigm,[222] stoic philosophy itself is "the primary influence on Smith's ethical thought."[223] Presumably the liberal ideology of sweetened men seemed sugar-watery to Adam Smith, for all of its usefulness, and presumably it lacked the nobility of the old school of thought, for his own words show Adam Smith as being less willing to break with classical humanism than the model of a decisive shift would lead us to believe.[224] When Adam Smith goes from the language of taste to the language of fortitude and self-command, he is not only infusing the new man with something like ancient virtue—not only dignifying the characteristically modern seclusion in private life with overtones of stoic with-drawal—but working within two rival paradigms competing for the loyalty of men of learning and affairs. Adam Smith's fixated language of fortitude and valor (language like "the real and solid glory of performing the greatest and most magnanimous actions") reflects the fixation of the liberal paradigm on its antagonist.

The civic and commercial ideologies struggled "at least down to the lifetimes of Adam Smith and John Millar," writes Pocock;[225] they struggle within the thought of Adam Smith, too. Similarly, we might say that in his contempt for luxury and his defense of a way of life built on the production and consumption of luxury goods, Adam Smith participates not only in the quarrel between ancients and moderns, but in the quarrel between two ancient styles of thought: the Ovidian style that welcomes luxury, sophis-tication, and the improvement of bare nature, and the Juvenalian style that sees all such adornment as corrupt and ruinous to manly simplicity.[226]

In a sense, the Scottish Enlightenment represented by Adam Smith spoke for improvement and refinement as against the retro-grade simplicity of the Juvenalian ideal. Schematically speaking, the Scots

> replaced the *polis* by politeness, the *oikos* by the economy. In place of the classical citizen, master of his land, family and arms, practising an austerely virtuous equality with his no less independent peers, appeared a fluid, histor-ical and transactional vision of *homo faber et mercator,* shaping himself through the stages of history by means of the division and specialization of labour, the diversification and refinement of the passions. The political image of man was replaced by a social and transactional image of man.[227]

This transactional figure being not a man of commerce as such but the Smithian man whose emotions respond to those of others. In theory, the classical value of independence and political person-ality belonged to a surpassed phase of history, and however noble the ideal of public spirit was, it "was not clear . . . that Lycurgus or Plato, Diogenes or Cato were figures to whom one should look back with overwhelming nostalgia. . . . [T]hey lacked politeness."[228] They were too Juvenalian.

And yet Adam Smith himself elegizes Cato in the *Theory of Moral Sentiments*:

> Cato, surrounded on all sides by his enemies, unable to resist them, disdaining to submit to them, and reduced, by the proud maxims of that age, to the necessity of destroying himself; yet never shrinking from his misfortunes, never supplicating with the lamentable voice of wretchedness, those miserable sympathetic tears which we are always so unwilling to give; but on the contrary, arming himself with manly fortitude, and the moment before he executes his fatal resolution, giving, with his usual tranquillity, all necessary orders for the safety of his friends; appears to Seneca, that great preacher of insensibility, a spectacle which even the gods themselves might behold with pleasure and admiration.[229] (*TMS*, p. 48)

It is somehow fitting that Cato, identified with the lost cause of republicanism, should be thus memorialized in a work of moral philosophy that reluctantly antiquates republican values in the name of new bywords like "trade" and "sympathy." There is something else of note in this homage to Cato: its purely honorific value. As stoicism teaches us "to aim at a perfection altogether beyond the reach of human nature" (*TMS*, p. 60n.), so Cato seems to belong among the gods. Human life as we know it is conducted along different lines. In practical terms, Adam Smith's homage to Cato changes nothing at all. He eulogizes Cato, who inveighed against luxury in the name of reason, in a work questioning the role of reason in human affairs and defending a way of life distinguished by an ever-expanding market for luxury goods. As though to underscore the point that Cato is to be contemplated with elegiac reverence but is not otherwise to have effect, Adam Smith later censures the practice of suicide (*TMS*, p. 287). The noblest of the republicans, performing the ultimate act of self-mastery, becomes a kind of fine irrelevance—an aesthetic object to elevate our minds. As an icon of "courage, self-control and public spirit," Cato helps to offset the lack of these masculine virtues in the social actor; at the same time, the loftiness of Adam Smith's language serves to raise the figure of Cato well above the kind of party wrangling in which he had been caught earlier in the century.[230] At one stroke, then, Adam Smith infuses traditional manhood into his argument and creates an elegiac mood in which political passions are hushed.

The case of Cato symbolizes the role of stoicism in *The Theory of Moral Sentiments*. By importing stoic language from a tradition whose "male bias . . . bordered on the absolute,"[231] Adam Smith was able to invest the polite male of commercial society with some of the dignity of the classical citizen, even while the modern goes about his business unaware that any such tradition as civic humanism ever existed; and so, ironically, stoicism fulfills its function of leaving things alone—of "noninterference." Stoicism is an especially apt choice to perform this ennobling role because its counsels of quietude bestow a certain dignity on the male who attends to his own concerns as though in observance of the stoic principle that "every man . . . is first and principally recommended to his own care" (*TMS*, p. 219). What the twilight republicanism of *The Theory of Moral Sentiments* obscures is that with the antiquating of the classical ideal of political personality, men had lost the one culturally authoritative model of themselves as actors in public life; thus men in *The Theory of Moral Sentiments* resemble women, shut out of the public world. If politics is a way of arguing out practices, Adam Smith prefers to entrust decisions not to politics but to the habitual sympathies and aversions of people—what John Stuart Mill would call the mere "likings and dislikings of society."[232]

If "empathy" is "culturally associated with women,"[233] Adam Smith's moral theory is founded on sympathy, which is about what we mean by empathy. If, as Mary Wollstonecraft argued, it is the paramount desire of women to be observed and admired,[234] if the craving for admiration was thought to be the characteristic female vice,[235] Adam Smith imputes this desire to men. If Pope's vainglorious Belinda tries to win "not love itself but the social status that comes from being admired,"[236] Adam Smith remarks explicitly that men slave to earn not wealth as such but the admiration that attends wealth. If women were taught good behavior and pleasing manners, isn't this the better part of virtue in the moral theory of Adam Smith? If according to Bentham a woman's affection doesn't extend to distant others,[237] Adam Smith says of men that it is right and proper that their affectionate concern doesn't extend to distant others, adding that every man is "much more deeply interested in whatever immediately concerns himself, than in what concerns any other man" (*TMS*, p. 83).[238] If women were deemed to be created to act within a small sphere, Smith's friend Hume finds that men are fitted to act only within a small sphere— and that we approve of the man who is "serviceable and useful within his sphere," a description that almost sounds like the domestic woman of the Victorians, and that Adam Smith himself might have written.[239] If women were seen as trifling and frivolous, prosperity itself demanded a society "trifling enough, but also rich and inventive enough, to bother about changing colours, materials and styles of costumes,"[240] matters traditionally associated with women and their love of show. If we have been taught to think of women as followers of fashion, Adam Smith depicts a social order in which the rich are worshiped "on the basis of taste and fashion rather than upon more substantial grounds."[241] And if women were thought to be unself-governing, lacking in autonomy and reason, where is the autonomy of men who trust to an Invisible Hand to steer their actions to ends they never intended? Ordinarily we act in self-interest (leaving it to the Hand to turn our action to the general good), but often virtue requires that we subordinate our interest to that of others. What is it, Adam Smith asks, that gives one the strength to do this? Not "the soft power of humanity," he answers, but the masculine principle, or what he calls "the man within" (*TMS*, p. 137). It is the man within who impresses us with the "love of what is honourable and noble, of the grandeur, and dignity, and superiority of our own characters" (*TMS*, p. 137). Thus the language of Roman manhood performs its ennobling mission—that of settling the male self on more substantial grounds—and men are left to pride themselves on the imaginary superiority of their characters to women's.[242]

It has been said that Hume "seeks in vain for a sure standard in anything. Knowledge, belief, ethics: all these have now been remorselessly 'feminized,' converted one by one to feeling, imagination, intuition."[243] Adam Smith completes the job and feminizes men themselves. They become creatures of feeling (exquisite sensibility), imagination (the spellbound brain of the poor man's son), intuition (sympathy, a sixth sense). And by means of the antique language of stoicism, Adam Smith preserves the illusion that the "sure standard" of male virtue still exists.

CHAPTER 3

Clashes of Opinion

A hundred years ago scholars in Germany identified "the Adam Smith problem," to wit the supposed inconsistency between the *Wealth of Nations,* with its defense of self-interest, and *The Theory of Moral Sentiments,* with its derivation of morality from the principle of sympathy. Self-interest and sympathy seem like contrary motives. Today the consensus is that no such Adam Smith problem exists. The author himself perceived no conflict between *The Theory of Moral Sentiments* (first edition, 1759) and the *Wealth of Nations* (1776), nor did he retract the former work upon the publication of the latter; indeed *The Theory of Moral Sentiments* itself grants legitimacy to self-interest, while conceding that this motive does not inspire the greatest actions, those "of the most heroic magnanimity and most extensive benevolence" (*TMS,* p. 293). "Regard to our own private happiness and interest . . . appear [sic] upon many occasions very laudable principles of action" (*TMS,* p. 304). The editors of the Glasgow edition of *The Theory of Moral Sentiments* conclude that Smith's two great works "complement each other."[1] If, as Joseph Addison says, trade "knits Mankind together,"[2] then it resembles sympathy, which performs the same office; a London merchant had once written, "traffic [trade] breeds affection."[3] And so believed Adam Smith.

As hard as it may be for us in the twentieth century to credit, Smith actually considered commerce a force for kindliness. "Commerce . . . ought naturally to be, among nations, as among individuals, a bond of union and friendship."[4] Indeed the thinkers of the Scottish Enlightenment, themselves knit together by bonds of intellectual sympathy, to some degree substituted an Addisonian image of man, as tasteful and sociable, for the uncouth figure of the classical citizen.[5] And as I have tried to show, the prudent man whose small virtues steadily—irresistibly—advance the wealth of the nation and the improvement of society, corresponds to the dutiful wife habitually performing the small duties of sympathy, exerting an improving influence not to be resisted. If in theory the domestic woman, that icon of sympathy, carries out her "lofty mission" within her "limited sphere," the prudent man carries out his historic role by religiously attending to his own business.[6]

Benjamin Franklin exhorted men who did not agree on points of religion to dedicate themselves with religious attention to their own "improvement." Thus they would be able to live fruitfully with one another without belonging to a single orthodoxy. Out of their differences would come the "philosophical good temper and moderation" that Adam Smith thought would result, and in Pennsylvania already had resulted, from tolerance.[7] Smith's idealization of conformity—"perfect concord" between spectator and actor (*TMS*, p. 16)—can be seen, similarly, as part of an agenda for trimming the power of the state and trusting mostly to social mechanisms and the laws of the marketplace to bring about "improvement." (A community of hearts is also a prettier thing to contemplate than a community of merchants with constricted views and a pharisaical respect for social rules.) From this point of view, *The Theory of Moral Sentiments,* far from contradicting the *Wealth of Nations,* sets forth those "natural" laws of action and passion that rule the social universe in a beneficent way, just as supply and demand rule the marketplace. As prices are now too high and now too low but generally seek and find their natural level, so emotions run too high or too low but tend to converge on the point of propriety (a point not discoverable by abstract speculation, but only by empirical observation and social experience). For Adam Smith seems to have believed that permitting men to act in their own interests would not decivilize them but on the contrary improve them—accustom them to the habits of moderation. Commerce, it seems, is a civilizing force. Before I act in my own interest, I learn that however vital my own good seems to me, it seems vastly less so to others. I act, then, with a chastened sense of the insignificance of my claims and with an exquisite awareness of others' judgments of me.

The Autonomous Male of Adam Smith

If "the Adam Smith problem" is framed as the inconsistency between the sympathy-principle of *The Theory of Moral Sentiments* and the profit-principle of the *Wealth of Nations,* the conflict is dissolved by that sentimentalization of the benefits of trade, that affirmation of the improving effects of a market civilization, which characterized the eighteenth-century ideology of commerce. Commerce improves men. By making them more interdependent, it makes them more sociable. "One of the principal reasons Smith favored the expansion of commerce was that by exposing men to the constant scrutiny of his [sic] neighbors [the] habit of subordinating the impulse of passion to the sentiments of others would be enhanced."[8] Perhaps passion can be "subordinated" out of existence, as seems to be happening in the case of the prudent man (*TMS,* p. 214), but Adam Smith would still defend the civilizing effects of commerce. On his terms, the profit-principle doesn't conflict with the sympathy-principle, but perhaps actually "enhances" it. Yet it seems to me that other Adam Smith problems exist, for example, the problem of how a man filled with contempt for wealth and status should have certified a commercial way of life in which, on his own showing, people strive for these things above all. Adam Smith's disdain for the scramble for happiness; his caustic view of social climbing; his lament over "the corruption of our moral sentiments" caused by the worship of the rich (*TMS,* p. 61); indeed his animosity toward merchants—such attitudes as these do not make for a very hearty and positive endorsement of the commercial way of life.

"It is notorious," write Istvan Hont and Michael Ignatieff,

> from his contemptuous references in the *Wealth of Nations* to the medieval lord's fascination for the "baubles and trinkets" of trade goods, and from his sardonic strictures in the *Theory of Moral Sentiments* on men's passion for accumulating objects of "frivolous utility," that [Adam Smith] believed material prosperity was purchased, more often than not, at the price of a measure of what he himself called "deception." At first sight, it is not an easy task to reconcile his evident distaste for the vulgar materialism of the "great scramble" of commercial society with his clear endorsement of economic growth.[9]

Not only at first sight. Adam Smith regards the bustle of the commercial way of life with a good measure of stoic dispassion, of ironic reserve. Another way to frame the Adam Smith problem I have isolated is, How is it that the language of stoicism informs

Adam Smith's analysis of moral life if he believed that stoicism belonged to a backward era characterized by poverty and slave-holding—that if we were to adopt stoicism, we would be consigning ourselves to a dungeon of "egalitarian barbarism"?[10] Stoicism can play only an honorific rule in *The Theory of Moral Sentiments* because if it were actually put into effect, humanity would sink to a lower plane. Modern society must proceed, regardless of stoicism. Thus Adam Smith diverts some of the prestige of stoic principles onto modern practices like frugality and industry,[11] even though the anxiety and the itch to get ahead that account for commercial activity cannot in truth be reconciled with stoicism. The stoic idiom of self-command, I find, serves *both* to index the author's scorn for the trumpery of wealth and status *and* to lend some moral authority to the life of hard work and self-denial, thereby saving the pursuit of happiness from disrepute and even dignifying it to a good degree. Adam Smith's effort to transfuse the masculine values of antiquity into the modern social actor is thus an awkward one. I believe he was led to make the attempt in the first place by the prospect that all the conformity, emulation, and desire for false goods written into his socioeconomic model would corrupt the self.

The prudent man is portrayed by Adam Smith as a rather petty conformist. Conformism, it seems, is prudent, useful, serving perhaps to paper over differences between parties who are not so much at one with each other as the language of sentimentality implies. (Thus Smith suggests that prudential behavior covers a lack of real social feeling, while J. S. Mill alleges that his prudential contemporaries conform not because they really believe the same old truths but because they do not.) Smith himself makes use of conformism in his moral theory, but his model of men as imitators styling their behavior to social rules, mimicking the corruption of others, so evidently threatens the standing of the self that he turns for relief to the stoic, sublimely indifferent to others. As a corrective to the social actor who adapts to the world, he invokes the legendary figure of the stoic who despises it. Thus his language moves back and forth between descriptions of minute conformism and monumental indifference. Missing is a third possibility: the agent who neither conforms sweetly to others, nor ignores others, but *argues,* as the author himself did so well in the *Wealth of Nations:* the political person. Wary as he was of faction, and dubious as he was of our ability to act as intentional political agents, Adam Smith in effect discourages political argument. The language of stoic disengagement enables Smith all at once to close off the active or political life; to channel men into the life of acquiescence and copying (for between modern sociability and a stony austerity is no choice at all); and nevertheless to dignify the male character as being more capable than that of women, even if the latter too are instructed to conform, to please, and to stay out of public affairs. [12]

The source of rightness in Adam Smith's moral universe is not the Bible or God's will or reason, but others—society. While in special cases one may appeal against social usages to natural principles of right (as Smith himself did when he argued against accepted practices like the regulation of apprentices), social usages remain in general the norm. [13] As a rule, right is what society, or good society, commends as right. I act right if I act in such a way that a spectator standing in for society in general commends me. Being sociable and wishing to please by nature, I fashion my conduct to the specifications of others. Because onlookers "cannot be expected to sympathize" with the urges of my body, I learn to keep them in check and not act them out (*TMS*, p. 27)—an example of that close watch over the "affects" of which Norbert Elias is a historian. [14] Indeed, not falling on one's food is the very model of moral conduct in *The Theory of Moral Sentiments*—such is the author's emphasis on sheer seemliness. A "keen and earnest attention to the propriety of our own conduct . . . constitutes the real essence of virtue" (*TMS*, p. 244).

In the rest of my conduct I follow the same principles as I do over my soup, carefully avoiding what gives displeasure or offense to a spectator, conducting myself in such a way that others find themselves "in perfect concord" with me (*TMS*, p. 16). If I cheat to advance my interests, "the indulgence of the spectators is entirely at an end" (*TMS*, p. 83); therefore, I do not cheat. Society is averse to cheating, and I respect the preferences and aversions of society. Not all preferences and aversions are so honorable, however. Society may be averse to Jews. Using the Smithian language of sympathy and the Burkean language of prejudice, Charles Lamb avowed his aversion toward that people: "I am . . . a bundle of prejudices—made up of likings and dislikings—the veriest thrall to sympathies, apathies, antipathies. . . . Old prejudices cling about me. I cannot shake off the story of Hugh of Lincoln [the libel that Jews ritually steal and kill Christian children]. . . . A Hebrew is nowhere congenial to me."[15] Here we get a sense of the dark side of the irrationalism that flows from Burke and Smith. In our own time H. L. A. Hart has exposed the menacing implications of the antirational claim that if the man in the Clapham bus, standing in for society—the Smithian spectator of the twentieth century—is moved to indignation or disgust at this or that, no argument can be made against him.[16] As I have said, there is a distinct antirational strain in Smith himself, just as Smithian theory opposes political rationalists like Mary Wollstonecraft, who defied certain norms of the community out loud. If society ordains the subordination of women, then in theory Smithian man believes in the subordination of women. Falling in with others gains him the "approbation" he craves as a sociable creature, and besides, if society, the determiner of right, believes in x, x is right. Richardson's Clarissa knows that rectitude depends strictly on "the inner intention of the believer," but that commercial society judges by outcomes, not intentions.[17] Adam Smith speaks for that society, for he agrees with its irrational verdict that rape "dishonours" the victim, no matter how innocent she may be (*TMS*, p. 332).[18]

The other-directed man may have been a discovery of the mid-twentieth century, but he was already written into one of the foundational texts of capitalism, *The Theory of Moral Sentiments*. For if Smithian man insisted on judging for himself, he would be too much like those Puritans who stressed rectitude of intention—and shook the state. Private judgment would make him too much like the Puritans (zealots to Smith), who claimed inner light. In Smithian man, therefore, all that is left of Puritanism is the religious avoidance of giving displeasure. Smith knew perfectly well that society's right and wrong may be nothing better than "rooted prejudices" (*TMS*, p. 233), but contending against those prejudices, as did Mary Wollstonecraft, using the same phrase as Smith[19]—as did Wordsworth, who deliberately affronted the prejudice in favor of sublime subjects[20]—has virtually no place in his theory of the well-lived life. "A man who challenges the 'group mind' and puts individual preferences before social norms will find himself an outsider, properly rejected by a society whose standards of propriety he has rejected."[21] Adam Smith's social actor does not challenge the spectator. He appeals to a higher spectator instead.

Apparently, after the publication of the first edition of the *Moral Sentiments* in 1759, a correspondent objected that if society determines right, then conscience, the voice of right, can never take issue with prevailing opinion; yet in point of fact conscience may with good reason take issue with prevailing opinion. Prevailing opinion may be mistaken, even corrupt (as Smith would concede in the last edition of the *Theory,* with its reference to the pervasive "corruption of our moral sentiments" [*TMS*, p. 61]). This argument impressed Adam Smith, prompting him to rarefy the spectator in the second edition and even to move toward the ideal of stoic indifference and insensibility, an ideal seemingly at the other pole from the man of feeling.[22]

Smith refines his spectatorial argument along these lines: We enter into the world with the "desire to please" (*TMS*, p. 129) and try to style our behavior to the wishes of those we depend on, but soon enough we learn that what pleases one person offends another. We learn that it is impossible to avoid crossing all people. Both as a way out of this bind and as an appeal from the "partial judgments" (*TMS*, p. 129) of those we offend, we turn to seeking the approval of an impartial or theoretical spectator rather than actual persons with all their biases and differences; the shift hints, perhaps, at the author's effort to abstract the ideal of sympathy from the intimate settings—confidential circles, clubs, private correspondence—in which it seems to flourish. Seeking the approval of real spectators, as real actors do, smacks of vanity,[23] a vice that society itself (the arbiter in all such matters) likes to associate with women and their falseness. A man sometimes courts compliments like a "woman who paints" (*TMS*, p. 115). Seeking the approval of the abstract spectator is open to no such imputation.

The abstract spectator Adam Smith likes to call "the man within" (e.g., *TMS*, p. 130); as his name suggests, he restores manhood to an agent who might otherwise have lost his moral standing to his love of "approbation." This point takes us right to a crux in the thought of Smith, for while there can be no doubt that he ranks the craving for "approbation" high in the order of human motives and that he ascribes genuine moral benefits to our wish to stand well with the world, still his stoic values pull in the other direction, and it is clear that at some level Smith thought so poorly of human beings as they are that he judged popular approval not worth seeking. A man of "real philosophy" knows that as long as he does what is right, "it is of little consequence though he be neither attended to, nor approved or" (*TMS*, p. 157). Not so much to be praised as to be praiseworthy is the desire of the virtuous man (*TMS*, p. 117). Of women Rousseau says the very opposite: "It is not enough that they be estimable; they must be esteemed."[24] Loving virtue for its own sake, Smith's man of stoic philosophy shows that he is no woman.

If the yearning to be admired like the rich corrupts our moral sentiments, the man within, speaking in the voice of "real philosophy," reminds us of the triviality and nothingness of human admiration. He gives us the fortitude to shut out the distorted judgments of the world—gives us something of the stoicism of the cellar. His verdicts outweigh all others': "if the man within condemns us, the loudest acclamations of mankind appear but as the noise of ignorance and folly" (*TMS*, p. 130). And so from being studious conformists and approval-seekers, we have become philosophers. Miraculously, all of the vanity, emulation, courting of favor—all of the "corruption of our moral sentiments" (*TMS*, p. 61)—built into Adam Smith's model of society vanishes, and there emerges a self-determining moral agent.

> To the extent that [a man] asserts that the habits promoted by the ethic of the middle ranks are approved not because they put one in mind of the way of life of the rich, but because they are right and just, to that extent he has also asserted the primacy of conscience over public opinion and rededicated himself to acting from a love of praiseworthiness and dread of blameworthiness.[25]

It seems that by becoming a really convinced conformist, the virtuous man proves himself superior to society. In other words, we are back to public opinion ("the ethic of the middle ranks"), now bronzed with a sort of Roman justification.

In the wondrous transformation from anxious copying to steady self-determination, nothing really has changed: stoicism changes nothing. The man within, that "demigod" (*TMS*, p. 131), is too much of a ghostly abstraction to be fully convincing.[26] Indeed, Adam Smith's more sociable view of men as courtiers of their own fellows, at once earnest to please, studious to conform, and keen for advantage—a view borne out by all those at the time who commented on the rage for emulation in a commercial society— runs right through *The Theory of Moral Sentiments* as though the "higher" view weren't there. Like Richardson's figure of male virtue, Sir Charles Grandison, who has been described as a fig- ment, a "nothing," the stoic seems to exist in absentia.[27] What is more, in his theoretically high disregard for the world, Adam Smith's moral agent leaves society just as it is. He leaves it to the corrupt pleasers, such as he himself once was. It would violate his philosophical composure to argue out his differences with soci- ety; morally speaking, he prefers the privacy of his cellar, or the society of intimates, to the clamor of voices in the public arena. The man within, speaking the language of stoicism, informs him that only his own virtue ought to concern him; the opinions of the world aren't worth fighting.[28] With his emphasis on etiquette and the seemly regulation of the passions, Adam Smith naturally dis- courages arguing in public (something seen as vulgar to this day), for arguments discompose our passions, especially in a time of "public discontent, faction and turmoil."[29] For all of the majestic virility of the man within, Adam Smith's theory scarcely allows for getting on one's feet and arguing—the essence of free political life. Significantly, Smith believed that the requisites of justice which he himself argued for could be secured in unfree states.[30]

I mean to say that Adam Smith's solution to the question left by the first edition of *The Theory of Moral Sentiments*—Can we never oppose the opinions of society?—is no solution at all. The social actor still agrees, and the man within is so ghostly, so idealized, that the world hardly knows he's there. In one sense, too, the sympathy of the social man and the apathy of the stoic work to the same effect. The bitter passions stirred by politics put the observer (the social man) out of sympathy; the stoic in his apathy subdues such passions in his own breast. In this respect sympathy and apathy both discourage political passions. Only so far do the so- cial man and the inner man differ. Although resonant, the lan- guage of the impartial spectator doesn't really modify the con- formism that was originally written into *The Theory of Moral Sentiments,* which is why I began this section by characterizing Adam Smith's theory as a morality of etiquette and imitation.

Wishing to please by nature, I seek the "approbation" of my

neighbor. What standard is to guide my conduct? My neighbor's. For this is what it means to act in such a way that others can go along with me, something Adam Smith often speaks of. But what standard is to guide my neighbor when it is his turn to act? His spectator's. And so on. In this way, the vital question of what is right and why gets passed down the line without ever receiving anything like a grounded answer; if the pattern of copying holds true, the question may never be posed. Adam Smith's own successor in the chair of moral philosophy at Glasgow, Thomas Reid, objected to Smith's attempt to resolve morality into conformity. Smith's moral theory, he claims, lacks "any Standard according to which either the Emotions of the Actor or the Sympathy of the Spectator is to be measured; all that is required is that they be in Harmony or Concord."[31] In our own century, Max Scheler has disputed Smith's notion that we take our right and wrong from others, arguing that at best it explains why witches came to believe the accusations against them.[32] (Hart argues convincingly that treating society's antipathies as a supreme law would condone the burning of witches.) It's ironic that Smith, wary of superstition and enthusiasm, should be associated with witch-burning in any way,[33] but the fact may remind us that he does ground his moral theory in a mechanism of sheer contagion: sympathy.

Bound to one another by deeper-than-rational ties of sympathy, Smithian people harmonize. They respect the "approved habitual associations" of their society.[34] They do what's done. Not doing what's done means behaving like a sow in a drawing room.[35] Presumably the worst kind of sow clashes with prevailing opinions, for this animal not only bumbles into the drawing room but orates about its right to be there. Doing what's done means following canons of propriety founded in habit and custom.[36] It means not questioning established norms with the sharp skepticism out of which the philosophy of habit and custom, the philosophy of Smith and Hume, arises. In particular the protagonist of commercial society, the prudent man, does what's done. For the most prudent way of gaining "approbation" is to behave perfectly conventionally. This is such a barren morality that two well-known readers of Adam Smith took issue with it: Mary Wollstonecraft and John Stuart Mill. I would like to trace some of the relations between these two dissenters and Adam Smith, and then shuttle back to a contemporary of Mary Wollstonecraft, Jane Austen, who speaks in a style of Smithian composure but is not really aloof from the clash of opinions.

In his brilliant poem "Mary," quite likely inspired by Mary Wollstonecraft, William Blake tells of a woman whose beauty sets her apart and who incurs the envy and hatred of the forces of conformity. Mary comes to the realization that "To be weak as a Lamb and smooth as a dove / And not to raise Envy is calld Christian Love / But if you raise Envy your Merits to blame / For planting such spite in the weak and the tame."[37] For Mary Wollstonecraft herself, a republic would be that political order where merit doesn't have to be hidden. Not passivity and obedience (the morality of "the weak and the tame") but active exertion would be the motto of a republic. The purpose of education wouldn't be to root out abilities and subject people to the rule of envy and fear, but to equip people with the power to think and act for themselves. As Adam Smith's teacher, the Commonwealthman Francis Hutcheson, deprecated the morality of passive obedience, extolled a vigorous ideal of liberty, and went some distance toward applying the same moral standards to men and women, so Mary Wollstonecraft, Commonwealthwoman, carried on the critique of a corrupt political establishment and claimed moral equality for women as rational beings.[38] Adam Smith, the middle term in this series, takes a position close to that of Mary Wollstonecraft when he argues that virtue which lies latent, for lack of the opportunity to act, doesn't count for much (*TMS*, p. 106). Thus Wollstonecraft contends that in order for women to achieve virtue, they must be free to act. Smith held no such unconventional views on gender, as though he saved all his challenges for the mercantile system. Nor indeed did he consider humans particularly rational beings. It is to be expected that Mary Wollstonecraft had some differences with a man who pronounced the present system of educating women perfect—Smith.[39]

Like the correspondent who objected to Smith's argument that society dictates right and wrong, Mary Wollstonecraft takes issue with Smith's claim that our moral sentiments are reflections of the moral sentiments of spectators. In her judgment, "if we pant after higher improvement and higher attainments, it is not sufficient to view ourselves as we suppose that we are viewed by others, though this has been ingeniously argued, as the foundation of our moral sentiments. Because each by-stander may have his own prejudices, besides the prejudices of his age or country."[40] This criticism is well aimed. It finds the weakness in the "foundation" of Adam Smith's moral theory. In a sense, indeed, Mary Wollstonecraft was truer to the skeptical premises underlying Smith's thought than Smith himself: working from the celebrated Humean principle that you cannot derive ought from is, she refutes the argument "that woman ought to be subjected because she has always been so."[41] Adam Smith, much friendlier to prejudice and habit, discourages such argumentative challenges to shared beliefs and beautifies agreement as a lovely concord of sentiments.

But adjusting my sentiments to your sentiments is a prescription for conformity, not moral conduct. Sooner or later this policy will turn us into mirror images (the identical men and women of J. S. Mill, who like Wollstonecraft speaks of suffocating confinement, the spirit of slavishness, the languishing of virtue). It creates a realm of reflections of reflections,[42] a theater of illusions in which we lose the stature of moral agents and act out a pretense of being. Something of the criticism that Mary Wollstonecraft makes of Rousseau can also be made of Adam Smith: styling our behavior so that it wins hearts (or earns the approbation of the spectator) makes Sophies of us. Reduced to correct manners and a yearning to conquer his judges, the economic man of Adam Smith has lost so much of the independence of an agent that it takes an injection of Roman self-command to give him seeming moral status. For her part, Mary Wollstonecraft despises the corrupt morality of conquering hearts, and prefers to imagine the stoic widow who bears adversity with fortitude, retires from sexual life, and rejects the mock heroic of coquetry in favor of the true heroic of republican duty.[43]

As we have seen, Mary Wollstonecraft misread *The Theory of Moral Sentiments* as claiming that the rich crave "to be observed, to be attended to, to be taken notice of with sympathy, complacency, and approbation" (*TMS*, p. 50). The text states that this motive runs through all ranks, presumably including the middle class, whose sentiments Wollstonecraft largely shares. But if she read Adam Smith wrong in one sense, she was right in another. By construing his statement of the dominant motive of social life as a reference to the morally effeminate rich,[44] she identified what it is in Adam Smith's theory that was offset by the hypermasculine language of fortitude that seems to ennoble his argument and raise it well above a morality of mere emulation.

With the help of Mary Wollstonecraft, we can see that Adam Smith had almost turned men into beings as vain as the women she detests. Where the woman of fashion affects to suffer from the phantoms of an unquiet mind—"the vapours"—the male economic actor chases illusions, or what economic theorists of the time called imaginary wants, and may even come under "the despotism of speculative fantasy."[45] Indeed, in castigating the "superficial weakness and trivial folly" of vain men (vanity being nothing less than the driving force of commercial society), Smith uses the same idiom that Mary Wollstonecraft applies over and over to women.[46] When Smith claims that women feel with others ("humanity"), while men possess a mastery of themselves that enables them to act for the good of others ("generosity"),[47] he reverses the thrust of his moral theory, which is to make *men* into beings who resonate sympathetically with others, beings who are so little the masters of themselves that their moral sentiments passively reflect society's, and who are apt to forgo generosity for self-interest. To preserve the ideal of manliness, Adam Smith fortifies his argument with a language of self-command that transports us far from the social theater of eighteenth-century England, as far as antiquity itself. As we have seen, in the argumentation of Adam Smith the figure or fiction of the man within serves to give weight to the values of bourgeois life and to invest negative liberty with some of the dignity of the classical tradition.

If Mary Wollstonecraft had approached Adam Smith in the critical spirit she brings to Rousseau, she might well have charged that his morality is false, that it is somehow founded both on the "sensibility" she despises and on the insensibility of the stoic, that the sonority of his language serves to conceal what is really a behavioral etiquette and a program of social copying. She might have objected that his morality of deference and envy still belongs to the old regime. She might have construed his many slights of reason as an affront to the dignity of rational beings and as a sort of admission that the old regime cannot defend itself before the bar of reason.[48] She might have drawn some connection between her strictures on "the fallacious light of sentiment"[49] and her reception of *The Theory of Moral Sentiments*. If she had carried out her intention of "teach[ing] women to recognize their essential affinities with men,"[50] she might well have pointed out how large a part sheer submission plays in the conduct of Smithian man, and how antirepublican he is, with his loyalty to the principle of hierarchy, his habit of submitting even to equals, his worship of privilege, his inability to "reason and dispute" with his masters (*TMS,* p. 53). And she might have recognized that the faulty reason of Smithian men, who confuse means for ends (a point emphasized both by Smith and his commentators as the very hinge of his theory of society), resembles the stunted reason imputed to women.

In the course of her extended argument with Rousseau in the *Vindication of the Rights of Woman,* Mary Wollstonecraft objects to her opponent's assertion that women possess only the kind of diminished, tactical reason that adapts means to ends but cannot determine ends themselves. She quotes Rousseau as saying, "Reason in women is a practical reason, capacitating them artfully to discover the means of attaining a known end, but which would never enable them to discover that end itself."[51] This pronouncement is cited without comment by Mary Wollstonecraft, though the page seethes with indignation. Denying women the possession of substantive reason, casting them as tacticians of the heart, Rousseau has confined their activity to crafty little pursuits, a kind of sexual needlepoint. As though there were something more to the republicans' worries about effeminacy than a mere fixation on an elegized past and a hereditary contempt for women and jealousy of male advantages (factors that were real enough), the case can be made that men too have turned their reason to the adjustment of means to ends, and lack the ability to evaluate ends as such. How if at all does a tactical reason differ from the instrumental reason that theorists from Max Weber forward have identified as a ruling concept of modern society—a reason that takes cognizance of means and not ends?[52]

Adam Smith claimed to have discovered the dissociation of means and ends, what becomes the very principle of instrumental reason. We are so enchanted (he theorizes) with the ingenuity of a watch, a government, or any other wondrous contrivance, that we come to value the thing itself in abstraction from the end it exists to serve. The watch is prized for its dainty workmanship, not its timekeeping properties; the government admired as a beautiful watch whose "wheels" move with "harmony and ease" (*TMS,* p. 185). As acts drift away from the ends or intentions of the actors, so things drift free of their use and become elegances, the market for elegances being open-ended, unlike that for mere necessities. The Invisible Hand that in the *Wealth of Nations* overrides the intentions of agents, turning their deeds to purposes they never had in mind, also turns men's appetites for elegances or "imaginary wants" to the service of higher goals. The law of displaced ends thus connects the author's ethics and his political economy.[53] Whether people lose sight of ends even in the pursuit of them (as in the story of the poor man's son) or the ends just don't bear looking into, in either case ends drop out of sight in Adam Smith's theory of society, in a clear anticipation of the instrumental reason that concerns itself with means to the exclusion of ends.

In modern commercial society there has risen to ascendancy a notion of reason which, "if it concerns itself at all with ends," takes only the narrowest view of them[54]—a reduced concept of reason that originates, in all likelihood, with Adam Smith's teacher Francis Hutcheson, and was expressed most memorably by Smith's friend Hume. Today ends are commonly decided for us by the organizations in which we function, at the same time that all questions of ends are theoretically private, viewed as lying outside the jurisdiction of reason altogether. (Hence our contradictory allegiance to the norms of technological rationality on the one hand and private choice on the other.) "The acceptability of ideals, the criteria for our actions and beliefs, the leading principles of ethics and politics, all our ultimate decisions are made to depend on factors other than reason,"[55] as though in keeping with the Smithian doctrine of the paltriness of reason. Having lost the ability to pass judgment on ends, reason is demoted to mere reasonableness, "which in turn points to conformity with reality as it is."[56]

How suggestively the prudent man, with his diminished reason and small frame of reference, corresponds with the image of woman that excites the anger of Mary Wollstonecraft—a human being trained in conformity, enslaved to a "practical reason," and confined in the private sphere. Voluntarily "confin[ing] himself" to narrow concerns (*TMS,* p. 215) and avoiding the clash of opinions, the prudent man still takes pride, perhaps, in his superiority to women, confined and excluded willy-nilly. The pride of Smithian man is the pride of a toy soldier in a cuckoo clock: not himself but the machinery behind him—"the secret wheels and springs" (*TMS,* p. 19)—is the wonder. The instrumental reason that has come to dominate commercial society, and is already on the verge of explicitness in *The Theory of Moral Sentiments,* occupies itself solely with the wheels and springs of things, as the rationalization of the world calls on men to perform their tasks like clockwork—a point brought out by an intellectual heir of Adam Smith, J. S. Mill.

According to perhaps the best interpreter of Adam Smith, J. Ralph Lindgren, Smith "would certainly be outraged if increased economic efficiency were achieved at the expense of the moral character of even the middle ranks of men."[57] John Stuart Mill's *On Liberty* indicts the moral character of the middle ranks of men, now seen as machines, engines of efficiency. While Mill inherited and broadened Smith's doctrine of noninterference, he evidently felt compelled to rethink the main conundrum of the Scottish Enlightenment—how men can maintain their "virtue" in a commercial society—for that is his topic in *On Liberty.* No more than Adam Ferguson, whom he read under the tutelage of his father, was Mill eager to extinguish to the virile ideals of classical republicanism. Sharing with Ferguson the characteristic civic humanist anxieties over the drooping of public spirit, the threat of bureaucracy, the mutilation of human beings by the division of labor, the corrupting effects of a standing army, Mill stands in an intriguing relation with his forebear in the negative liberty tradition, Adam Smith. *On Liberty* might be read, indeed, as an exposé of the degrading effects of the conformism written into Adam Smith's moral theory of heart beating to heart.

Where Smith would have us defer to the habitual preferences and aversions of the community, Mill calls into question the mere "likings and dislikings" of society.[58] Where the philosophy of Smith, like that of Hume, is grounded in habit and custom, Mill tends to consider habit and custom stultifying routines. Where propriety is the better part of virtue in the *Moral Sentiments,* Mill was healed and nourished by the poetry of Wordsworth, written in rebellion against the norm of propriety itself. Where Smith thinks the advancement of society is well worth the corruption of the individual,[59] the strengthening of society at the cost of the individual gives Mill cause for alarm. Where Smith frames a thoroughly ironic defense of a way of life wherein people imitate the imitators of the rich, Mill sees in this copying nothing but a loss of self. Perhaps the model of all such ruinous imitation is the nobleman who bankrupts himself to keep up with the newly rich imitating *him*. [60] Both Smith and Mill knew that such moral habits of the old regime carried into the commercial order, which they both defended in spite of its corruption.

Adam Smith, theorist of negative liberty, leads straight to John Stuart Mill, theorist of negative liberty; but in another sense, Smith's reliance on the chilling eye of society (the all-observant "impartial spectator") leads straight to Mill's protest against living under "the eye of a hostile and dreaded censorship."[61] It is as though Mill argued that the ideology of diverting men from public strife into private betterment had succeeded far too well, producing an individual at once pacified, lacking in public spirit, incapable of arguing with effect, and given over to the small-mindedness that Smith himself appears to have associated with the mercantile classes.[62] The emulation identified by eighteenth-century commentators as the very mechanism of commercial society Mill views with contempt:

> Not only in what concerns others, but in what concerns only themselves, the individual or the family do not ask themselves—what do I prefer? or, what would suit my character and disposition? or, what would allow the best and highest in me to have fair play, and enable it to grow and thrive? They ask themselves, what is suitable to my position? what is usually done by persons of my station and pecuniary circumstances? or (worse still) what is usually done by persons of a station and circumstances superior to mine?[63]

The parenthetical "worse still" conveys Mill's scorn for the life of envious imitation, an attitude Adam Smith shares in his more disenchanted moments. Mill brings out the debit side of the ideology of "gentle commerce." Celebrated as a theorist of laissez-faire, he nevertheless disputes the first principle of the ideology of commerce, that dependence is good for men, or in the words of the Encyclopedist Forbonnais, that "Infinite Providence, the creator of nature, intended to make men dependent on each other" through commerce.[64] (The stoic ideal of independence appealed to Mill as it did to Adam Smith.) And where Smith thought subjecting men to "the constant scrutiny of [their] neighbours" would have the good effect of making them more restrained and sociable, Mill believes that very process has destroyed the moral fiber of the middle class in which Smith vested his hopes for the improvement of society.[65]

Those virtues of abstinence and self-denial that were to be so signalized by the Victorians, Adam Smith actually regarded as second best. Indeed, the effect, and intent,[66] of *The Theory of Moral Sentiments* is to make over some of the prestige of the great or "public" virtues to prudent conduct.

> It is from the unremitting steadiness of those gentler exertions of self-command, that the amiable virtue of chastity, that the respectable virtues of industry and frugality, derive all that somber lustre which attends them. The conduct of all those who are contented to walk in the humble paths of peaceable and private life, derives from the same principle the greater part of the beauty and grace which belong to it; a beauty and grace, which, though much less dazzling, is not always less pleasing than those which accompany the more splendid actions of the hero, the statesman, or the legislator. (*TMS*, p. 242)

Adam Smith has put the "public" virtues out of reach—raised them to the level of legend—and enabled people to get on with their daily pursuits. While men go about their business with the "beauty and grace" of women,[67] avoiding clashes of opinion, they can tell themselves they are carrying on the great tradition of heroic virtue, which endows their actions with a certain radiance. Those "contented to walk in the humble paths of peaceable and private life"—who are they but the sheep J. S. Mill portrays in *On Liberty*? And if the essence of Mill's case in *On Liberty* is that the individual has been reduced to submissiveness and innocence and timidity, has lost the capacity for public life, what does this mean but that in Mill's opinion men have actually become like the Victorian woman they themselves celebrate for her feebleness and her exclusion from the public world?

This image of men as something less than vigorous agents is already latent in Adam Smith's portrayal of them as being tightly bound by the littlest rules of propriety and as dependent on others for their judgments. I have theorized that Adam Smith tried to impart some of the prestige of positive liberty to the socioeconomic actor, a figure as yet in need of stature. In page after page of *The Theory of Moral Sentiments,* Adam Smith labors to invest this figure with more dignity than his cravings and lack of independence might otherwise entitle him to. In Mill's *On Liberty* we get a sense of what the socioeconomic actor might look like without his toga of dignity; as it turns out, he possesses the same "narrowness, meanness, and . . . selfish disposition," the same smallness of soul, that Smith himself seems to have found in men of commerce.[68] At the same time, as I have argued elsewhere, Mill's boldness comes down more or less to the counsels of noninterference already followed by Adam Smith's prudent man, "not a meddler in other people's affairs" (*TMS*, p. 215).[69]

Lamenting the dwindling of moral courage and public spirit, which he valued as highly as Adam Ferguson, Mill alleges that conventional, that is, Christian, morality teaches an ideal

> negative rather than positive; passive rather than active; [an ideal of] Innocence rather than Nobleness; Abstinence from Evil, rather than energetic Pursuit of Good; in its precepts . . . "thou shalt not" predominates unduly over "thou shalt." . . . It is essentially a doctrine of passive obedience; it inculcates submission to all authorities found to be established. . . . What little recognition the idea of obligation to the public obtains in modern morality, is derived from Greek and Roman sources, not Christian.[70]

The "negative virtue" of refraining from injury that is stressed by Adam Smith[71] evolves into the morality of abstinence and blamelessness that is the object of attack in *On Liberty*. Such is the duality of Mill's position that the main underwriter of his laissez-faire principles is also the authority, as it were, behind the very morality that Mill opposes. Never did Mill reconcile his love of public spirit and even martial virtue with the pursuit of private happiness. Indeed, while he accuses his contemporaries of feebleness and degeneracy in the tradition of the eighteenth-century critics of "luxury,"[72] his remedy of free consumption is the very "luxury" they inveighed against. (As David McNally has persuasively demonstrated, neither did Adam Smith reconcile his profoundly mixed feelings about commerce—the same commerce that Mill believed had sapped all valor and public spirit.) Abundant evidence shows, in any case, that Mill cherished republican values that call us out of the little sphere of merely private interests, the sphere he himself stockaded in *On Liberty*. Mill could never wholly bring himself to believe that the public good would come about by itself if only men renounced their capacity for public life, avoided public contention, looked to their interests with diligence, and altogether forgot about more expansive notions of virtue.

Like those republicans from Machiavelli on who spoke of the need to return the polity to its original principles, Mill looks back to moments of inception when practices were fresh and hadn't yet sunk into corruption and routine—whereas the Smithian doctrine of unintended consequences may imply the very reverse, that practices originate in blindness and folly but become wise as they play themselves out in time.[73] In the republican spirit of the Encyclopedist who wrote that where luxury goes unchecked by civic duty, "the people will grow weak, lazy, listless, and discouraged,"[74] Mill portrays the English as spiritless and feeble and complains of the dying out of a sense of civic duty. In the spirit of republicanism, too, Mill deplores the confinement of men in "the narrow circle of personal and family selfishness,"[75] as though men themselves showed some of the same debilities they impute so insistently to women, discouraged or barred from participation in "all the things which are of general and not solely of private interest."[76]

In the *Subjection of Women* Mill criticizes the morality preached to women as "principally negative."[77] Though he draws no connections, almost certainly it is close kin to the morality of "thou shalt not" that (as we have seen) cows men, a morality descended in turn from Adam Smith's doctrine of propriety and inoffensiveness. Similarly, when Mill complains in the *Subjection of Women* that education instills in women no sense of the public interest,[78] he shows no recognition of ever having said that men fail their "obligation to the public" and have even lost the idea of it. As he echoes *On Liberty* in unacknowledged ways, so he recalls the thinking of the Scottish Enlightenment. Remarking in the *Subjection of Women* that the influence of women is "encouraging to the softer virtues, discouraging to the sterner,"[79] Mill reminds us of the Scottish theorists who found that commercial society itself works to the same effect, snuffing out virtues like valor and nourishing instead habits of sentiment. Thus, for example, Adam Smith judges that modern civilization fosters the virtues of humanity. "Humanity is the virtue of a woman, generosity of a man," he writes (*TMS, p.* 190), meaning by generosity the magnanimity, the greatness of soul, of a man in charge of himself. It is the decline of generosity or magnanimity that John Stuart Mill deplores when he speaks of the "energetic Pursuit of Good." (Of magnanimity Hume says that it seeks out opposition and is roused by opposition.[80] If this is so, the "sympathetic" society where heart beats to heart is no climate for magnanimity, nor is the pacified society where opposition is choked.)

No more than Adam Smith was John Stuart Mill able to forget about classical republicanism. So strong was the hold exerted on the imagination by the figure of the man in charge of himself that each of the two principal theorists of negative liberty retains an image of male virtue from the classical tradition. But while republicanism was deeply biased against women (as was Mill's father, himself under the influence of the Scottish Enlightenment), Mill attacked the falsity of conventional gender distinctions, as between men governed by themselves—the man within—and women governed by others. *On Liberty* portrays men incapable of self-governance, men whose claim to be the natural and appointed governors of women therefore collapses.

More than any other English writer, perhaps, Jane Austen is known for avoiding issues of public contention. In a time of "public discontent, faction, and disorder" (*TMS*, p. 231), she writes a prose of composure. She generally defends the existing order in spite of her ironic insight into its nature, like Adam Smith; and like Smith she approves class stratification while judging merit without respect to class. She "endorses both the individualistic perspective inherent in the bourgeois system *and* the authoritarian hierarchy retained from traditional paternalistic society";[81] he endorses individual liberty while preserving deference and privilege. Indeed the Smithian morality of seemly behavior, sympathetic understanding, corrected passions, and wry acceptance bears a curious relation to the ethic of Jane Austen. (To enrich the analogy, Smith was something of an artist himself, writing in a style of maddeningly serene irony and working vignettes, parables like that of the poor man's son, and "homely Addisonian illustrations"[82] into the structure of his discourse.) In that the tempering of the passions, underscored in *The Theory of Moral Sentiments,* guards against distempers of the polity, the concord of sentiments is a sort of vision of tranquillity. But the tranquillity of Jane Austen can be overstated. In fact it has been argued that she is a party on one side or another to the "war of ideas" that came to a head in the French Revolution and that Adam Smith referred to as disorder.[83] Here I want to trace out a faint line of affinity between Jane Austen, famed for composed passions and the avoidance of public questions, and Mary Wollstonecraft, famed for discomposed passions and public combat.

As Adam Smith makes much of the process of lowering our passions for presentation to society, so in *Pride and Prejudice* the mighty Darcy undergoes an education of the emotions that brings *him* down to the social level. The author makes a social being of him, breaches the stoic fortress of his self. She teaches him manners. One might have thought that with the sorry roster of men in *Pride and Prejudice* who lack character—the impotent Mr. Bennet; the servile Collins; Bingley, an amiable nobody; Wickham, a sociopath—Jane Austen would have been more lenient toward the one male with character. As it is, she makes Darcy learn what women learn: how to please. The incomparable delight that *Pride and Prejudice* offers its readers may reflect its uniqueness as a light revenge fantasy, with Darcy, a seignorial power, being made to learn something of the care for manners and appearances that was constantly preached to women. It is as though the Smithian man within—he who despises "groundless applause" (*TMS,* p. 115) and impresses on us a sacred regard for "the grandeur, and dignity, and superiority of our own characters" (*TMS,* p. 137)—were tempered into human shape, introduced to social being, and painfully taught the "desire to please" that Smith says we bring with us into the world (*TMS,* p. 129) and that Mary Wollstonecraft angrily argues is impressed on women as the one thing needful. In *Pride and Prejudice* the man within must drink of the same cup as women.

Implicitly, without employing the confrontational style of Mary Wollstonecraft, Jane Austen criticizes the system of education that makes women into coquettes (Lydia) and idiots (Mrs. Bennet). By chastening Darcy and making him learn to his pain what women were taught above all else—"the science of being agreeable"[84]—she turns the tables. I would stress the author's wry implicit handling of the same general issues that Mary Wollstonecraft treats polemically. *Pride and Prejudice* is connected to the *Vindication of the Rights of Woman* by a fine thread, hard to see but strong for all that. In the famous opening scene, for example, we are introduced to a woman so witless, so without conscious dignity that she might illustrate Mary Wollstonecraft's notion of the woman taught simply to please. The mother of Elizabeth Bennet represents the end product of the education that Mary Wollstonecraft detests. Taught to captivate and taught nothing else, she conquered the young Mr. Bennet; soon enough her attractions went to dust, and exactly in accordance with Mary Wollstonecraft's predictions, she revealed herself as an empty-headed woman of no charm at all, unfit to be the equal or friend of her husband, who in turn is left to console himself with ironic philosophy for ever having bound himself to this ninny. Rather than polemicizing against the educational double standard, however, Jane Austen evens it out fictionally by teaching Darcy (with all of his sense of "the grandeur, and dignity, and superiority" of his own character) if not piano and drawing, at least some social graces.

In his proposal to Elizabeth Bennet, "Darcy says what is on his mind and in his heart as plainly as anyone could say it, and yet he is misconstrued."[85] He is misconstrued as Elizabeth Bennet was misconstrued by Collins when she gave him her negative. When Collins remains unwilling to credit her refusal, she exits in silence, resolved to ask her father to reject the imbecile in her name, for her father's word "could not be mistaken for the affectation and coquetry of an elegant female."[86] Mary Wollstonecraft herself could not have more emphatically rejected the image of women as artful dissimulators with no claim to the status of moral agents. Indeed, when Elizabeth enjoins Collins to consider her " 'a rational creature speaking the truth from her heart' " (which is just how Mary Wollstonecraft demands to be considered), she uses the idiom of the *Vindication.*[87] "Let [women] be taught to respect themselves as rational creatures."[88]

Speaking plainly and being misconstrued, Darcy is made to suffer something of what a woman suffers, made to drink of the same cup. More than this, in being shown that he can't ignore the proprieties and spring his meaning on his audience, Darcy is instructed in that modesty of verbal dress, or address, that his society requires in women. The precepts of modesty were codified in works like Fordyce's *Sermons to Young Women,* the same Fordyce whom Mary Wollstonecraft challenges in the *Vindication of the Rights of Woman.* Collins chooses to read Fordyce's *Sermons* to the Bennet family. It is a sufficient, though implicit, comment on the book that its pieties and prescriptions endear it to that ass, at once abjectly servile and filled with a sense of his own majesty. While Mary Wollstonecraft argues in declamatory style, Jane Austen refutes Fordyce with hardly a word spoken.

In the view of Adam Smith, society improves as the division of labor renders men more dependent on the activities of others, and as the progress of manners impresses on men their dependence on the good opinion of others. Jane Austen has Darcy, an independent power, improve as he learns a care for the opinions that are held of him, such as Elizabeth Bennet's. But if the mighty Darcy learns to seek "approbation" like a proper member of Smithian society, Elizabeth Bennet, his destined other, distinguishes herself by scorning to seek the "approbation" of Darcy. As heartily as Darcy himself, and perhaps much in the spirit of Mary Wollstonecraft, she despises women who sue for his favor, " 'always speaking and looking, and thinking for *your* approbation alone. I roused, and interested you, because I was so unlike *them*!' "[89] Elizabeth scorns the courting of "approbation," a motive that figures centrally in the moral theory of Adam Smith, and a skill that Wickham possesses to perfection. His winning ways earn him "the general approbation of the neighbourhood."[90] At one point they earn him Elizabeth Bennet's "approbation" too.

In Smithian terms, Wickham is vain—a pretender who "sees the respect which is paid to rank and fortune, and wishes to usurp this respect" (*TMS*, p. 256)—and Darcy proud.[91] "The proud man," Adam Smith writes, "is commonly too well contented with himself to think that his character requires any amendment. The man who feels himself all-perfect, naturally enough despises all further improvement. His self-sufficiency and absurd conceit of his own superiority, commonly attend him from his youth to his most advanced age" (*TMS*, pp. 258–59). In *Pride and Prejudice*, then, a figure who despises all further improvement is made to undergo improvement, like it or not; is saved from lifelong incivility. Learning the art of sweetness, he transforms from a Caliban into a gentleman. Actually, though, Darcy isn't the monster he seems to society, Lady Catherine being the true colossus of conceit in *Pride and Prejudice*—a compound of all the imbecilic privilege and prejudice that Mary Wollstonecraft wants swept away. Again, while pride is a famous vice, there exists a pride that imposes on its possessor higher standards of conduct than the social average, and this even Adam Smith classes as a virtue. In the superior, he writes, "pride is frequently attended with many respectable virtues; with truth, with integrity, with a high sense of honour, with cordial and steady friendship, with the most inflexible firmness and resolution" (*TMS,* p. 258). There exists a healthy pride. A healthy pride fires Elizabeth Bennet when she rejects Collins. Although Darcy's contempt for disguise and his desire that his character speak for itself seem like conceit (or prejudice us against pride), reflection convinces us that both of these motives inspire and ennoble Elizabeth Bennet in her encounter with that suitor. It is here that she claims the rights of a rational creature, an act Mary Wollstonecraft would surely applaud.

Darcy is a good match for Elizabeth Bennet because he is proud in the complimentary sense, like her, as well as being merely conceited. "We frequently say of a man, that he is too proud, or that he has too much noble pride, ever to suffer himself to do a mean thing" (*TMS,* p. 258), and Darcy is "not so mean as to resent" having been rebuffed by Elizabeth Bennet.[92] He possesses a high sense of honor. He bears Wickham's libels with silent scorn[93] until his love of Elizabeth Bennet breaks down his indifference to opinions that are held of him. He is disgusted by flattery and servility. As a master and landlord he is generous, but he doesn't care to publicize his virtue to the world. Possibly he is the kind of public-spirited landowner whom Adam Smith, with his agrarian bias, saw as a natural aristocrat, fit to rule Britain and able to save it from the mean designs of merchants.[94] Where Mary Wollstonecraft inveighs against the unnaturalness of the aristocracy and of the women brought up in its image, Jane Austen creates as it were a natural aristocracy of two—Darcy, who frees himself of the hereditary prejudice seen in Lady Catherine, and who has the liberality to undergo with good grace the chastening the novel deals him; and Elizabeth Bennet, a commoner the equal of the great.

I have suggested that Jane Austen speaks by implication where Mary Wollstonecraft does so by declamation and polemic. The novels of Jane Austen speak of politics with a kind of artful muteness, politics belonging to a list of embattled topics including "war, . . . religion, business, [and] the life of the working classes."[95] Perhaps we are apt to confuse Jane Austen's composure and serenity for the composure and serenity of the well-armed sovereign to whom public discontent gives "little disturbance" and who can therefore ignore clamoring mobs and preserve his policy of tolerance.[96] Jane Austen is not above the clash of opinions. Nevertheless, she prefers to speak implicitly—to speak, as it were, under the noise—silently (but tellingly) declaring her differences, for example, with the same Fordyce whom Mary Wollstonecraft debates by name in the *Vindication of the Rights of Woman.*

Jane Austen avoids outright polemic and keeps her partisanship in "an active war of ideas"[97] unannounced. For his part, Adam Smith, author of the highly polemical *Wealth of Nations,* seems to ignore the political agitation of the day. Smith takes a most guarded view of political speech. Having authored what he rightly considered a "very violent attack" on Britain's commercial system,[98] he did not, perhaps, want to open the gates to more violence of this kind.[99] In theory, therefore, Smithian man shuns confrontation and polemic, seeks concord of sentiments, is just as cautious of voiced political utterance as Jane Austen (although without speaking by eloquent implication), and concerns himself with public affairs as little as people did when an attack like Smith's could never have been penned—when by and large people considered government "as natural as any other social institution . . . when [they] discussed it at all."[100] Put somewhat differently, ideological strife presents such openings for "the turbulence and disorder of faction" (*TMS,* p. 232) that Adam Smith's "hero"—the prudent man—is at once too cautious and too timid to get mixed up in public affairs. How must Adam Smith, philosopher of frugality, have felt about elections where money was thrown around in bibulous entertainments and open bribery?

In eighteenth-century England there sprang up clubs toasting mutual benevolence, fiscal probity, free trade, sturdy independence (as opposed to sycophancy and corruption), and political radicalism.[101] According to Adam Smith, the prudent man shuns "convivial societies" like these (*TMS,* p. 214), an aversion that Smith reads as a sign of a certain frigidity. Smith would have backed the clubs on every point except their radicalism. I have argued that stoicism, with its precepts of quietude and submission to the order of things, helps Adam Smith shut politics out of human life in the *Moral Sentiments,* as Jane Austen was traditionally said to do.[102] "Stoicism . . . invites us to stand *against* the world of physical and political circumstance at the very same time that it requires us to act in conformity with nature."[103] The stoic ideal commemorates, as it were, the collapse of the ancient polis; in that respect it is unpolitical of its nature and well fitted to the uses to which Smith puts it. Being a citizen of the world, the stoic is perhaps not a citizen of his own state.[104]

Yet Smith himself speaks well of the love of country in *The Theory of Moral Sentiments* (pp. 227–31), just as he reviles stateless merchants in the *Wealth of Nations.*[105] Perhaps he believed that as long as the tradesman pursues his private interests with resolute ("stoic") constancy, he does well, but that as soon as he tries to get public policy slanted in his favor by playing on the love of country—the narrow partiality for one's own nation (*TMS*, p. 228) underwriting the mercantile system—he perverts the public good. The good tradesman sticks to his work. Like Defoe, who advises upholsterers to stay out of political clubs,[106] Smith finds that the prudent man keeps out of politics (*TMS*, pp. 215–16), and even if the author considers this figure inferior to the heroes of Rome, as well as deficient in conviviality and feeling, there can be no doubt that he is the protagonist of Smith's theory of society or that Smith himself championed the prudential virtues of frugality and industry. Besides, upholsterers make bad patriots. In the *Wealth of Nations* Smith heaps contempt on the Americans who from shopkeepers turn men of politics and start "contriving a new form of government."[107]

Similarly, perhaps in response to the French Revolution—one of those subjects Jane Austen passes over in silence—Adam Smith sternly cautions in the last edition of *The Theory of Moral Sentiments* against those who would "new-model" the constitution (*TMS*, p. 232) and idealizes that singular man like himself who carefully leaves the orders of society as they are while using "reason and persuasion" to make changes one by one (*TMS*, p. 233). (Not reason and persuasion but the glacial advance of history moves society from one stage to the next, in Smith's view, men being dubiously rational anyway.) This single deeply reluctant endorsement of political speech—the author's wariness being understandable in view of his ancestral distrust of the many, his belief that our actions outrun our intentions, his strong allegiance to the institution of property, and the spectacle of the French Revolution—is the extent of Adam Smith's concession to the defininition of the human being as a political animal.[108] In the end Smith does not think of men as together making decisions that shape the way they live. The writer whose presentation of himself as a spectator at once sympathetic and impartial anticipates the Smithian spectator as well as the fictional narrator, Joseph Addison, liked to think of man as a "sociable," not a political animal;[109] Smith followed his lead. Smith would have been dismayed to see his model of spectatorial sympathy, subdued passions, and political quiet turned inside out in Kant's exclamation that the French Revolution "finds, in the minds of all spectators, a sympathy very near to enthusiasm."[110]

The stoic in his pride learns to ignore the opinions of "the great mob" (*TMS*, p. 226). The sociable person surrenders to the prejudices of others, in dread of losing their goodwill. In this sense, both pride and prejudice shun the clash of opinions. The stoic knows his place as a citizen of the universe; the social man, undisputatious by nature, knows his place in a stratified society and performs its duties. The first withdraws from a corrupt world into the fortress of his own rectitude; the second, while presenting the appearance of moral chastity, nevertheless partakes of the general corruption of moral sentiments. The missing possibility is the political person who argues out his or her opinions, standing the risks and responsibilities of public speech, and as need be tries to change the order of things, as Adam Smith himself did when he refuted the doctrines of mercantilism. Smithian man does not act like a citizen but accepts a political order based on deference and subordination while trying to better his own lot. He considers himself free even if living under absolute monarchy, provided his property is secure.[111] Equality too is foreign to him. He is obsequious to his own equals.[112] In *The Theory of Moral Sentiments* the political principle of equality is diluted into a sentimental vision of a community of souls experiencing the same pitch of the same emotion; that is, the equality actually being sought by claimants like Mary Wollstonecraft is depoliticized. The idealization of equality flows from stoicism itself, one of whose most celebrated exponents—Epictetus—was born a slave, while another—Marcus Aurelius—was an emperor.

As equality in the *Moral Sentiments* lacks political meaning, so also does self-government. When Smith speaks of self-government (*TMS*, p. 23), he means deportment. The term calls up no political meaning whatever, no thought of citizens who both rule and are ruled, indeed no thought of the large numbers of radicals at the time who agitated for a say in government. Self-government in Adam Smith is "that reserved, that silent and majestic sorrow, which discovers itself only in the swelling of the eyes, in the quivering of the lips and cheeks, and in the distant, but affecting, coldness of the whole behaviour" (*TMS*, p. 24). Thus the political sense of self-government melts away in a beautiful Arthurian image of mastered passions. And the mastery of the passions on which Adam Smith lays such stress particularly implies, as I have argued, the quieting of political passions, the most dangerous of all.

Addison, *Spectator* essayist, endeavored to turn minds away from the hostile passions of politics. Hume discouraged changes in established institutions and warned against charlatans and fanatics selling quack political remedies.[113] The neostoicism of Dr. Johnson was recommended as an antidote to dangerous political passions.[114] Jane Austen keeps her politics unvoiced, in contrast to Mary Wollstonecraft. Wordsworth gave up the hopes inspired by the French Revolution and turned within. As stoicism teaches that the really free man cannot be enslaved, so quietists like Wordsworth came to believe that people really enslaved—people whose minds are enthralled to error—cannot politically be freed.[115] Writing during the Paris revolution of 1830, Carlyle prescribed a "strenuous economic activism" that is strangely consistent, however, with political quietism.[116] Adam Smith's prudent man stays out of politics and dedicates himself instead to the chaste desire for "sympathy" and esteem, almost in the manner of the Victorian wife "removed from the actual collision of political contests, and screened from the passions which such engender."[117]

Behind the prudent shunning of confrontation lies, perhaps, a bitter truth: that argumentation (Smith's "reason and persuasion") avails little against ideas as deeply held, as furiously defended, and indeed as impregnable to reason as traditional prejudices like those against commerce and luxury, the latter inveterately associated with women.[118] Such beliefs, verging on manias, aren't so much refuted as swept away. The prejudice against commerce was conquered not so much by argument as by commerce itself. By avoiding contention, Smithian man allows the processes of commerce to do their work and keeps from disturbing society more than it already is, lest the old regime of belief should fall in its entirety. As a theorist of the slow action of commerce, Adam Smith perhaps can be classified as Jane Austen is by an acute reader—as "moderately progressive."[119]

Bernard Mandeville, who like Adam Smith believed that private consumption yields public benefits, considered the tradition of the virtuous citizen a hoax, a piece of statecraft. Mandeville favors the new way of hedonism. He denies that luxury weakens a nation militarily,[120] contending in fact that a love of finery and ribbons makes the soldier fight. He denies too the need for civic virtue, persuaded as he is that government works pretty well by itself even if officeholders possess no shining qualities. Civic participation makes no sense to him either. In such an advanced commercial society as England, people may justly forget about the austere "aristocratic and classical virtues recommended in civic humanist ideology" and dedicate themselves to pursuing what they really want, happiness.[121] The consumer way of life makes for civility, better clothes and bread, and the banishment of the repressive, or Catonian, ideal of virtue. Mandeville mocks stoicism by name in his *Fable of the Bees*. Adam Smith censures Mandeville by name in *The Theory of Moral Sentiments* (*TMS,* pp. 308–13).

Adam Smith is not prepared to renounce republican virtue in the manner of Mandeville, being too much attached to the classical values that seemed like pious frauds to the latter. Instead of repudiating those values outright, Adam Smith assigns men a vestige of the classical ideals that according to Mandeville make no sense in commercial society. He assigns them self-command. As it happens, though, self-command enjoins on men something like the patience and constancy, the faultless manners and avoidance of strife, that homilists such as James Fordyce prescribed to women. "When you show a sweet solicitude to please by every decent, gentle, unaffected attraction," writes Fordyce, preceptor of women, "we are soothed, we are subdued, we yield ourselves your willing slaves."[122] According to Adam Smith, theorist of subdued passions, the moral universe coheres by virtue of a natural force of attraction called sympathy, while the decency and diligence of the prudent man improve society gently, as by a sort of irresistible influence. In a newly economic version of the old argument that patience vanquishes, Smith envisions the patient accumulator of wealth vanquishing obstacles by his humble perseverance and, what is more, improving the tone of life in society as women were said, by Addison, Fordyce, and the Victorian homilists, to shed an improving grace over the world.[123] As, in the ethos of romance, the patience and guile of the weak overcome the strong, so the patience of the prudent man triumphs, aided by ruses of history like the Invisible Hand. As, in romance, virtuous women redeem men and lead them to higher things, so commercial society celebrates female "virtue" and redemptive power—most markedly, perhaps, in the heavily romantic discourse of the Victorians.[124]

The good woman, says Fordyce, doesn't haunt public places, preferring a more sheltered locale. "She loves the shade. There she finds herself most secure from the blights of calumny and the heats of temptation."[125] So does the prudent man love the shade, and for the same reason: in it he finds security. Deep down he likes nothing so much as "the undisturbed enjoyment of secure tranquillity" (*TMS*, p. 216). And as we have seen, he is averse to the risks and the glare of politics. If the good woman is "unambitious of appearing," this is precisely true of the prudent man as well.[126] Where women were constantly reminded of their immense influence—their unbounded power to act through others but not in their own person—the man of prudence is loath to act in his own person, preferring to leave that to others. Keeping his station, the prudent man carries forward the traditional ethic of a ranked society, "my station and its duties," thus slowing the dissolution of the ways of deference in a commercial order. Unlike pretenders to public notice—men who have hit on a quick way to make their fortune—the prudent man makes his fortune by slow degrees. Unlike the importunate merchants who claim favors from Parliament and in so doing corrupt public policy, he keeps away from scenes of public contention. And the prudent man is no minor player in Smith's drama. Really he has the leading role, for it is his steady habits that have built up the wealth of the nation in spite of the malfeasance of monopolists, the errors of legislators, the idiocy of the rich.[127] Carefully submissive to established norms,[128] averse to crossing others, the accumulator of capital is nevertheless a man within, and it is this inner man who gives him the steadiness needed to carry out his historic work.

CHAPTER 4

The Domestic Woman

The conventions of Adam Smith's time define the good woman as quiet, modest, dutiful, inoffensive, and pleasing, an image of woman that looks toward the Victorian angel presiding over the domestic sphere. Curiously, though, in the opinion of Smith a wife doesn't have to actually love her husband in order to perform the part of the good woman, just as the man of prudence doesn't have to feel much sympathy in order to act correctly. If it happens that a woman cannot find it in herself to love her husband, she must simply act as if she did:

> A wife . . . may sometimes not feel that tender regard for her husband which is suitable to the relation that subsists between them. If she has been virtuously educated, however, she will endeavour to act as if she felt it, to be careful, officious, faithful, and sincere, and to be deficient in none of those attentions which the sentiment of conjugal affection could have prompted her to perform. (*TMS*, p. 162)[1]

Tellingly, this "character" of the good wife illustrates the author's discussion of *men* who act purely out of obedience to social rules. Indeed, the careful wife and the prudent man are mirror images. In her, lack of conjugal affection in no way blocks the performance of conjugal duties; in him, lack of social affection in no way blocks the punctilious observance of "all the established decorums and ceremonials of society."[2] In both is seen a formality, an inhibition of sentiment, a frigid propriety that seem to disappoint the author but that he certainly prefers to loose behavior. Somehow the emotional constriction of the prudent man assures his steady conduct, while the passionlessness of the careful wife proves she is not the dangerous creature of passion that women were so often said to be.

This wife whose life has become an act of "sincere" dissimulation—what is she "careful" of? Presumably she is careful not to displease her husband; probably, too, she watches carefully over the management of the household. Where a strong and well-enshrined antifeminist tradition once pictured women themselves as the worst of men's cares, Adam Smith speaks for a more decorous but also rather official view of women as being the antithesis of those dangerous and deceitful creatures that men liked to rail about. Never having married, Smith does not write in the strains of the old antimatrimonial tradition warning that women ruin men and consume men's substance (although he does claim that romantic love, with its "jealousy and folly," compares poorly to friendship between men of virtue [*TMS*, p. 225]). Instead he writes for a social consensus that affirms both marriage and the diligent accumulation of small property—a consensus of men who feel that their dearest possessions are safe in a woman's hands, provided she is proper. Security of private property means, after all, security in the hands of women. I want to reflect on the displacement of the once-dominant view of women as unruly and untrue by the faithful domestic of Adam Smith and the Victorians.[3]

For Montesquieu, the advance of civilization "requires the domestication of women; in a more advanced society, women will be sure to occupy their proper place. The domestic woman is accommodated to her new surroundings, [and] her narcissistic vanity and licentious use of freedom are curbed."[4] So too Adam Smith believed, unquestionably. And yet he himself identified the narcissistic vanity of *men,* their corrupt craving for admiration, as the driving force of commercial society. This was a remarkable transference, for the association of women with luxury and show was so strong, so culturally constant, that medievals and moderns, preachers and pamphleteers, republicans and men of God, Catholics and Protestants, mercantilists and nonmercantilists, libertines and homilists, all traded on the language of female vanity. By a grand irony, then, Smithian society is planted on the "imaginary wants" that men imputed to women with manic insistence. Indeed we might take a woman—Pope's Belinda in all her narcissistic vanity—as the symbol of a consumer Britannia.

An empress of commerce, a titan of littleness surrounded by jewels, combs, and all the other trinkets, minutiae, and spoils of the consumer way of life—Belinda personifies a consumer society that fancies itself the center of the world.[5] If, as Adam Smith affirms, consumption is the end of production, Belinda as consumer is the end-all of her private universe, the "final point in a vast nexus of enterprise."[6] (And if, as Smith thinks, we consume for vanity's sake, Belinda is a paragon of vanity.) In an economic but still faintly prurient sense, all the world ends up in Belinda's boudoir. In "The Rape of the Lock" the obscenity of a female port engorged with the offerings of men is muted into the image of Belinda furnished with imported goods and drinking up the world's regard with the keen desire of a true narcissist.[7] Analogously, as commercial society comes to trade on the "imaginary wants"— the wandering imagination and swollen desires—traditionally associated with women, the scandal of woman seems to be muted. The silencing of the scandalous and the obscene is a mark of bourgeois morality, the expurgation of the scandal of female consumption being complete in the Victorian ideal of the wife, a "pure" consumer in the double sense of being sealed off from the world of production and of being untainted by the corrupt appetites that were imputed to women by the Western tradition (especially its Juvenalian strain) and that are still somehow visible through the diaphanous veil of "The Rape of the Lock." If women themselves are credited with improving men, with inducting men into "a more advanced society," then improvement itself presupposes a certain cleansing or expurgation of the reputation of women.[8]

By the middle of the eighteenth century, when the first edition of *The Theory of Moral Sentiments* appeared, the vitriol of the antifeminist tradition had subsided into a tamer kind of satire. As though in keeping with the moderation of the passions that figures centrally in the moral theory of Adam Smith, the chastisers of women tempered the traditional style of Juvenalian invective.[9] One possibility is that the long tradition of antifeminism sank of its own excess and absurdity; it had in fact been something in the nature of a joke among men, and of the hundreds of literary and subliterary artifacts in the inventory of antifeminism, a good many seem spoofs.[10] Additionally, the tempering of the emotions that has been remarked by many from Adam Smith to Max Weber to

Norbert Elias, and that formed part of what came to be known as improvement, would have dampened the sheer mania of antifeminism as well as its mood swings from jest to curse; the antifeminism of Pope, polite, expertly modulated, but still prurient and malicious, stands as it were partway between traditional woman-hatred and the goodly image of woman that was later instituted. "Improvement" itself tames (domesticates) the image of woman.[11] Nietzsche, an ultrareactionary on the subject of women, insists on their essential wildness. He also sneers at the careful tuning of the emotions that Adam Smith describes so meticulously and that made for the suppression of the free and open, even gleeful woman-hatred seen in earlier centuries.[12]

If "improvement" tended to suppress the wild image of woman as scandalous and coarse, perhaps too the very resemblance that allows Smith to liken "many men" to a dutiful wife (*TMS,* p. 162) —that allows Mandeville to picture men with all the unbounded desires, obsessive vanity, and corruption that for centuries had been said to be women's by nature[13]—enabled more men to see women as members of the human species (even if beautifully subordinate) rather than as a monstrous species of their own. And if it is true that "as soon as peacetime values prevail, women's status rises,"[14] then the "improved" society based on the genteel enjoyment of the spoils of trade, the civilized consumption of the loot of empire—a society that seemed to Adam Smith to have lost all martial valor—might have discouraged the image of woman as a traitor to men who fights with guile because she lacks courage. That stability which gives life the even tone observed by Adam Smith among others and which is conveyed by the word "Augustan"; that security of property which is so much a theme of British thought; that more general security which shields us moderns against "the more brutal strokes of fate" that fall in less pacified societies[15]—all this must have made against the idea that men contend against a malicious irrational force of which woman is somehow the image. As a man of the Enlightenment, Adam Smith could not credit such a superstition. As he tells the story in the *Wealth of Nations,* the feudal landlords squandered their own power—consumed their own substance. "And thus, for the gratification of the most childish, the meanest and the most sordid of all vanities, they gradually bartered their whole power and authority."[16] No woman ruined the feudal magnate. He ruined himself.

The proverbial rise of the middle class (closely twined with the decline of the feudal way of life) also has a part, surely, in the creation of the Domestic Woman. As early as the fourteenth century, homiletic literature in English promoted the housewifely ideal.[17] In Shakespeare's most middle-class play, *The Merry Wives of Windsor,* the wives are the chaste guardians of their own virtue and their husbands' treasure, a reversal of their celebrated role as lewd betrayers. Bound up with the institution of middle-class values over time, and as responsible as anything for the repression of the ancestral view of woman as a wild thing never to be trusted, is the "modern" view of the seeking and holding of wealth. As the drive to better oneself comes to be seen less as an unruly appetite and more as a decent and sociable (or "Smithian") sentiment, as the decency and innocence of the desire to possess and enjoy things are proclaimed, so the figure of the dangerously appetitive woman is upstaged by the sentimental domestic.[18]

By the same token, the outraged opponents of commercial society—traditionalists who saw it as releasing base appetites and subverting truth and order—could pour into their diatribes something of the fury, zest, obsessive repetition, and fantastic excess that marked the antifeminist tradition at its height.[19] To those like Adam Smith who preferred to connect the rise of commerce with the consolidation (not the subversion) of order and the improvement (not the depravity) of manners, rants against commerce and against women might have sounded equally uncouth. In spite of the riotous depravity it was sometimes charged with, commercial society itself promulgated an image of woman as neither riotous nor depraved. A tradesman's credit being, as Defoe says, "the same thing in its nature as the virtue of a lady,"[20] the rise of a credit economy (an economy in which the reputation for probity stands surety for a man's debts) brings with it an idealization of feminine "virtue." For it seems axiomatic that in order for men to accumulate capital, they cannot be married to one whose nature it is to devour men's capital. There can be no accumulation of capital—the foundation of things must crumble—if women "dissipate their husband's patrimony in riotous and unnecessary expences," as for centuries they were said to do.[21] And as the getting of wealth took on in theory the regularity of clockwork, so the love of luxury and display that was obsessively condemned in women became in Adam Smith's theory the motive of commercial society itself, reducing the traditional complaint to a hypocritical cavil.

By rights, the usual diatribes against women should have fallen silent in a society where men themselves were seen to be given to vanity, luxury, fashion.[22] How could women be reviled as before for excessive desires when the economic system itself presupposed unbounded desires in men? How could women be reviled as before for exciting the desires of men when manufacturers themselves "constantly titillated" men's urge to consume?[23] How could women be caricatured as consumers—wasters, destroyers—when men themselves belonged to a consumer society? How could women be blamed for magnifying the petty when an entire empire was maintained for the sake of a "little" extra profit?[24] But beliefs don't fall dead of their own irrationality. While the commercialization of society cut the ground from under traditional misogyny, and made an idol of the domestic woman, the old habit of thought was not all at once extinguished. (To this day one hears it said that men earn money and women spend it.) The fear that women would revert as it were to their natures still found expression. The antifeminist image of woman lies not far behind Adam Smith, and lives on, being called up, for example, in the Victorian image of a hardworking man tormented "by the artificial wants and insatiable demands of his wife and daughters"—as though theorists the century before had not established that commercial society itself stimulates "imaginary wants" without end.[25]

Indeed, Smith himself significantly, and twice, omits the wife from the list of those nearest and dearest to a man, as though he still partook of the ancestral distrust of woman, however much he theorizes about the security of property.[26] During and after Smith's time moralists still warned of the voracity of woman (for no man could enjoy his property in security married to a devourer), but their preachments were generally less violent and more veiled than they would have been in the heyday of antifeminism, and promoted a cult of domesticity that went far beyond the praise of frugal women heard in earlier centuries. Much as the channeling of men's efforts into the steady and rational pursuit of wealth was thought "to weaken and tame" their more dangerous passions, so the angelic image of the domestic woman was itself used to tame and subdue the feared appetites of women (as for speech, sex, and money) as well as to displace the long-standing image of woman as an animal of desire. The comparatively weak passion for gain vanquishes the stormier passions of men's nature; women for their part come to be seen as possessing an all-vanquishing weakness.[27]

Let me first sketch the antifeminist view of women, which associates them with the *ir*rationality of economic pursuits and blames them for consuming men's wealth. With the rationalization of the seeking of wealth (as seen in the diligent habits of Adam Smith's prudent man) and the institution of the family as consumer, the antifeminist image of the consuming woman loses much of its force and point.

The antifeminist conception of woman finds expression in Chaucer's Merchant's Tale, a good source for our purposes because of its reliance on traditional materials; that is, the sentiments of the tale's teller do not belong to him alone, but come from the fund of antifeminist lore. Toward the beginning of the tale the Merchant presents a heavily sarcastic tribute to marriage and women:

> How myghte a man han [have] any adversitee
> That hath a wyf? Certes [certainly] I kan nat seye.
> The blisse which that is bitwixe hem tweye [two]
> Ther may no tonge telle, or herte thynke.
> If he be pore, she helpeth hym to swynke [work];
> She kepeth [cares for] his good [goods] and wasteth never a deel [not a bit];
> Al that hire [her] housbonde lust [wishes], hire [she] liketh weel;
> She seith nat ones [once] "nay," what he seith "ye."
> "Do this," seith he; "Al redy, sire," seith she.[28]

Recall that this is a mock encomium. The teller believes that women are anything but the solace and sustainers of men, and illustrates his point in the character of May, a lewd and not-to-be-trusted "yong thyng"[29] who betrays her mate and possesses herself of his estate: women consume men's substance.[30]

In fine, the Merchant's idea of woman runs exactly contrary to the careful wife of *The Theory of Moral Sentiments*. Where the latter watches over her own conduct to make sure she doesn't fail in her duties, the former watches for her chance, her husband being blind. Where the latter exercises care over the household, which means over the husband's laboriously acquired wealth, the former bleeds her mate. Only in acidic sarcasm can the Merchant speak of a woman carefully tending her husband's wealth. ("She kepeth his good, and wasteth never a deel.") He envisions women as serpents or creatures of prey, lying in wait to ruin men. A wife "waiteth ay [always] / After thy good,"[31] a line playing on men's fear that women look forward to the day that they claim the goods of their dead husbands (as the Wife of Bath has done over and over again). Where the dutiful woman of *The Theory of Moral Sentiments* acts the part of the loving wife even if she feels no "tender regard" for her husband—a dim reminder of the old theme that men marry their worst enemy—May in the Merchant's Tale is pictured as an accomplished feigner. In fact, the tale mockingly purports to explain how it is that women got their ability to dissimulate, the power that the good wife of *The Theory of Moral Sentiments* puts to such commendable uses.

In all the Merchant portrays women, in keeping with the antifeminist tradition, as creatures dangerous in their appetites and treacherous in their designs.[32] The beatification of the domestic woman, the Angel in the House, carries a usually silent warning to women that they had better take care of their virtue, on pain of being considered the kind of whore that medieval and Renaissance women were so often branded. The property of men resting on the propriety of women, the former can enjoy their goods in security only if the reputedly hereditary nature of the latter is suppressed—as in the angelic image of woman. Prescriptive writers of the eighteenth and nineteenth centuries still declaim against women who show off and wander, as though at some level women remained those figures of lewdness that medieval preachers used to condemn for gadding about in provocative dress; the difference is that the modern woman is also said to possess a "higher" nature, in which capacity she does not ruin men but sustains and improves them, does not devour their property but secures and blesses it. The literature scolding Victorian women for imitating the fashions of the kind of female who "excites attention,"[33] pictures women as possessing two natures—that of a carnal being who makes herself seen in order to arouse the lust of men (the eternal woman of antifeminism) and that of a shamefaced being to whom that very behavior is disgusting and sinful.

Ironically, though, no less an authority than Adam Smith had pictured men as corrupted imitators, followers of fashion, lovers of attention, an understanding shared at the time by hucksters high and low who themselves excited the attention of a new society of consumers. (Henry James was to say that in a society with a taste for luxury—the kind of improving society envisioned by Adam Smith—men and women partake of the same faults and follies.)[34] Another irony is that up to our own century, whores themselves have conventionally been seen as guardians of virtue, sinning so that wives may be pure. In the figure of the whore watching over the virtue of society, the image of woman as caretaker reaches an ironic conclusion.[35] And if whores sin to keep others from sin, the Catholic Church ("the whore of Rome") was condemned for its luxury and gaudy shows, which made the rational prosperity and social theater of the English look decent by comparison.[36]

While there must surely have been companionate marriages no matter what the poison pens of men say, still the tradition of antifeminism had power, like the clerical culture of which it was part, and certainly pervaded society to some degree. And the long tirade of antifeminism predates Chaucer and extends beyond Chaucer; he is just a node in a tradition that persistently imagines luxury as a woman ruinous to men's character (virility) and wealth.[37] Before Chaucer, although not by much, came Eustache Deschamps, whose *Mirror of Marriage* contains ironic praise of the woman who takes care of her husband's wealth. Richard de Bury complains of women who would sell their husbands' books, that is destroy their substance, in order to get money for gowns and furs.[38] Clearly the theme of woman as the pillager of men is a commonplace. Centuries before, St. Jerome had quoted the Greek Theophrastus as saying that a man who entrusts the management of his house to a wife becomes her slave. If he tries to keep control of his property, "she will have the poison ready."[39] Rather than being the loyal guardian of a man's goods (like the famous Penelope, the exception that proves the rule),[40] the woman of the antifeminist tradition needs a keeper herself, except that she is so wild by nature that no man, however watchful, can manage her. (The Wife of Bath boasts that even Argus with his hundred eyes couldn't have kept her in line.) The giant of the antifeminist tradition is Juvenal, the same whose tenth Satire underlies Dr. Johnson's stoic reflections on the "Vanity of Human Wishes." From Juvenal's obscene invectives to the polite image of woman in the neo-Roman *Theory of Moral Sentiments* is a great leap. In the eyes of Juvenal trade is depraved, as are women, who themselves lust for money; Adam Smith extols fair trade and what he calls "the fair sex."

The objection that envenomed portrayals of women by authors like Juvenal are "just literature" has some force, but underrates the authority of the pen and ignores the power of "totally imaginary" things on the order of shared beliefs to structure human life. Why were women subjected to the rule of a husband, even in the more companionate marriages of the seventeenth and eighteenth centuries, if not because they were thought to possess a trespassing nature? The least we can say is that the impolite view of women as whores who cost men dearly, a view still so pronounced in Shakespeare,[41] had to lose its high status if the polite view of women as the tenders of men was to be instituted. When men begin to say that "To thrive one must wive"[42]—a direct reversal of the commonplace that women are the ruin of men—the idealization of the domestic woman becomes theoretically possible. Similarly, with the bourgeois maxim that promiscuity in a man is a waste of precious time and money,[43] it is as though men took some responsibility for ruining themselves instead of rejoicing in the portrayal of women as their despoiler. Defoe preaches that time is money; he also deals a blow to the stereotype of the riotous wife. Instead of blaming spendthrift wives for ruining their husbands (the traditional line), he blames secretive husbands for not informing their wives of the truth of their financial condition and so fostering the illusion of riches; if such a man comes to ruin, let him bear the blame himself.[44] In this sense among others, the more regular and steady (or Smithian) pursuit of wealth seems to have worked against antifeminism, or rather to have suppressed the rude violence of antifeminism in favor of the polite hypocrisies of an "improved" age. In his treatise on *The Sublime and the Beautiful,* Adam Smith's admirer Burke likens beautiful women to ornamental furniture and lovely birds, the secret of beauty in all these cases being smooth lines and imperceptible transitions; thus the beautiful woman is a human emblem of the perfectly gradual advance of society as it reaches the commercial or Smithian stage,[45] the stage at which men themselves "rise gradually and gently"[46] in the social scale. But the aesthetic woman didn't replace the monster of tradition all at once; antifeminism has deep historical roots.

The antifeminist caricature of woman was after all embedded deeply enough that it survived the crisis of clerical authority in the Renaissance and passed into secular culture, satires on woman exciting "the laughter of the man in the street."[47] According to Ian Maclean, the dominant notion of woman in the Renaissance was of a being weak in reason, strong in passion, and stained with vice.[48] Not that this view went undisputed. Chaucer himself had recorded the stories of "good women," and defenses of woman were published in the Renaissance; surely Renaissance idealizations of the piety and economy of the good wife help to make possible the Victorian cult of the home.[49] It was one of the more bizarre irrationalities of the antifeminist tradition that while it assigned women to the domestic sphere (women having been excluded from public life by ancient prohibition), it warned of how dangerous they are there, out of sight and in charge of a man's goods; the image of the thrifty, pious wife must have been a comfort to men who heard women reviled as caged beasts. Yet such is the vigor of antifeminist invective as opposed to pallid sanctifications of the good woman, and such the persistence of the old caricatures, that defenses of the good woman seem to call up an antithetical image, as in the false encomium of the Merchant's Tale or in English Renaissance debate. (Linda Woodbridge argues that defenses brought forth calumnies of women in the English pamphlet wars.) One such reactionary performance is the early seventeenth-century *Araignment of Lewde, idle, froward, and vnconstant women* by a Joseph Swetnam. In this popular work of the early modern era, ancestral misogyny survives at full strength. Swetnam delights to represent woman as the wildest of all beasts: "A Bucke may be inclosed in a Parke, a bridle rules a horse, a Woolfe may be tyed, a Tyger may be tamed, but a froward woman will neuer be tamed, no spur will make hir goe, nor no bridle will holde hir backe." As we would expect, unruliness is only one of a fixed cluster of traits including deceit, garrulity, and homicide. This is the woman, too, who ruins men by spending their wealth. "Man must be at all the cost and yet liue by the losse, a man must take all the paines and women will spend all the gaines, a man must watch and ward, fight and defe[n]d, till the ground, labour in the vineyard, and looke what hee getteth in seauen yeares, a woman will spread it abroad with a forke in one yeare."[50] Women pick men's pockets, empty their purses, and cut their throats: these are old sentiments that men apparently loved to hear reiterated obsessively. Swetnam's satire stands for a thousand. Before Adam Smith can write of the slow and steady accumulation of wealth, the image of the woman who balks men's labor and prevents the accumulation of wealth must be dethroned. Or as we might say, with his image of the constant wife who backs her husband in his constant pursuit of wealth, Adam Smith himself helps to bury the memory of an antithetical tradition of representation that somehow possessed both the stature of high culture and the scurrility of the gutter. That tradition hovers quite visibly behind Hume's teasing essay "Of Love and Marriage," and survives in Pope's epistle "To a Lady," which sparkles with malice and uses dirty arguments.

If the domestic woman secures her husband's gains, the wandering woman of antifeminist lore haunts markets, possesses the deceitful appeal of goods that are sold there, and confounds men just as truth and quackery, real wants and "imaginary wants," the wellborn and the baseborn are themselves confounded in this public place. Those in Adam Smith's time who insisted that commerce made women of men remind us that before commerce was discovered to be a reputable and "improving" activity, it was irrationally (therefore deeply) associated with the least reputable and most ruinous human traits—with women.

No one in English literature embodies the spirit of commerce as vividly as that archwoman, the Wife of Bath. Alan Macfarlane has argued that many of the conditions of capitalism were in place in Chaucer's time, among them private property (especially including property rights over one's own body), contract, mobility, "constant choice and weighing of advantage," and marriage "on an open market."[51] Every one of these factors is instanced with stunning clarity in the Wife of Bath. When she refers to "my profit and myn ese," "my body and my good [goods]," "my land,"[52] she strikes a note of defiant individualism (insisting on her right to make whatever deals she wants with her own property) that is audible at the distance of many centuries and that must have been the more so in a society whose official ideology assigned every individual a role subordinate to the common good. At once widow, wife, and whore, insubordinate by nature, Alice of Bath crosses up the very idea of an assigned role or status. In marrying one man after another, she dramatizes the notorious mutability of economic things; while Boethian/stoic values define the good as stable and eternal, she partakes of all that is shifting, false, and corrupt. Such are her tricks, though, that she actually invokes the stoic tradition ("Redeth Senek, and redeth eek [also] Boece"),[53] affording Adam Smith a dubious precedent for the use of stoic values in the service of commercial interests. The Wife presents, indeed, an unparalleled example of the kind of riot, or "luxury," that the opponents of commerce ranted about centuries later. So too her orality, signified both by the torrential flow of her speech and by her habit of devouring men, illustrates the reputedly all-consuming nature of female desire. In order for the consumer way of life to become respectable, it had to be cleared of incriminating associations with the voracity of women, a trait seen at its most sensational, or perhaps comical, in the Wife of Bath. In order for commerce to become respectable, it had to be cleared of its association with the corruption and craft of women, said to be the first sellers of all. Patriarchy makes much of the difference between legitimate and illegitimate birth; capitalism is itself of base birth—a sort of illegitimate child of patriarchal culture.

As Jews came to be associated with money markets, probably because they were barred from holding wealth in the more stable form of land,[54] so women, with their legendary instability, were traditionally associated with markets (an association neatly concealing the fact that women themselves had been traded, dealt, held). Like Jews, too, women have been depicted as the secret governors of the world and the spreaders of corruption. Thus, for example, Werner Sombart alleges that "women seized the reins of the world" when the production of decadent luxury goods quickened.[55] Adam Smith fears that merchants hold the reins. The merchants he rails against in the *Wealth of Nations*—stateless, insidious, conspiratorial, greedy—all too clearly bear the traditional image of the Jew.[56] Intruding into public affairs and seducing the nation with the siren song of their false arguments (their "interested sophistry"),[57] they less visibly resemble the bad or public woman whose nature it is to mislead, seduce, corrupt, usurp, and go where she doesn't belong. What seals the association of women with commerce is that commercial relations can be "dissolved by the fancy of the parties,"[58] women themselves being identified by ancient habit with shifting fancy, changefulness, and the threat of moral dissolution. In Adam Smith's time the enemies of commercial society, seeing in it the threat and even the fact of moral dissolution, railed against it in much the same terms and tone that had been used for centuries in antifeminist invective. Such, it seems, is the kinship of women and commerce—as in Milton's image of the sexually regal Dalila as a grand trading ship—that denigrators of commerce, men like Juvenal and Boethius, once portrayed women as fickle, bestial or lewd; as visiting a moneylender was likened to visiting a whore;[59] as the moralizing of trade in the seventeenth century somewhat enhances the reputation of women;[60] as Defoe took up the cause of women and trade, both historically slighted; as Adam Smith's discovery of the Newtonian nature of the economic universe makes for the Victorian cult of the angel.

But before the getting of wealth could be rationalized, the commonplace of Fortune as an irrational woman/force presiding over the affairs of men had to fade.[61] In the process, the official image of woman becomes less capricious and whorish, more constant and proper. The harlotry of Fortune (standing for the insecurity of worldly goods and gains) gives way to the decency of the domestic woman (standing watch over property). Fortune presides over the shifting goods of the wide world; the domestic woman presides with blessed constancy over the private realm and confers that security of possession without which (Adam Smith believes) men's efforts at self-improvement are apt to come to nothing. When Smith speaks of our abiding desire for an "augmentation of fortune,"[62] Fortune possesses none of the old scandalous connotations; when David Hume repeats the adage "Fortune commonly favors the bold and enterprizing,"[63] we may or may not discern the Machiavellian image of Fortune as a woman who loves to be physically mastered. Similarly, Hume's notion that philosophical reflection vanquishes the "changeable, weak, and irregular" principles of the mind,[64] not only conserves the manhood of the mind, but hints of the mastery of Fortune (notoriously changeable and irregular)—and still more faintly hints of the regularity of economic pursuits once felt to be more or less subject to Fortune.

Perhaps the locus classicus of the image of Fortune as a female bringing men to ruin is the immensely influential *Consolation of Philosophy* of Boethius, a man of stoic sentiments. Under the tutelage of Lady Philosophy, Boethius learns to vanquish the weakness of his own mind. And Philosophy teaches that Fortune possesses the proverbial character of woman: she spins her wheel, changes, and betrays men. "I am well acquainted," says Philosophy, "with the many deceptions of that monster Fortune. She pretends to be friendly to those she intends to cheat, and disappoints those she unexpectedly leaves with intolerable sorrow. If you will recall her nature and habits, you will be convinced that you had nothing of much value when she was with you and you have not lost anything now that she is gone."[65] This conception of Fortune as a treacherous woman permeated the literature of the Middle Ages, as in this thoroughly conventional Middle English lyric: "The Levedy [Lady] Fortune is bothe frend and fo: / Of pore she maket [maketh] riche, of riche pore also. / She turneth wo into wele, and wele all into wo; / No triste no man [Let no man trust] to this wele, the whel it turnet [turneth] so."[66] As Lear's Fool says, "Fortune, that arrant whore."[67] As Hamlet says, "In the secret parts of Fortune? O, most true, she is a strumpet."[68]

It seems to me that the commonplace of Fortune as a treacherous woman was bound up with the notion that wealth comes and goes, that "weal" can't be trusted because it is subject to Fortune's "wheel," that the accumulation of capital is nothing like as steady and regular as it is in the theory of Adam Smith, that wealth circulates among men like a public woman. In the Grimms' fairy tales there is really no such thing as the gradual accumulation of wealth; wealth appears or fails to appear or disappears, but is not predictably brought into being by labor.[69] Adam Smith would probably have considered such beliefs as superstitions begotten in an age when property was insecure. His entire theory of society is erected on the notion of steady gains and secure possession; that theory also suppresses the notion of the witchery of women that is written into the fairy tales and is bound up as well with the image of Fortune as a woman who frustrates the designs of men.[70]

It is a sign of the belatedness and sentimentality of Adam Smith's stoicism that it does not, as in Boethius, discredit economic striving, but to the contrary, somehow accredits it. Somehow the stoic self-command that Philosophy tries to instill in Boethius is made over to the man industriously laying up gains. Somehow the "steadiness" imparted by Philosophy is made over to the very pursuit of wealth (*TMS*, p. 242). Moreover, instead of adopting a circular model of human life based on Fortune's female changes (from woe to weal, from weal to woe), Adam Smith uses a linear model of the progress of human society from the hunting stage to the commercial stage, a model popularized in the Victorian creed of progress. All the same, the older idea of life as a struggle with Fortune lies just behind Adam Smith. Hume's essay on stoicism treats of Fortune in the same language as Boethius, while the republican tradition, with which Smith has affinities, took over the stoic principle of virtue conquering Fortune; as J. G. A. Pocock has demonstrated, republicans were persuaded that the polity must overcome Fortune if it is to escape the cycle of ruin.[71]

At least into the eighteenth century, republicans were reading in Machiavelli that a prince had better be able to withstand Fortune's sudden changes and that Fortune itself has the nature of a woman: "I conclude, then, that so long as Fortune varies and men stand still, they will prosper while they suit the times, and fail when they do not. But I do feel this: that it is better to be rash than timid, for Fortune is a woman, and the man who wants to hold her down must beat and bully her."[72] Machiavelli is a scandal, of course, and language like this could have no place in the official discourse of an "improved" society, but the notion that women overthrow men nevertheless found licit ways of expressing itself. A noteworthy example appears in two of the *Spectator* papers of the amiable Addison, the man whose ideology of gentleness and commerce so recommended itself to the Scots trying to remedy the backwardness and inhumanity of the republican tradition. In *Spectator* No. 561 (1714) we read of a fictitious club made up of man-devouring widows who together attempt to corner the marriage market and so assure a constant supply of well-to-do men they can marry, drain of their estates, and survive. The president of this club, a woman "who has disposed of six husbands," is a true daughter of the Wife of Bath. *Spectator* No. 573 reveals how her various husbands met their end—one fox-hunting, one dueling, one by apoplexy brought on by his wife's purchase of a two-thousand-pound necklace.[73] In sociable essays that establish the very meaning of taste, Addison manages to play on the dark tradition of antifeminism. Delicately he awakens men's fears that women will survive them and devour their estates, or indeed that women look forward to the day of their death, as in the comment in *The Beggar's Opera*, "The comfortable estate of widowhood, is the only hope that keeps up a wife's spirits."[74]

Marrying in order to be widowed and playing the widow in order to marry, Mrs. President is like Fortune, circular, constant only in her changes, ruinous to men. In order to appear in the *Spectator*, misogyny took the guise of humor. And in order for the cult of the domestic woman to be established, men had to suppress the ancestral notion that women were Fortune-like and had to believe that the seeking of wealth was a rational proceeding nothing like committing oneself into the hands of a strumpet. Fear of women might still come out. As Norbert Elias reminds us that the security of our persons and the evenness of our "affects" are of comparatively recent date, so Addison reveals that not too far behind the image of the home as an island of tranquillity may lie man's old fear of woman as the devourer of his goods, his powers, and his life. Such a devourer is Anthony Trollope's Lizzie Eustace, who captures a rich husband, in short order survives him, possesses herself of the family jewels, and for the bulk of *The Eustace Diamonds* tries to decide whether to exchange widowhood for marriage as she exchanged marriage for widowhood. A perverse despoiler, Lizzie Eustace is a Fortune-figure.[75]

Like Fortune, opinion shifts and is not to be trusted; as we say, "fame and fortune." (In point here is Chaucer's depiction of Fame as a supremely capricious female.) Stoicism inculcates a contempt for opinion, as in Lady Philosophy's disdain for the false judgments of the many; Machiavelli's advice on the manipulation of public opinion;[76] or Adam Smith's own contempt for "the noise of ignorance and folly" (*TMS*, p. 130n.).[77] But it is the essence of the ideology of "gentle commerce" that men are improved both by a respectful submission to the opinions of society and by the diligent and purposeful pursuit of wealth. Smith's friend Benjamin Franklin takes the reformed view of Fortune: a respectable woman, she rewards the constant suitor with her hand; for the virtuous husband she is a faithful wife. As we might expect, Franklin also takes the reformed view of opinion. He preaches a regard for opinion and warns against crossing the opinions of others. In the view of Franklin, it is good for men to court the favor of their neighbors—and to the tradesman, the franchise of the community is life and death. Franklin, then, is with those who believe that the best hope for human improvement lies in the right cultivation of our passion for gain, a passion that includes, however, a yearning for the esteem and "sympathy" that gain brings. Thus he recommends socially licit conduct as the surest way of pleasing others and gaining their good will, and furthermore as a sort of behavioral common language for a community not bound by a single religious orthodoxy or joined in awe before the visible hand of authority. And Franklin likes the thought of the frugal wife taking care of her husband's wealth. In his thought grotesque woman is turning into a domestic being.

Adam Smith, similarly, would use education to discourage dangerously "wanton" and "capricious" opinions, much as men of trade took defensive measures against the threat of gossip and loose opinions to their credit.[78] As Smith proposes to stabilize opinion, so he stabilizes the proverbial unruliness and caprice of women in the figure of the domestic woman. As the modern state is supported by opinion, so the economic male is supported by his wife.

Rousseau would subject women to society's opinion even while he despises opinion and cleaves to the stoic ideal of a man superior to Fortune and opinion; Benjamin Franklin serves to remind us that the cult of the domestic woman not only pictured woman as crowning the gains of men (gains secured in a process improving to men themselves) but pictured opinion as a worthy agency far unlike the false and shifting thing it had once been. No longer a force as corrupt and unstable as Fortune to be mastered by "virtuous" (that is, virile) men, opinion is a steady and well-founded consensus to which all, both men and women, are supposed to submit. Thus is opinion upgraded from a figure of female caprice to a worthy agency.

In the course of "improvement," gain, too, was moralized (trade being bound up with opinion, as shopkeepers depended on a reputation of probity). To Joseph Addison, man of taste, merchants seemed like the most useful of men, and he watched their dealings on the Royal Exchange with pleasure. In Ben Jonson's *Epicoene,* written a century before, the Exchange is coupled with Bed'lem as a place where gadding women go;[79] it has not yet been moralized, just as the old tricks of managing husbands—the Wife of

Bath's brand of husbandry—have not been upgraded into the bourgeois art of household management. The Wife of Bath herself doesn't get rich by any rational, morally improving process of capital accumulation so much as by the death of her husbands one after the other. It seems to me that the Wife is loaded with the worst traits of the merchant class of her time: profiteering, guile, pushiness, love of status and precedence. Just as she makes the most of St. Paul's reluctant concessions to human frailty in the matter of marriage, so she lustily exploits the Church's reluctant tolerance of economic gain.[80] Another way to say this is that in the Wife of Bath economic motives figure as female rapacity. Where medieval officialdom regards the lust for gain as "a *pudendum*,"[81] the Wife boasts of her pudenda (literally "things to be ashamed of"), manifesting the lack of shame, the perverted reason, and the appetitive nature that were said to be inborn in women long before the lust for gain was moralized, and with it women's sociocultural role.

With the complete accreditation of middle-class values over time and the establishment of a middle-class culture of consumption, economic motives lose much of the association they once had with the depravity of women (imagined as consumers of men), whose reputation in turn is somewhat cleansed in the process. Thus we come to forget that men had been warned against the love of money as against a temptress who lures men to ruin.[82] We come to forget, too, that the love of luxury and display which Adam Smith sees as the very mechanism of commercial society, and Defoe as its habitual vice, was for centuries catalogued among the most arrant vices of women.[83] As though "luxury," "consumption" and "woman" were bound together in a single cluster of meaning (women having been charged with luxurious appetites and ruinous consumption), the more sensational meanings of all three terms were contested during the life of Adam Smith. The shift that the term "luxury" underwent—the partial purgation of its scandalous meaning—is recorded in a tract written by one Joseph Harris in 1757, where we read, "The word luxury hath usually annexed to it, a kind of opprobrious idea; but so far as it encourages the arts, whets the inventions of men, and finds employments for more of our own people, its influence is benign . . . to the whole society."[84] However, the "opprobrious" connotations of luxury, a word redolent of lust and corruption, lingered even in a society given to the production and consumption of luxury goods as never before. Or rather, the acceleration of commerce itself provoked diatribes against luxury, diatribes that rose to a frenzied rant similar in tone to antifeminism at its most feverish. Commerce and modernity prevailed, although Adam Smith himself, among others, particularly men of classical persuasion, continued to worry about the luxury and "effeminacy" of modern society.[85]

The modern concept of luxury goods (as innocent enjoyments, boons to commerce, badges of status) eclipses the older concept of luxury (as the indulgence of corrupt desires) that lies behind it. Similarly, not far behind Adam Smith's portrayal of men as driven by the desire "to be observed, to be attended to, to be taken notice of with sympathy, complacency, and approbation" (*TMS*, p. 50) lies a tradition of castigation of female vanity, and in particular of scarlet women like the Wife of Bath who are given to competitive emulation and insist on making a show of themselves. Long before Adam Smith wrote of exhibitionistic men whose dearest desire is to smite the hearts of their audience, preachers railed against "women that busieth hem [themselves] aboute gay apparaile to schewe hem with to menis [men's] sight."[86] Margery Kempe, the fifteenth-century visionary, describes her unregenerate self in just these terms, saying that she wore loud clothing "that it schuld be the mor staryng to mennis sygth [sight]" and that "Alle hir desyr was for to be worshepd [admired] of the pepul."[87] In Smithian society, men themselves take up that desire. Indeed, it becomes the master motive of their activity. They desire nothing so much as to be stared at in admiration. Like the poor man's son who labors in the hope of one day stunning society with his wealth, the Smithian actor busies himself to acquire things whose value is show. And so Adam Smith's contempt of the sheer vanity that by his own account drives commercial society, resembles the eighteenth-century novelist's censure of "romance" and its glittering illusions: both are committed to what they condemn.

When Mandeville floats the idea that men's love of dressing in scarlet keeps multitudes employed and makes for a wealthy nation, he gives a new turn to the evocative theme of the scarlet woman: not only does the Mandevillian thesis direct our attention to the appetitive male rather than the appetitive female, but it calls into question the supposedly ruinous effects of those once-female habits of depravity.[88] While men had railed for generations against the insatiable desires of woman,[89] Mandeville insists that men's love of luxury knows no limit, and moreover keeps commercial society in motion. While men had once complained of the fickleness of Fortune, Mandeville claims that changing tastes and fashions—"fickleness," in fact—is "the very wheel that turn'd the trade."[90] If Fernand Braudel is right, modern Western civilization has the ironic distinction of being the only civilization erected on instability itself—erected on "fickle" whims that its own traditions pronounced trivial and worse.[91] He might have added that instability and shifting desire were identified with women by the whole weight of the same tradition that moderns began to repudiate.

Mandeville was one such repudiator. He had his detractors, among them Adam Smith, but by advancing the idea that luxury (a word with overtones of lust and effeminacy) was a public benefactor, and by endowing men so richly with the most celebrated vices of women (vanity, luxury, craftiness, unbounded desire), he dashed men's pretensions wonderfully. Mandeville felt that a commercial society that rested on men's vanity and corruption rested on a perfectly "solid basis."[92] I think Smith would have recoiled from this notion as he recoiled from Mandeville's roguery generally, and I have reasoned that he looked to stoic principles to give his own theory a "solid" basis. The idea of basing society on something as baseless and imagistic as the love of admiration was too much even for Adam Smith's sense of irony.

When Smith says that men behave like aldermen's wives (*TMS,* p. 57)—meaning that men are given to petty rivalry and parade, like the citizens' wives of the General Prologue of the *Canterbury Tales,* or like the Wife of Bath herself[93]—we realize that he knows as well as Mandeville the role played in commercial society by envious emulation and amour-propre. His argument plays off traditional antifeminism. In portraying the rich as creatures of fashion who value gold principally for purposes of show and "ornament,"[94] Adam Smith makes over to them, and their innumerable imitators, something of the character of the traditional adorned woman, corrupted by luxury; by the same token, though, his caustic analysis destroys men's claim to superiority over women. (Hence stoicism: it establishes men's superiority, puts it on solid ground after all.) Complaints about the effeminacy of society; jibes at ladies' men, effete aristocrats and their imitators, and foppery in general in eighteenth-century England—these things suggest a crisis of gender distinctions. A crisis occasioned, it may be, by the "feminization" of a market society that so institutionalized traits long catalogued as female vices, that by the time the *Wealth of Nations* was published, there existed some three or four hundred hairstyles for the elegant man.[95]

Hence Smith's scorn of "that impertinent and foolish thing called a man of fashion" (*TMS,* p. 63), as of a kind of neuter. Hence his finding that men like aldermen's wives, rivals for social distinction, keep commercial society going (*TMS,* p. 57). With the institution of the domestic woman, women "paradoxically" go from "embodying the disorder that men fear to embodying the values men seek";[96] as, in the thinking of Francis Hutcheson, consumption paradoxically goes from dramatizing the rapacity and sensuality of women (consumers of man's substance) to exemplifying the workings of the "moral sense" itself;[97] as the vices so long castigated in women—unbounded desire, self-love, envious rivalry, love of display—paradoxically go from being threats to the social order to being the very ground of that order, a shift illustrated by the moral theory of Adam Smith. For centuries men poured vitriol on the insubordinate woman, that profoundly evocative figure dressing above her station and roaming about parading her "luxury";[98] paradoxically, the emulation of the rich, the taste for luxury, and (as we learn from Adam Smith) even the urge to display become the very mechanism of a consumer society.

In the essays of Addison, consumption in the old sense of riotous indulgence is turning into taste, and women from figures of license and ruin into fellow humans. Hence the "paradox" that a devourer of men whom traditional satirists would portray as a she-demon becomes in Addison a human being (or almost one) who does what's done in a commercial society. The man-consuming widow of Addison's *Spectator* No. 573 is nothing so much as a speculator. She speculates on husbands, guessing on their characters and the time remaining to them and investing the spoils of the preceding marriage on each new venture. Traditional antifeminism takes on a more human image in Mrs. President, who is really no worse than men, once perceived as appetitive creatures given to the love of show. Mandeville perceives men in these terms; ironist that he is, he doesn't deny that women consume men's substance, but simply claims that their expensive habits are socially availing and add greatly to the wealth of the nation.[99] Adam Smith knows that the multiplication and indulgence of "imaginary wants" enhance the wealth of the nation, but unlike Mandeville strains to save the dignity of men even so. It needs saving because the trendsetter in the multiplication of wants is the fop who tries to distinguish himself "by the multitude and variety" of his costumes.[100]

With her fantastic costume and wandering ways, the Wife of Bath fits the description of the showy woman. I bring her up not only because men inveighed against the public woman in obsessively constant terms from the Middle Ages through and beyond the lifetime of Adam Smith, but because she bears so closely on the process that moralized the culturally official reputation of both women and the pursuit of wealth and status. If negative liberty means being unrestricted, free to do as you like, the Wife of Bath clamors for negative liberty outright, which is to say that negative liberty is as yet associated with the license and caprice of women. The Wife gets her fifth husband to say, "Do as thee lust," Do as you like;[101] and so negative liberty is seen as a comical-monstrous expression of women's wild nature. What is now liberty was once license, and that license was concentrated in women. Swetnam takes up the theme in the Renaissance, arguing that women are mad to go where they want, say what they please, and have what they will.[102] (Of course men want the same privileges; but women make a polemic of it. They are too vocal and clamorous, which makes their doctrine of negative liberty absurd.) The association of liberty with license and willfulness carries into the thought of Adam Smith himself: thus his argument that a standing army makes the sovereign secure enough that he doesn't have to crack down on the "licentious liberty" of mobs.[103] As a rule, though, Adam Smith thinks of liberty not as wild but as lawlike, not as clamorous but as quiet and respectable. Left to itself, the system of "natural" or negative liberty functions with the regularity of a law of Nature, predictably raising the level of wealth and civility in society. And as liberty becomes unlicentious, women become "the fair sex." When John Stuart Mill argued out the case for noninterference (or negative liberty), he was in one sense codifying rather than challenging the doctrines of the Victorian middle class, a class that had determined that the freedom to pursue social and economic gains and enjoy them in security had nothing of scandal in it. Once that freedom had been associated with the scandal of woman. Now the dominant ideology cast women themselves not as beasts beneath the level of men (wilder than tigers, according to Swetnam) but as higher beings who could raise men above their own animal nature.

So far I have suggested that the displacement of the traditional image of woman as a threat to man and his goods owed much to the elevation of the pursuit of wealth to the status of a reasonable and edifying process. Traditionally women had been accused of buying their beauty and selling their virtue and gadding about the markets, as though all the disrepute of commerce were specially concentrated in them; as we have seen, they were also associated through the figure of Fortune with an irrational force working to the ruin of men. The upgrading of economic pursuits to a theoretically Newtonian level of regularity[104] did much to deprive the traditional ranting language of antifeminism of its authority. (Theoretically "unalterable" in her principles, the domestic woman represents a kind of proof that the commercial way of life is grounded in the unchangeable nature of things.) As trade became more godly and morally beneficial, as in the thought of Benjamin Franklin, women came to be pictured less, perhaps, as creatures who conduct commerce through their ports and more as persons called to "economy" in the original sense of household management.

Ideally the prudent man feels his possessions are *so* secure in the hands of his economical wife that he loses the need to cheat other men in the world of business to make up for a wife's depredations. So it is that the domestic woman sheds an improving influence over capitalism. "In [his wife's] personal honour and fidelity, and also in her oeconomy and prudence with regard to all affairs at home, her husband reposes such perfect confidence that he can go abroad, and attend to public business, without the smallest anxiety about his domestic concerns, or the least temptation to enrich himself at the expense of other men."[105] If the measure of progress is security of private property, then the highest form of society is that which has most decisively suppressed the idea that the wealth of men is in the hands of a never-to-be-trusted female, and which has most officially idealized women themselves as watchers over the secret places where men's wealth is. A medieval or Renaissance writer likening women to the moon would probably be pointing up their proverbial fickleness; a popular Victorian homilist likens domestic women to the moon in a passage celebrating their "unalterable principles."[106] In Chaucer, if women are likened to kept birds, it is to make the point that they are wild by nature; Edmund Burke likens the beautiful woman to a beautiful dove, both of them displaying gradually swelling lines, both of them emblematic of a social order of fine gradations, imperceptible changes, and gradually augmenting wealth.[107]

By the time of the full ascendancy of the middle class in the Victorian era, the woman of the house performed nothing like the role of producer (churning, spinning, and so on) that middling women had played not so long before. One function of ideology, Eve Kosofsky Sedgwick theorizes, is to justify a given system in terms of the values it has overthrown. Thus Adam Smith justifies commercial society in the name of stoic values that, by his own analysis, belong to a surpassed stage of civilization. Thus Defoe defends the valor of a commercial society whose men no longer go to war. Thus Fordyce idealizes the good woman who labors with her own hands and delights in the work. Thus, too, the heavily ideological notion of the family "strengthens as the jurisdiction and the private material basis of the family itself become weaker and more internally contradictory, under the atomizing effects of early [that is, eighteenth-century] capitalism."[108] The ideologizing of the family, the magnifying of its sentimental importance, rises as its economic importance as a locus of production recedes. And of course it is the domestic woman, supremely without a role in production, who of all beings is the most sentimentalized.[109] This suggests that the cult of the domestic angel becomes possible as the Smithian division of labor reaches the point where producers are sharply divided from consumers.

Indeed, the division of labor—the starting point of Adam Smith's analysis in the *Wealth of Nations*—could take on the status of a sacred ordinance for those who believed that men and women were meant to perform different duties, the domestic sphere being assigned to the latter.[110] But if the division of labor in this sense domesticates woman, it also leaves the domestic woman without enough tasks to occupy her hours; thus Dr. Johnson observes that unless women used up their time in make-work and decorative arts, there is no telling what mischief they would wreak on men.[111] And in theory, the decorative life is infinitely pleasing. If, as Terry Eagleton claims, coercion "aestheticized" doesn't feel like coercion,[112] then the male fancy of a woman leading an aesthetic (non-utilitarian) existence in a pleasure cage would seem to be the height of the aesthetic. For his part, Adam Smith observes that there are many who aestheticize power—who discourse on the beauties of "the great system of public police [order]" (*TMS,* p. 186) and encourage a kind of delicious contemplation of government rather than training attention directly on the ends government exists to serve. This habit of sweetening power and idealizing the harmonies of the system of subordination—a habit Smith himself seems to consider corrupt—prepares for the ideology of the "aesthetic" or nonproducing woman who feels not coerced but blessed.

If women become "pure" consumers, it is no longer an article of a ruling creed that they consume a man's substance. One reason may simply be that it is so obviously children and not wives who eat up wealth. As Alan Macfarlane has shown, in nuclear families of the British or American kind, children cost their parents heavily, and this with no sure expectation on the parents' side that their huge investment will be repaid even in part. (Think of the tumbling children and improvident parents in Dickens.) Adam Smith himself finds "parental tenderness a much stronger affection than filial piety" (*TMS,* p. 142). This he judges a wise dispensation of Nature, which makes children dependent on parents but not the reverse, as though there were no cultures where grown children took care of their parents.[113] In any case, the evidence Macfarlane compiles suggests, too, that men were well enough aware of the costs of children. Having sold his land to support seven children, an eighteenth-century gentleman nevertheless remarries when his wife dies. He finds " 'I have got a house full of fine children, and straitened circumstances,' though he loyally wrote that he would 'a thousand times rather choose this situation, than be bound for life to a person I could not love, though in the midst of affluence and worldly prosperity.' That people were faced with the choice of either affluence or children is the crucial fact."[114]

One transformation wrought by capitalism, writes Macfarlane, "is to make children seem a problem, a burden, a cost."[115] Thus Hume argues, in justification of the double standard, that men need to believe their children are theirs if they are to take on such an onerous expense willingly; thus Mary Wollstonecraft observes that no man is keen to marry a widow encumbered with children—

no man wants to support another's offspring. Considering that during Adam Smith's lifetime, middle-ranking parents spent as never before on schools, toys, books, nurses, clothes for children, it makes sense that children began to be considered a cost. Eighteenth-century England may not have invented the child, but it did invent the child as consumer.[116] In a family with a number of children, all of whom consume and need to be kept unworking if the family is to be respectable, and all of whom will one day leave the family without making any economic return, it becomes simply pointless to sing the old song about wives devouring men's wealth.[117] Anyway, in the case just cited the wife died.

With the distinct separation of production and consumption, and the sentimentalization of the family on the consuming side, the notion of "consuming" lost most of the ravaging connotations that it had when women were officially vilified for consuming man's substance. In Chaucer's time the word "consume" carries a negative valence, meaning "to destroy, to use up, to waste, to exhaust"[118] (a meaning activated by today's critics of the profligacy of consumer society). The Wife of Bath consumes her husbands. If "aggressive consumption lies at the heart of successful bourgeois society,"[119] the bourgeois Wife brings out, or as we might say de-expurgates, the meaning of aggressive consumption, with its implication of desire that is not quenched but actually kindled on being satisfied. In theory the domestic woman consumes decently and serves as proof and crown of her man's prosperity. Where wealth was once displayed in great entertainments and liveried retainers, the domestic woman is, as it were, the sole retainer of the bourgeois male—King Lear's last knight. Her leisure, her attentions, her status as consumer shower credit on him.

In the change from feudal to bourgeois modes of production and display that Adam Smith sees as a turning point of history, the consuming woman changes, then, approximately from a figure of riot to a figure of order. The words "consume" and "luxury" undergo a similar change of meaning during the life of Smith himself, outgrowing some of the foul associations they once had with women and their corrupt appetites.[120] When Charlotte Perkins Gilman laments that the condition of the late-nineteenth-century wife is to "consume food, to consume clothes, to consume houses and furniture and amusements, to take and take and take forever,"[121] she revives the old discourse of the riot and rapacity of women, but attributes those traits now to women's exclusion from the world of production. It is as though Gilman exploded the Victorian myth by portraying the female consumer all over again as a creature of appetites both boundless and foul. Producing nothing and consuming wantonly, the "over-sexed" Victorian woman is a "sink into which human labor vanishes without any return,"[122] the image evoking an obscene pit, at once mouth, genital cavern, and privy. Interestingly, Gilman finds the domestic woman given over to "all that is luxurious and enervating,"[123] which is exactly the idiom that men of republican sentiment, like Adam Smith and John Stuart Mill, used to express their fears of the depraving effects of commercial society on *men*. Perhaps Victorian men preserved their manliness—that favored Victorian term—by creating the ideal of a feeble woman who would carry the ill effects that were predicted of the commercial way of life by its own best theorists.

The Victorian ideal of "manliness" is after all heavily nostalgic, calling up as it does Agincourt, country squires, physical gallantry, good bloodlines—a way of life totally outside of commerce. With its shifting contractual relations, commerce outmoded the idea of old blood living on that the cultists of "manliness" celebrated, much as the narrow regulation of the passions demanded by the commercial way of life (and underscored by Adam Smith) ruled out the robust physicality and bold imprudence of "manliness." Like Edmund Burke's vision of true men of chivalric spirit, Victorian "manliness" was infused with archaism.[124] Summoning up a way of life "neither Puritan nor mercantile,"[125] the romance of "manliness" represents a sort of wishful escape from the realities of middle-class life. The "manliness" of the mercantile male is a fiction, an illusion in need of shoring up. The Victorian woman, who was to make men look sturdy and vigorous by comparison, shored it up.

Rather than accept the Victorian conception of a binary universe wherein "male hardness" confronts "female benevolence,"[126] I incline to the idea that men were more like women than they liked to admit—women's secret sharers. This resemblance comes out with clarity in a passage in Conrad's *Heart of Darkness,* a tale in which men are consumers, the consumers of Africa. On his journey into the Belgian Congo, Marlow meets his company's chief accountant, who, in an environment of murder and rapine (thus ends the myth of the gentleness of trade) keeps his books in perfect order and even maintains the impeccable appearance of "a hairdresser's dummy." Who better than a good accountant to illustrate the bourgeois virtues of probity and fiscal exactitude? Bourgeois values in turn envisioned women as inferior beings, disqualified by reason of their weakness from going out into the strife of the world; something of this notion is written into *Heart of Darkness* itself. But in effect our accountant is that woman. His exact way with his books is the exactitude of a good housewife who accounts for everything. His mannequinesque appearance likens him to the decorative beings that women were rumored to be, as well as to the inanimate men of Mill's *On Liberty*. He bears a certain resemblance to the fashion dolls that at one time set the standard of taste in women's hairstyles and clothing. His evident vanity is a reputedly female vice. He even blushes like a woman and speaks "modestly":

> I respected the fellow [says Marlow]. Yes; I respected his collars, his vast cuffs, his brushed hair. His appearance was certainly that of a hairdresser's dummy; but in the great demoralisation of the land he kept up his appearance. That's backbone. His starched collars and got-up shirt-fronts were achievements of character. He had been out nearly three years; and, later, I could not help asking him how he managed to sport such linen. He had just the faintest blush, and said modestly, "I've been teaching one of the native women about the station. It was difficult. She had a distaste for the work." Thus this man had verily accomplished something. And he was devoted to his books, which were in apple-pie order.[127]

This man's creation in the middle of the jungle of a little sanctuary where order reigns, likens him to the wife who presides over a little church (the home) in the midst of a violent and nasty world. He has a native woman take care of his clothes, the wife superintends servants who do such work. His completely private frame of reference, another officially female trait, is shown by his ability to block out what is going on all around him. Where the Victorian woman was thought to civilize her man, the accountant purportedly carries the blessings of civilization to the jungle of Africa. (In fact, the trading company deals glass beads to the natives, an exact equivalent of the trinkets and baubles that the men of commercial society busy themselves to possess, according to Adam Smith.) In a sense, this "hairdresser's dummy" represents the finished product of a code of values that represents a close attention to private gain—the sort of diligence the accountant exhibits—as a civilizing influence. An incarnation of those "inferior" virtues of prudence, circumspection, constancy, steadiness, in which Adam Smith put his hopes, he descends directly from *The Theory of Moral Sentiments*.

CHAPTER 5

Conclusion

In the moral theory of Adam Smith men bear a family resemblance to women, traditionally barred from public life chiefly because of an alleged defect of reason. Smith openly depreciates the reason of men and deems it much better for them to attend closely to the getting of wealth, follow custom and habit, and busy themselves with baubles than to employ such faulty reason as they possess to call shaky structures into question and embitter public discourse. He settles, therefore, for the prudent man: a man of reduced passions and decent manners who combines assiduous effort with political quietism. In a lesser version of the story of heroism conquering Fortune, Smith envisions prudent men whose "inferior" virtues (*TMS*, p. 304) and sheer constancy build the wealth of the nation. Implied but not actually stated by Smith is that the common good is best promoted less by traditional masculine virtues than by virtues associated with female propriety, such as diligence, seemliness, quiet, and in particular the avoidance of public contention. If as J. G. A. Pocock remarks economic man was seen in Adam Smith's time "as on the whole a feminised, even an effeminate being" ruled by appetite and fantasy,[1] Smith's more decorous male reflects the process that tamed such ruinous "female" forces as Luxury and Fortune to make possible the stable accumulation of wealth. In the society where wealth builds steadily, the proper woman calms the passions of men (unlike Luxury and Fortune, who play on them) while the prudent man calms the polity itself by abstaining from public questions.

Smith belongs, then, among those wary of political remedies

and passions. Of this group Edmund Burke, who thought so highly of Smith's *Moral Sentiments,* is the most forceful. Burke hates and dreads the spirit of contention and in his heart prefers that commoners know nothing of political matters, as he prefers the deep shade of the great oaks of tradition to enlightenment. It is not for us, he insists, to throw into question what is bequeathed by the past. Burke is more abusive than Smith, and more of a glorifier of the past and of the beauties of subordination, but as to the dangers of political innovation, they were at one—both men reprobating the idea of tearing down the existing order to raise a new one on a foundation of reason. "The age of chivalry is gone," laments Burke, "and sophisters, economists and calculators have taken over."[2] In the Arthurian language of *The Theory of Moral Sentiments,* the greatest of the economists seems to say that calculation need not be the end of chivalry, and the fiction of manhood informing this work is indeed nothing but one of those "pleasing illusions"[3] identified by Burke as the saving graces of life.

Burke was on guard against the risks of the political imagination, understood as wanton and volatile. Believing as he did that ambition and rapine spring from overheated imagination (*TMS,* p. 57), Smith, too, appreciated the threat of imagination, and it is as though he tried to civilize that wild force by confining it to civil pursuits. He defused the dangers of imagination by dedicating men to the pursuit of "imaginary" goods he considered neither better nor worse than toys. Thus, while Burke descants on the "false ideas and vain expectations" entertained by men "destined to travel in the obscure walks of laborious life,"[4] the other tells of a poor man's son whose head buzzes with false ideas and vain hopes (a precursor of Pip in Dickens's *Great Expectations*) but who presents no threat to the political order, enslaving himself as he does to a life of numbing fatigue and power-worship. And though Smith heaps ridicule on the poor man's son, that seeker is no more beguiled than anyone else, even a man of prudence, who yearns for imaginary goods. At a time when it was widely believed that reason must check the vagrancy of the imagination, the prudence of the prudent man makes him look rational even while his motions are driven not by rational self-interest but by the desire for illusory goods like status.[5] Thus imagination is diverted from political endeavor into the life of patient labor. Even as the old regime is demystified (and Smith well knew how groundless the worship of political superiors really was), even as tradition begins to be called habit, the polity continues to stand and wealth builds. If men pursue their imaginary wants with regularity and obey the regularities of the groups they find themselves in, society predictably gains. Through frivolous desires and blind miscalculations—through the incapacity of reason proclaimed by conservatives—comes the progress proclaimed by liberals.

What Hazlitt said of Burke (an economic liberal himself) holds equally true of Smith: he believed a man "must be chiefly interested in those things which are nearest to him, and with which he is best acquainted, since his understanding cannot reach equally to every thing; because he must be most attached to those objects which he has known the longest . . . that is, because he is by nature the creature of habit and feeling."[6] The feebleness of reason; the corresponding importance of habit and sentiment; the centrality of self-interest—many Smithian principles are implied here. In spite of the familiar antithesis of the Enlightenment and the romantic reaction, it seems that Smith, a member of the Scottish Enlightenment, has much in common with the Burkean strain of romantic feeling. In time this joint romanticism made for the ideal of the Victorian woman, romantic in weakness, performing her role in a sexual division of labor founded in turn on the division of labor Smith identified as the secret of progress. The influential homilist Sarah Ellis discusses the duties of woman in Burkean language, poeticizing the sphere of closest acquaintance and endowing women with a kind of chivalric fealty. When all was well, women's "sphere of action was at their own fireside, and the world in which they moved was one where pleasure of the highest, purest order, naturally and necessarily arises out of acts of duty faithfully performed."[7] Heightened with the beauty of the feminine, memories of chivalry, and the aura of sublimated eros, Smithian values are romanticized in Sarah Ellis's portrait of woman. The wealth of nations is romantically transfigured into the "nation's moral wealth," of which woman is guardian.[8] And as though in illustration of the bond between Burke and Smith, woman's chivalric love of duty prepares her man for the rigors of economic competition. Men live in a bruising world ruled by utility; women (says Ellis) inhabit the realm of feeling, and it is their calling to bring the balm of kindness to men. Here the lines of our own society, "romantic in its private and imaginative life and utilitarian or instrumentalist in its public, effective life,"[9] are already drawn. The realms of production and consumption are officially split.

In Adam Smith's doctrine that production exists to supply the largely specious pleasures of consumption, we discern a clear augury of the technical reason that now prevails—the reason that fits means to ends but does not apply to ends themselves.[10] It is usual to trace instrumental reason back to the Puritan principle of ascetic labor, but no Puritan, I imagine, ever alleged that ends lie in some realm of choice outside the jurisdiction of reason. "Reason is but choosing," says Milton.[11] The maxim that reason is and ought to be the slave of the passions Milton would have fought with all his strength, but in Smith's economic version of this maxim—his theory that the ingenuity of production goes to serve vacuous and trivial ends of consumption, or in other words that men slave away with "the most unrelenting industry" to achieve empty goals (*TMS*, p. 181)—instrumental reason as we know it takes shape.

Instrumental reason produces, like the pin-factory immortalized at the beginning of the *Wealth of Nations*. But if we want to know what uses those pins, such perfect emblems of triviality, are destined to serve, or where they end up, maybe the place to look is the dressing table of Belinda in Pope's "Rape of the Lock," with its "files of pins." If, as Smith says, we produce for the sake of consumption, and in turn consume for vanity's sake ("to be observed, to be attended to . . ." [*TMS*, p. 50]), who can outdo Belinda in vanity as she contemplates her own divine image in a mirror, accepts the tributes of commerce, and unknown to herself enjoys the admiring attentions of the spirits of the air? In the figure of this "demanding consumer" is illustrated the traditional association of women with consumption—the same that led Smith's French contemporaries to identify women with overconsumption and that got women typed "as creatures of consumption par excellence."[12] In effect, with his thoroughly ironic defense of the luxury consumption that jumped to a new level in his century, Adam Smith converted the exorbitant desire and wandering imagination commonly imputed to women from a threat into a prop of order. His doctrine that consumption, by its nature endless, "is the sole end and purpose of all production"[13] not only outlines the instrumental reason of today; it implies that the defective reason, the excessive desire that men share with women can be steered away from dangerous channels and into civil and innocent channels of consumption in a society economically busy and politically quiet. The consumer who mistakes utility and the subject whose loyalty does not depend on calculations of utility (*TMS*, p. 52) are one person.

Although he despises the fops of the upper class who set the standard of consumption, Smith would prefer that they were not overthrown. As contemptuous as he is of the delights of consumption, his theory envisions the popularizing of the consumer habits of the rich. This is the only "democratization" it allows.[14] Smith would rather see the elite's monopoly undermined slowly by the market than all at once by the concerted action of political-minded men or women. He affirms subordination and the duties of one's station. In part, he affirms this commonplace just because it *is* a commonplace and not something that people "reason and dispute" about (*TMS*, p. 53). A pure case of an unreflecting response is cited very near the beginning of *The Theory of Moral Sentiments,* as though the principle somehow grounded the author's argument: when we watch the rope walker in the circus, we gyrate naturally, without having to think about it (*TMS*, p. 10). The poor man's son gives himself up body and soul to the unthinking pursuit of the glittering images that fascinate everyone else. While Smithian theory does ask us to reflect (for example, to consider what is likely to offend), it also accords a considerable role to trancelike responses akin to the swoons of sentimental literature, unreasoned attachments, states of delusion, hypnotic effects, "waking dreams and idle reveries" (*TMS*, p. 52), like Burke's waking romance of chivalry. As a corrective to the political rationalism Burke found so menacing, it is as if Smith prescribed a moderate irrationalism.

We must abandon, then, the schematic theory that the romantic movement asserts all those values of a "patriarchal or feudal" world threatened by the march of capitalist rationalism,[15] for the most renowned theorist of commerce—Adam Smith—distrusted abstract rationalism severely, was much admired by the same Burke claimed by the romantics, and preserved the beautiful Burkean fiction of the patriarchal rule of the self over the self: stoicism. Just as Burke defends collective prejudices as superior to the puny "stock of reason" that we possess in isolation,[16] so in Smithian theory the feebleness of our reason as consumers is redeemed by the ingenuity and power of the apparatus of production; implicitly the "liberal" Smith offers an economic version of the "conservative" precept that the species is wise, the individual foolish. For all that is said about the exaltation of reason in the Enlightenment, such is the reduction of reason in the Smithian moral universe that its central moral mechanism, sympathy, holds us in its sway like a trance; starts up at times without reflection; and possesses the automatism of habit. (Sarah Ellis was to say that the moral being of women is fulfilled as the performance of their duties of sympathy cements into habit.) In time, the almost hypnotic sympathy that binds the Smithian moral universe becomes the almost hypnotic images and phrases that bind millions of "atomized" political consumers.[17] As Kenneth Burke, quoting one of Adam Smith's favorite authorities, says of newspaper headlines, "Subtly, they act by the principle of empathy (for, as Cicero reminds us, in the mere representation of an emotion there is something which invites the beholder to participate in it.)"[18]

Adam Smith presents a searching analysis of society that terminates in counsels of submission—a skeptical account that commits us to such unskeptical actions as social reflex and unreasoned habit. The breaking of social norms Smith's theory does not countenance. Faced with, say, Mary Wollstonecraft's public attack on the enfeebling ideal of womanhood then current,[19] a Smithian might play up the conventional aspects of her argument in the interest of protecting social consensus. In point of fact, as though in accordance with the Smithian principle that what is approved is approved, critical opinion at the time applauded those positions Mary Wollstonecraft took that were already canonical, and ignored or slighted the rest.[20] Nor does the meticulous antirationalism of Smith allow for Wollstonecraft's argument that women have rational souls (her own being demonstrated by her war on sophistical reasoning) and that reason equips us to sweep away the idiocy of prejudice. The clash between the rationalism of Mary Wollstonecraft and the irrationalism of Adam Smith, both of them nourished by the Commonwealth tradition, is ironic in that she shared his contempt for the fashionable and partiality for the middle class, and actually quoted Smith at length and with approval in the *Vindication of the Rights of Woman*. And it seems to me that Mary Wollstonecraft did well not to yield unreflectingly to the norms of her society. She dissented, in spite of traditional prohibitions on women's entry into the public realm, in spite of the dogma that quiet and habit are infinitely superior to contention. She could not have written as she did if she had approved of what was approved, or done what was done, in Smithian style. The argument that argument is sterile and futile goes from Bacon to Locke, informs Smith's vision of the concord of sentiments, and is reflected to this day in popular contempt for what is called rhetoric as opposed to the real goods delivered by the system of production. But in the case of Mary Wollstonecraft's polemic against the enfeeblement of women, argument was neither groundless nor pointless.

As a defender of commerce, Adam Smith had to face the question of how men could preserve their autonomy and moral standing in spite of the corruption and yearning for false goods—in eighteenth-century terms, the vanity and luxury—that prevail in commercial society. His solution at the level of theory was to install a man within men, a stoic governor or monitor who keeps down passions and calibrates conduct to social requirements; in effect, autonomy itself is made an instrument of compliance. Smith's writing resonates with the language of stoicism, and to the degree that he steers men away from the one model they have of participation in public life (the classical model) in favor of the more fruitful way of trade and sympathy, Smith in effect echoes the history of the stoic ideal, which survived the collapse of the ancient polis and was written into the antipolitical ethos of Christianity. If at one time stoicism affirmed the man "active in his political capacity," the republicanism of Cicero, Smith's favorite ancient, is already commemorative, idealizing what no longer is, while the Smithian man of prudence does not act in a political capacity, that role having been idealized out of existence.[21] The distinctly quietistic strain in stoicism, moreover, discourages the sort of battling undertaken by Mary Wollstonecraft, many of whose positions, as has been noted, were actually close to Smith's; in this respect it is as though stoicism offered Smith a security against the riskier implications that might have been drawn from his premises, such as that a political order where foppery and not merit rules does not deserve to stand.[22]

Additionally, stoicism affords Adam Smith a vantage point of ironic detachment from which to survey the follies of men. In the cool dispassion with which he views the prizes of consumption, in his own stoic temperament, we discern something of the indifference to ends that comes to characterize the instrumental reason prevailing in the commercial order. Means drift away from ends— the gap that distinguishes instrumental reason opens—when the ends of men's efforts are so trivial that reason dissociates itself from them. "Of such mighty importance," Smith observes ironically, "does it appear to be, in the imaginations of men, to stand in that situation which sets them most in the view of general sympathy and attention. And thus, place, that great object which divides the wives of aldermen, is the *end* of half the labours of human life" (*TMS*, p. 57; my emphasis). The idiom of heroic triviality ("mighty importance," "great object") recalls "The Rape of the Lock," although it may be that Smith's irony exceeds even Pope's. Of Wordsworth, Hazlitt said that, in the spirit of the French Revolution, he brought low the mighty and "rais[ed] trifles into importance."[23] It seems to have been Adam Smith's hope that by occupying themselves mightily with trifles, the men of consumer society would at least divert their imagination from the political attempts that lay behind Hazlitt's remark.

I have argued that the love of false goods, the competition for social eminence, the anxious seeking and itching envy, the imitation of corrupt others—the very conditions that seem to call for an infusion of Roman self-mastery into Smithian man—rule out stoicism. Stoicism cuts down desires, and as the theorists of trade recognized and stated, commercial society expands them; the multiplication of wants is the correlative of the division of labor. From Smith's observations on the motives driving economic actors, Isaac Kramnick composes a sketch of a figure who is anything but stoic, a man "obsessive and anxious," haunted by "insecurity" and the dread of losing status.[24] The language of stoicism puts some firm ground under this figure—or at least the illusion of ground. With Adam Smith's sentimental fiction of male nobility, we are on our way to the equally sentimental fictions that today seem to rule public discourse. Perhaps our equivalent of the spectral stoicism of the *Moral Sentiments* is the fantasy language in which "masculine" businessmen save the nation from politicians.[25]

The moral standing of men in commercial society cannot be vested in stoicism. As an ideal of desperate austerity, stoicism has no place in a society of consumers, which is probably why Mandeville debunked it. Not the regulation of the passions to social standards but the power of disputing those standards if need be; not the traditional morality of submission and resignation, dignified as stoicism, but the questioning of that morality itself, is the mark of autonomy. Like Hume, Smith was himself a questioner, and his highly contentious *Wealth of Nations* a masterpiece of polemic. Maybe he thought that once natural liberty of trade was established, no such argumentative assault would have to be launched again. Maybe he thought of the *Wealth of Nations* what Burke thought of the Revolution of 1688: that it was an act that would never have to be repeated.

Notes

Chapter 1

1. The theory that the end of men's efforts is display corresponds to the view, frequently voiced in the eighteenth century, that the end-point of trade is the adorned woman, showcase of luxury goods that come to her from the four corners of the earth.

2. I use the variorum edition of *The Theory of Moral Sentiments,* eds. D. D. Raphael and A. L. Macfie (Indianapolis: Liberty Classics, 1982). On irrational sympathy for the ruling class as the cement of the political order, see pp. 51–52; cf. p. 62. "Aldermen's wives": p. 57. "That foolish and impertinent thing called a man of fashion": p. 63. Vanity as the ruling passion of commercial society: p. 50. The vanity of the "weak man": p. 117. Henceforth references to *TMS* appear in my text.

3. Mary Wollstonecraft herself cites *The Theory of Moral Sentiments,* the last edition of which was published some two years before the *Vindication.* See *A Vindication of the Rights of Woman,* ed. Carol Poston (New York: Norton, 1988), pp. 58–59, 133, 135, 188. On the corruption of English society, see, e.g., p. 40: thanks to luxurious women, "licentiousness is spread through the whole aggregate of society." Like Adam Smith, who also finds society pervasively corrupt, Mary Wollstonecraft nevertheless thinks of the middle class as virtuous (pp. 9, 57). On the author's loathing of effeminate men, see, e.g., her comments on "equivocal beings" and their male lovers (p. 138), her scorn of "vain" and "weak" men (?) of the upper class who pollute society (p. 9), and her opinion of the system of education that makes boys "vain and effeminate" (p. 158). On Mary Wollstonecraft as champion of manliness, see Terry Eagleton, *The Ideology of the Aesthetic* (Oxford: Basil Blackwell, 1990), pp. 56, 61.

4. See Thorstein Veblen, *The Theory of the Leisure Class* (New York: Random House, 1934), p. 54.

5. David Hume, *A Treatise of Human Nature* (Harmondsworth, Middlesex: Penguin, 1985), p. 622.

6. Hume, *Treatise of Human Nature,* p. 586. My emphasis.

7. John Brown, *An Estimate of the Manners and Principles of the Times* (London, 1757), vol. 1, p. 29.

8. On ostentatious aristocrats, see Fernand Braudel, *Civilization and Capitalism, 15th–18th Century,* vol. 2: *The Wheels of Commerce,* trans. Siân Reynolds (New York: Harper and Row, 1979), pp. 488–93. On public women and the old regime, see Joan Landes, *Women and the Public Sphere in the Age of the French Revolution* (Ithaca: Cornell University Press, 1988). If women were traditionally thought prone to vanity, Adam Smith found the aristocracy vain in the sense that it presented itself for public admiration without possessing merit. Mary Wollstonecraft (citing Adam Smith) took the same view. When Smith adverts to the aristocratic habits of "vanity and expence," of "luxury and extravagance" in the non-English colonies of the New World, he names traits that for centuries came together in the highly charged image of the sumptuous woman (Milton's Dalila and her variants), ruinous to men. No doubt his language implies the corruption of those colonies. See Smith, *An Inquiry into the Nature and Causes of the Wealth of Nations* (New York: Modern Library, 1937), p. 541. A typical statement of Smith's perfect contempt for the fashionable "of both sexes" appears on p. 649 of the *Wealth of Nations:* in commercial society, the rich "not being able to distinguish themselves by the expence of any one dress, will naturally endeavour to do so by the multitude and variety of their dresses."

9. The soldier does not fit in commercial society because his idle habits and loose morals disqualify him for work: Smith, *Wealth of Nations,* p. 437. By the same token, however, the soldier becomes a romantic figure, an exception to the rule of humdrum and self-seeking in commercial society, a fine archaism. On the whole Smith takes a romantic view of soldiering (e.g., *TMS,* p. 239).

10. D. A. Reisman, *Adam Smith's Sociological Economics* (London: Croom Helm, 1976), p. 73. Cf. Hiram Caton, "The Preindustrial Economics of Adam Smith," *Journal of Economic History* 45 (1985): 840n.: "The core of Smith's anthropology is the conformist principle."

11. Stuart Ewen, *All Consuming Images: The Politics of Style in Contemporary Culture* (New York: Basic, 1988), p. 129.

12. Werner Sombart, *Luxury and Capitalism,* trans. W. R. Dittmar (Ann Arbor: University of Michigan Press, 1967), p. 2. Orig. pub. 1913. Sombart is close to Adam Smith in concluding that feudal magnates dissipated their fortunes in trying to keep up with ostentatious parvenus—that is, in imitating the imitators of the nobility—a shining example of the corruption of the imitative mechanism still at work in Smithian society. Sombart cites Smith himself on pp. 91 and 95. Smith in turn reads like Sombart when he states that a palace "may serve to promote luxury, and set the example of the dissolution of manners" (*TMS,* p. 35).

13. "The disposition to admire, and almost to worship, the rich and the powerful, and to despise, or, at least, to neglect persons of poor and mean condition . . . [is] the great and most universal cause of the corruption of our moral sentiments" (*TMS,* p. 61).

14. John Sekora, *Luxury: The Concept in Western Thought, Eden to Smollett* (Baltimore: Johns Hopkins University Press, 1977), e.g., p. 26. Luxury as the original sin of Eve: p. 24.

15. On imaginary versus natural wants, see, e.g., Brown, *Estimate of the Manners and Principles of the Times,* vol. 1, p. 155: "The Passion for Money, being founded, not in Sense, but Imagination, admits of no Satiety: like Those which are called the natural Passions." The fairy tale of "The Fisherman and His Wife" illustrates female desire that swells to outrageous size on being satisfied.

16. Introduction to *TMS,* p. 9.

17. Louis Schneider, ed., *The Scottish Moralists: On Human Nature and Society* (Chicago: University of Chicago Press, 1967), p. xxx.

18. On the blindness of merchants toward the public interest, see *Wealth of Nations,* p. 250.

19. Smith, *Wealth of Nations,* p. 739. Mill applies the language of mutilation and deformity to the middle class in *On Liberty.*

20. Daniel Defoe, *The Complete English Tradesman* (New York: Burt Franklin, 1970), vol. 1, p. 151.

21. The prudent man "never rashly or unnecessarily obtrudes his opinion," he is "an exact observer" of the proprieties, and he "is willing to place himself rather below than above his equals" (*TMS,* p. 214).

22. See Hume, *Treatise of Human Nature,* pp. 622, 533.

23. For a salutary warning against the gothic excesses of theory, see David Cannadine's essay "Through the Keyhole" in *The New York Review of Books,* 21 Nov. 1991. I cannot agree, however, that ideological constructs such as the domestic woman simply had no force.

24. On sympathizing with we know not what, see *TMS,* p. 11.

25. Jacob Viner, *The Role of Providence in the Social Order: An Essay in Intellectual History* (Philadelphia: American Philosophical Society, 1972), pp. 84–85: "Before the 1750's, *laissez-faire* played no significant role in any of the predominant systems of religious, or ethical, or political thought. Systematic economic thought had not yet really appeared. To most writers of the period, as of earlier periods, government, at least after the Fall of Man, was as natural as any other social institution."

26. Karl Mannheim, *Essays on Sociology and Social Knowledge* (New York: Oxford University Press, 1953), p. 86.

27. See Smith's scathing commentary on public education in the *Wealth of Nations,* pp. 733–34: the minds of young men are crammed with "a mere useless and pedantic heap of sophistry and nonsense." Women, however, not being eligible for public education, learn "nothing useless, absurd, or fantastical in the common course of their education." Smith's views on women are narrow and conventional; the passage in question shows that Smithian men may take on infamous traits of women (in this case triviality and unreason) and still somehow retain their hereditary title of superiority.

28. Smith, *Wealth of Nations,* p. 391.

29. *Wealth of Nations,* p. 391. On the shift of landed to mobile property, see the work of J. G. A. Pocock, for example *Politics, Language and Time: Essays on Political Thought and History* (New York: Atheneum, 1973), chap. 3.

30. *Wealth of Nations,* p. 673.

31. See, e.g., Jane Rendall, *The Origins of the Scottish Enlightenment* (London: Macmillan, 1978), p. 9.

32. See, e.g., Kenneth Burke, *A Rhetoric of Motives* (Berkeley: University of California Press, 1969), p. 96.

33. See, e.g., Mannheim, *Essays on Sociology,* pp. 292–93; Ernst Cassirer, *The Myth of the State* (New Haven, Conn.: Yale University Press, 1946), p. 103.

34. On the place of stoic values in a republican discourse whose male bias "bordered on the absolute," see J. G. A. Pocock, "Cambridge Paradigms and Scotch Philosophers: A Study of the Relations Between the Civic Humanist and the Civil Jurisprudential Interpretation of Eighteenth-Century Thought," in *Wealth and Virtue: The Shaping of Political Economy in the Scottish Enlightenment,* eds. Istvan Hont and Michael Ignatieff (Cambridge: Cambridge University Press, 1983), pp. 237, 235.

35. *Wealth of Nations,* p. 556.

36. Among mercantile people "narrowness, meanness, and a selfish disposition" prevail (*Wealth of Nations,* p. 633). This phrase occurs in Smith's exposition of the principles of Physiocracy, and might be read as reporting a view that Smith himself does not share. However, in expressing a qualified dissent from Physiocracy, Smith nowhere claims that the French school misreads the moral sentiments of men of commerce. He claims that men of commerce are more productive than the French school allows. This of course does not mean that their moral sentiments can't be shabby, for the divine irony of unintended results often brings forth good outcomes from mean intentions. Smith's severely skeptical attitude toward men of commerce is emphasized by David McNally, *Political Economy and the Rise of Capitalism: A Reinterpretation* (Berkeley: University of California Press, 1988). J. S. Mill's *On Liberty* voices a protest against the mental narrowness, the meanness and selfishness, of the mercantile class. In fact this work can be read as yet one more effort to resolve the central question of the Scottish Enlightenment, how men can preserve virtù in the midst of a commercial society.

37. Felicity Nussbaum, *The Brink of All We Hate: English Satires on Women, 1660–1750* (Lexington: University Press of Kentucky, 1984), p. 5.

38. David Marshall, *The Figure of Theater: Shaftesbury, Defoe, Adam Smith, and George Eliot* (New York: Columbia University Press, 1986), p. 184. In turn, the importance of habitual association in the Smithian universe is underscored by Reisman, *Smith's Sociological Economics.*

39. Adam Smith, *Lectures on Justice, Police, Revenue and Arms* (New York: Kelley and Millman, 1956), p. 258. On the male bias of the *Moral Sentiments,* see Lucinda Coles, "(Anti)feminist Sympathies: The Politics of Relationship in Smith, Wollstonecraft, and More," *ELH* 58 (Spring 1991): 107–40.

40. Edmund Burke, *Reflections on the Revolution in France* (Indianapolis: Library of Liberal Arts, 1955), p. 39. The rhetoric of Burke is ripe for deflation, which it received in effect from Wordsworth's portrayal of the sublimity of the commonplace; on which, see M. H. Abrams, *Natural Supernaturalism: Tradition and Revolution in Romantic Literature* (New York: Norton, 1973), e.g., pp. 391–92. Where Wordsworth attacks the rottenness of class values poetically, Smith upholds a class system he knows to be corrupt.

41. Rosalind Williams, *Dream Worlds: Mass Consumption in Late Nineteenth-Century France* (Berkeley: University of California Press, 1982), pp. 250–51. The theorist is J. G. Courcelle-Seneuil. In his catalog of received ideas, Flaubert

includes an entry on "Stoicism," reading simply, "Not feasible." Conventional though this opinion may be, it has more than a little truth in it. See Gustave Flaubert, *The Dictionary of Accepted Ideas,* trans. Jacques Barzun (New York: New Directions, 1968), p. 83.

42. McNally, *Political Economy and the Rise of Capitalism,* p. 163. On "ethical life" as another term for "military spirit," see p. 175.

43. On stoic influence in England, see Colin Campbell, *The Romantic Ethic and the Spirit of Modern Consumerism* (Oxford: Basil Blackwell, 1987), p. 165.

44. Sekora, *Luxury,* p. 44: in literature, "almost all personifications of luxury are feminine."

45. Isaac Kramnick, *Republicanism and Bourgeois Radicalism: Political Ideology in Late Eighteenth-Century England and America* (Ithaca: Cornell University Press, 1990), p. 13. On anxiety as a middle-class affliction, see Ewen, *All Consuming Images,* p. 67.

46. A. L. Macfie, *The Individual in Society: Papers on Adam Smith* (London: George Allen and Unwin, 1967), p. 58; cf. pp. 22, 52. Utter resignation Smith would have considered a cause of economic inactivity and backwardness; in theory, Smithian or sentimental stoicism makes for political quiet while allowing for the economic striving censured by religious fanatics of Scotland the century before. See R. H. Campbell, "The Enlightenment and the Economy" in *The Origins and Nature of the Scottish Enlightenment,* eds. R. H. Campbell and Andrew Skinner (Edinburgh: John Donald, 1982), p. 13.

47. On the inapplicability of stoicism, see *TMS,* p. 292. On the "association" of the prudential virtues with their noble stoic ancestor, see the introduction to *TMS,* p. 9. Burke's own comment on the sublimity of *The Theory of Moral Sentiments* figures stoicism as a kind of poetic fiction. Particularly sublime in his opinion is "that fine Picture of the Stoic Philosophy towards the end of your first part which is dressed out in all the grandeur and Pomp that becomes that magnificent delusion." See Burke's letter to Smith of 10 September 1759 in *The Correspondence of Adam Smith,* eds. Ernest Mossner and Ian Ross (Oxford: Clarendon Press, 1977).

48. Williams, *Dream Worlds,* p. 253. On the reputedly insatiable desires of women, see p. 258. When a critic of luxury rages against the Eiffel Tower as a foul "siren"; when another declaims against exhibitions that "appeal to all that glitters and seduces," they play on the ancient image of woman as a temptress of corrupt beauty. See Williams, pp. 260-61.

49. *On Duties* in Marcus Tullius Cicero, *Brutus; On the Nature of the Gods; On Divination; On Duties,* trans. Hubert Poteat (Chicago: University of Chicago Press, 1950), p. 516. On Cicero and the Enlightenment, see Peter Gay, *The Enlightenment: An Interpretation* (New York: Knopf, 1966), pp. 105-9. If upon the fall of the Roman Republic, Cicero "continued to idealize a dying political system" (p. 109), Adam Smith's republicanism is doubly belated—sentimental. And if according to the Ciceronian ideal man is "active in his political role" (p. 107), Smithian man does not act in a political capacity, his political role having been "idealized" out of existence.

50. On stoicism and natural law, see Alasdair MacIntyre, *After Virtue: A Study in Moral Theory* (Notre Dame: University of Notre Dame Press, 1981), pp. 157-58. See also the incessant references to acting conformably with nature in

The Moral Discourses of Epictetus, trans. Elizabeth Carter (London: J. M. Dent, 1910). The "system of natural liberty": *Wealth of Nations,* p. 651.

51. John Rist, "The Stoic Concept of Detachment" in *The Stoics,* ed. John Rist (Berkeley: University of California Press, 1978), p. 263.

52. David Hume, "The Stoic" in *Essays Moral, Political, and Literary* (Indianapolis: Liberty Classics, 1987), p. 149.

53. Daniel Defoe, *The Complete English Tradesman* (New York: Burt Franklin, 1970), vol. 2, 90.

54. "All these moralities that address themselves to the individual, for the sake of his 'happiness,' as one says . . . All of it is, measured intellectually, worth very little and not by a long shot 'science,' much less 'wisdom,' but rather, to say it once more, three times more, prudence, prudence, prudence, mixed with stupidity, stupidity, stupidity—whether it be that indifference and statue coldness against the hot-headed folly of the affects which the Stoics advised and administered; . . . or that tuning down of the affects to a harmless mean according to which they may be satisfied, the Aristotelianism of morals." Nietzsche, *Beyond Good and Evil: Prelude to a Philosophy of the Future,* trans. Walter Kaufmann (New York: Vintage, 1966), p. 109.

55. Albert Hirschman, *The Passions and the Interests: Political Arguments for Capitalism before Its Triumph* (Princeton: Princeton University Press, 1977).

56. Addison uses the phrase in *Spectator* No. 201. Edward and Lillian Bloom consider it "a journalistic generality" covering a range of meanings from politeness and submission to courage and honesty to the serenity that goes with getting rich. See Bloom and Bloom, *Joseph Addison's Sociable Animal* (Providence: Brown University Press, 1971), pp. 162–63.

57. On habitual deference and the theatrical glories of power, see, e.g., *TMS,* pp. 51–52.

58. On "narcissistic overinvestment in the image," see Landes, *Women and the Public Sphere in the Age of the French Revolution,* p. 72. On the culture of narcissism, see Christopher Lasch, *The Culture of Narcissism: American Life in an Age of Diminishing Expectations* (New York: Warner, 1979). Vain men who in imagining themselves "are struck with the highest admiration for their own persons" (*TMS,* p. 115) are described by Adam Smith as narcissists, although not in any psychoanalytic sense. On the emergence of consumer society in eighteenth-century England, see Neil McKendrick, John Brewer, and J. H. Plumb, *The Birth of a Consumer Society: The Commercialization of Eighteenth-Century England* (Bloomington: Indiana University Press, 1982).

59. "The luminaries, their clothes and cars and villas and vacation yachts, represent a consumerized interpretation of personal freedom—a 'middle class' ideal—multiplied exponentially; beyond comprehension, but never so far as to undermine a glimmer of hope in the mind of the spectator" (Ewen, *All Consuming Images,* pp. 99–100). At least twice in the *Moral Sentiments* Smith portrays spectators enthralled with the spectacle of high consumption (pp. 51–52; 181), and he identifies the worship of glittering elites as the cause of the pervasive corruption of moral sentiments (p. 61).

60. Reisman, *Smith's Sociological Economics,* p. 112.

61. See J. H. Plumb, "Political Man" in *Man Versus Society in Eighteenth-Century Britain: Six Points of View,* ed. James Clifford (Cambridge: Cambridge

University Press, 1968). Burke recoiled in horror from the sight of political clubs in England; his *Reflections on the Revolution in France* was published in the same year as the last edition of the *Moral Sentiments*, 1790. The Victorian Sarah Ellis, whose theory of womanhood represents an evolution of Smithian morality, believes that if women were better, men would stay home, rather than being "increasingly attracted by the political associations, and the public calls, now leading them away from those domestic scenes which offer little to excite attention, or fascinate the mind." Sarah Ellis, *The Women of England, Their Social Duties and Domestic Habits* (London, 1839[?]), p. 353. If this statement offers any sort of evidence of political stirrings in middle-class men, it also evidences the antipolitical thrust of Smithian morality.

62. *Coleridge's Writings, Volume 1: On Politics and Society,* ed. John Morrow (Princeton: Princeton University Press, 1991), p. 56.

63. Kramnick, *Republicanism and Bourgeois Radicalism,* chap. 1.

64. See John Brewer, "Commercialization and Politics" in McKendrick et al., *Birth of a Consumer Society.* Interestingly, Smith marks it down to the discredit of the prudent man that he takes no part in "convivial societies" (*TMS,* p. 214).

65. Mary Poovey, *Uneven Developments: The Ideological Work of Gender in Mid-Victorian England* (Chicago: University of Chicago Press, 1988), p. 12.

66. Ellis, *Women of England,* p. 13.

67. Smith, *Wealth of Nations,* p. 822.

68. Ellis, *Women of England,* pp. 106, 122. Ellis's judgment that "a splendidly dressed woman entering the parlour of a farm-house, or a tradesman's drawing room, bursts upon the sight as an astounding and almost monstrous spectacle" (pp. 97–98) corresponds with the Smithian maxim that a sow in a drawing room is ridiculous, a principle of such moment in Smith's thought that it runs like a refrain through Reisman's excellent study, *Smith's Sociological Economics.* This canon of propriety was deliberately breached by Wordsworth, almost as though it received its highest expression and most polemical violation at once; see Abrams, *Natural Supernaturalism,* pp. 390–99.

69. "We approve pursuing the public good. For what reason? Or what is the truth for conformity to which we call it a reasonable end? I fancy we can find none . . . more than we could give for our liking any pleasant fruit." Francis Hutcheson, *Illustrations on the Moral Sense* (Cambridge: Harvard University Press, 1971), p. 129. Cf. pp. 229–30.

70. Smith, *Wealth of Nations,* p. 625.

71. On the removal of consumers from producers, see Joyce Appleby, *Economic Thought and Ideology in Seventeenth-Century England* (Princeton: Princeton University Press, 1978), e.g., p. 79. According to Raymond Williams, the consumer as abstraction dates from the mid-eighteenth-century discourse of political economy. *Keywords: A Vocabulary of Culture and Society* (New York: Oxford University Press, 1976), p. 69. Williams may be late, but in any case what makes the consumer an abstraction (as opposed, say, to a female figure of grotesque particularity) is the removal of production and consumption into different spheres. This separation hardens into a virtual gender distinction. By our century, "The distinction between producer and consumer was largely equivalent to the distinction between male and female." Williams, *Dream Worlds,* p. 307.

72. Hume, *Treatise of Human Nature*, p. 539.

73. See Ruth Bottigheimer, *Grimms' Bad Girls and Bold Boys: The Moral and Social Vision of the Tales* (New Haven: Yale University Press, 1987), p. 170.

74. The ideology of gentle commerce can perhaps be read as a transformation of the romance principle of a happy guile enabling the weak (frequently women) to conquer the strong. The overcoming of violent passions by weak ones, the belief in benign ruses like the Invisible Hand, the displacement of the heroic ideal, and the triumph of what are hostilely called effeminate values—all broadly characteristic of the ideology of commerce—have analogues in romance, which emerged from the "mercantile ethos" of Greek New Comedy. See Northrop Frye, *The Secular Scripture: A Study of the Structure of Romance* (Cambridge: Harvard University Press, 1976), p. 71 and chap. 3 generally. On the invisible hand of woman, p. 75.

75. On the gentleness of commerce, see Hirschman, *The Passions and the Interests*. On the dominion of the calm passions over the stormy ones in the philosophy of Smith's teacher Francis Hutcheson, see Jane Rendall, "Virtue and Commerce: Women in the Making of Adam Smith's Political Economy" in Ellen Kennedy and Susan Mendus, eds., *Women in Western Political Philosophy: Kant to Nietzsche* (New York: St. Martin's, 1987), pp. 53, 56.

76. Mary Poovey, *The Proper Lady and the Woman Writer: Ideology as Style in the Works of Mary Wollstonecraft, Mary Shelley, and Jane Austen* (Chicago: University of Chicago Press, 1984), p. 61. Emphasis in the original. Invisibility: the prudent man "is averse to all the quackish arts by which other people so frequently thrust themselves into public notice and reputation" (*TMS*, p. 213); he wants no part of public business (p. 216). Inoffensiveness: his conversation "is always perfectly inoffensive" (p. 214). Etc.

77. See *TMS*, p. 214. On the frigidity of the prudent man, cf. *Wealth of Nations*, p. 633: the men of commerce tend to be "averse to all social pleasure and enjoyment." Cf. the author's observation that the morals of dissenters are strict to the point of being "rather disagreeably rigorous and unsocial" (*Wealth of Nations*, p. 748).

78. Again and again Smith depreciates the power of reason, for example on p. 53 of *TMS:* that kings may rightfully be overthrown "is the doctrine or reason and philosophy; but it is not the doctrine of Nature" and thus the idea does not really speak to people. Smith characterizes reason as a kind of slow, artful construction.

79. "Waking dreams": *TMS*, p. 52. Enchantment: *TMS*, p. 181. The second passage refers to a "poor man's son," but I will argue that it applies generally.

80. Cited in Cassirer, *Myth of the State*, p. 178. See also Hannah Arendt, *Lectures on Kant's Political Philosophy* (Chicago: University of Chicago Press, 1982).

81. See David Miller, *Philosophy and Ideology in Hume's Political Thought* (Oxford: Clarendon Press, 1981), p. 200.

82. See Garry Wills, *Inventing America: Jefferson's Declaration of Independence* (Garden City: Doubleday, 1978); and Douglass Adair, " 'That Politics May Be Reduced to a Science': David Hume, James Madison, and the Tenth *Federalist*," *Huntington Library Quarterly* 20 (1957): 343–60.

83. F. A. Hayek, *The Counter-Revolution of Science: Studies on the Abuse of Reason* (Glencoe, Ill.: Free Press, 1952), p. 87.

Chapter 2

1. Isaiah Berlin, *Four Essays on Liberty* (New York: Oxford University Press, 1969), p. 122.

2. John Stuart Mill, *On Liberty,* ed. David Spitz (New York: Norton, 1975), p. 6.

3. Mary Poovey, *The Proper Lady and the Woman Writer: Ideology as Style in the Works of Mary Wollstonecraft, Mary Shelley, and Jane Austen* (Chicago: University of Chicago Press, 1984), p. 60.

4. On the shabbiness of the man of commerce, see Adam Smith, *An Inquiry into the Nature and Causes of the Wealth of Nations* (New York: Modern Library, 1937), p. 633: among mercantile men "narrowness, meanness, and a selfish disposition" prevail.

5. See J. G. A. Pocock, "Gibbon's *Decline and Fall* and the World View of the Late Enlightenment," *Eighteenth-Century Studies* 10 (1977): 292.

6. Cf. Ruth Bloch, "The Gendered Meanings of Virtue in Revolutionary America," *Signs* 13 (1987): 56: in America around the time of the publication of the last edition of *The Theory of Moral Sentiments,* "virtue, if still regarded as essential to the public good in a republican state, became ever more difficult to distinguish from private benevolence, personal manners, and female sexual propriety."

7. Letters of 10 October 1759 and 9 November 1776 in *The Correspondence of Adam Smith,* eds. Ernest Mossner and Ian Ross (Oxford: Clarendon Press, 1977), pp. 56, 218.

8. Berlin, p. 135. Epictetus repeats this argument obsessively, as though having arrived at bedrock, there were no place farther to go. In passages like the following, Epictetus speaks for positive liberty: "I have ranged my pursuits under the direction of God. Is it his will that I should have a fever? It is my will too. Is it his will that I should pursue anything? It is my will too. . . . Is it his will that I should be tortured? Then it is my will to be tortured. Is it his will that I should die? Then it is my will to die. Who can any longer restrain or compel me contrary to my own opinion?" Not being subject to coercion or restraint, the stoic is therefore free. See *The Moral Discourses of Epictetus,* trans. Elizabeth Carter (London: J. M. Dent, 1910), p. 208.

9. On Smith's library: A. L. Macfie, *The Individual in Society: Papers on Adam Smith* (London: George Allen and Unwin, 1967), p. 29. "Primary influence": *TMS* introduction, p. 5.

10. On the pivotal role played by corrupt tastes, petty vanity, and childish judgments in Smithian society, see Nathan Rosenberg, "Adam Smith, Consumer Tastes, and Economic Growth," *Journal of Political Economy* 76 (1968): 361–73. "Diamond buckles": *Wealth of Nations,* p. 389. In Smith's theory, the true patriarch—the lord who does *not* squander his authority—is the chieftain in the

society of shepherds. The state of society offers this man no "trinkets or baubles of any kind" to sell his position for; hence wealth remains in his family for generations, undissipated; hence the mystique of long lineage. See *Wealth of Nations,* pp. 671–73. This figure evidently equals the biblical patriarch, and the threat that luxury "of any kind" would pose to him helps to makes sense of the biblical hostility to "luxury"; on which, see John Sekora, *Luxury: The Concept in Western Thought, Eden to Smollett* (Baltimore: Johns Hopkins University Press, 1977), chap. 1. Sekora's subject is the attack on luxury in the name of hierarchy; Smith's word for "hierarchy" is "subordination"—instituted, he claims, during the shepherd phase (*Wealth of Nations,* p. 674).

11. Smith, *Wealth of Nations,* p. 332. Smith describes the male consumer, with his love of "jewels" and "trinkets," as possessing "not only a trifling, but a base and selfish disposition" (p. 332).

12. The "weak man" is guilty of "the most contemptible vanity" (*TMS,* p. 117); but vanity in turn is the ruling passion of commercial society (*TMS,* p. 50). In some sense, then, the weak man is Everyman.

13. James Fordyce, *Sermons to Young Women* (London, 1766), vol. 1, p. 25. In *Pride and Prejudice,* when the unctuous Collins visits the Bennets, he is requested to read to the family. Rejecting novels with shock and horror, he chooses instead Fordyce's *Sermons.* Lydia Bennet actually gapes as he opens the volume. When Mary Wollstonecraft concludes her refutation of Rousseau in the *Vindication of the Rights of Woman,* she turns to Fordyce.

14. Cf. Edmund Burke, *Reflections on the Revolution in France* (Indianapolis: Library of Liberal Arts, 1955), p. 39: by virtue of its noble ancestry, British liberty "carries an imposing and majestic aspect. . . . It has its bearings and its ensigns armorial. It has its gallery of portraits, its monumental inscriptions." As I have said, the stoic is the noble ancestor of Adam Smith's modern.

15. Cf. Hume's argument in "Of Commerce" that because Roman principles "are too disinterested and too difficult to support, it is requisite to govern men by other passions, and animate them with a spirit of avarice and industry, art and luxury." David Hume, *Essays Moral, Political, and Literary* (Indianapolis: Liberty Classics, 1987), p. 263. Mandeville makes the same case in his own fashion in the *Fable of the Bees,* debunking the "haughty pretences" of stoic philosophy. See Bernard Mandeville, *The Fable of the Bees; or, Private Vices, Publick Benefits* (Edinburgh, 1772), p. 106.

16. *Wealth of Nations,* pp. 358–59.

17. See Hiram Caton, "The Preindustrial Economics of Adam Smith," *Journal of Economic History* 45 (1985): 833–53. On Smith's fondness for agriculture, see also David McNally, *Political Economy and the Rise of Capitalism: A Reinterpretation* (Berkeley: University of California Press, 1988), chaps. 4 and 5. Smith hoped to see country gentlemen at the head of the political order—incorruptible landowners who could shield the polity from the designs of merchants. That his hope came to nothing we may judge from J. S. Mill's comments on the imbecility of the ruling class and its complete lack of the Harringtonian virtù that Adam Smith looked for.

18. Eve Kosofsky Sedgwick, *Between Men: English Literature and Male Homosocial Desire* (New York: Columbia University Press, 1985), p. 14. The archetype of "manly" pursuits is war, and until recently the language of war-

making has been heavily antique and feudal—heavily ideological—talking of swords and steeds while soldiers were being butchered most unchivalrically by modern methods. On feudal language and modern warfare, see Paul Fussell, *The Great War and Modern Memory* (New York: Oxford University Press, 1976). That the dead language of feudal valor survived even World War I we can infer from some of Orwell's criticisms of ornate diction.

19. Letter from Burke to Smith, in *Correspondence of Adam Smith,* eds. Mossner and Ross, p. 47: *TMS* "is often sublime, too, particularly in that fine Picture of the Stoic Philosophy towards the end of your first part which is dressed out in all the grandeur and Pomp that becomes that magnificent delusion."

20. *Wealth of Nations*, p. 423. In a notable example of unintended effects, the Puritans, with all their hatred of luxury and ostentation, helped to set in motion the economic forces that would produce luxury goods as never before. On this irony, see Rogers Brubaker, *The Limits of Rationality: As Essay on the Social and Moral Thought of Max Weber* (London: George Allen and Unwin, 1984), pp. 25–26, 29. (This work also explores the dry concept of rationality in industrial capitalism, citing Hume's diminution of the role of reason as a sort of foretaste of Max Weber.) Smith was not alone in his appreciation of the divine irony of unintended consequences. On the shared understanding of unintended consequences among the thinkers of the Scottish Enlightenment, see Louis Schneider, ed., *The Scottish Moralists: On Human Nature and Society* (Chicago: University of Chicago Press, 1967), xxix–xlvii. Gibbon concluded that the Septennial Act, "so vicious in its origin," proved its wisdom in the end. (See Edward Bloom and Lillian Bloom, *Joseph Addison's Sociable Animal* [Providence: Brown University Press, 1971], p. 130.) To "superintend" the universe is thus to override the intentions of human actors. The fact that stoicism itself gives a kind of backing to the idea of an invisible hand (see Introduction to *TMS*, p. 8) enables Adam Smith to make use of stoic values even while antiquating them.

21. Hume, *Essays Moral, Political, and Literary,* p. 153. Hume too considers stoic sentiment "sublime": see pp. 146, 153. Mandeville classes the stoic among those "lofty high-spirited creatures" who "aimed at no less than the public welfare, and the conquest of their own passions" (*Fable of the Bees,* p. 23). He considers the majestic concept of virtue puffery, and is ready to argue that the indulgence of our passions advances the public good, and the wealth of the nation, in ways that the conquest of them never could. On the inadvertent promotion of the public good, see Francis Hutcheson, *Illustrations on the Moral Sense* (Cambridge: Harvard University Press, 1971), p. 160: "It is probable, indeed, no man would approve as virtuous an action publicly useful, to which the agent was excited only by self-love, without any kind affection." Yet Smithian man specializes in just such actions; so it is, perhaps, that Smith describes the prudent man as distinctly frigid, lacking in kind affection (*TMS,* p. 214).

22. See *Moral Discourses of Epictetus,* e.g., p. 182: "For in what doth the exhortatory manner consist? In being able to show to one and all . . . that they care for everything rather than what they mean to care for."

23. Cf. Daniel Defoe, *The Complete English Tradesman* (New York: Burt Franklin, 1970), vol. 1, pp. 149–51: "Credit is so much a tradesman's blessing, that it is the choicest ware he deals in. . . . In a word, it is the life and soul of his trade, and it requires his utmost vigilance to preserve it. . . . A tradesman's

credit and a maid's virtue ought to be equally sacred from evil tongues. . . . The credit of a tradesman . . . is the same thing in its nature as the virtue of a lady."

24. See, for example, *TMS*, p. 52: "in spite of all that reason and experience can tell us to the contrary"; p. 53: "the doctrine of reason . . . is not the doctrine of Nature": p. 77: "the slow and uncertain determinations of our reason"; p. 320: "it is altogether absurd and unintelligible to suppose that the first perceptions of right and wrong can be derived from reason." On Smith's doctrine of the incompetence of reason, see Hiram Caton, "The Preindustrial Economics of Adam Smith," p. 839. Jacob Viner, *The Role of Providence in the Social Order: An Essay in Intellectual History* (Philadelphia: American Philosophical Society, 1972), p. 78, reminds readers of Smith "how low down on [Smith's] scale reason enters into the picture as a factor influencing social behavior." Cf. p. 47: "Adam Smith has puzzled many commentators by his attribution of the origin of commerce to a subrational propensity to truck and barter, rather than to a rational pursuit of economic benefit." On the doubt of reason among the thinkers of the Scottish Enlightenment, see Schneider, ed., *The Scottish Moralists*, pp. xvii–xxi. Cf. Edmund Burke, *A Philosophical Enquiry into the Origin of our Ideas of the Sublime and the Beautiful* (London: Routledge and Kegan Paul, 1958), p. 107: "the languid and precarious operation of our reason." Cf. Dr. Johnson's "Vanity of Human Wishes," line 11: "How rarely Reason guides the stubborn choice . . ." Sheldon Wolin, *Politics and Vision: Continuity and Innovation in Western Political Thought* (Boston: Little, Brown, 1960), p. 293, finds that both Hume and Smith are "distinguished by a profound respect for the limits of reason and the pervasiveness of irrational factors in man and society." On Hume's demotion of reason, see Wolin, "Hume and Conservatism," *American Political Science Review* 48 (1954): 999–1016. See also David Miller, *Philosophy and Ideology in Hume's Political Thought* (Oxford: Clarendon Press, 1981), p. 24: "The most striking feature of Hume's theory of judgement is the reduced role assigned in it to reason." In Hume's reading of English history, Adam Smith would also have found confirmation of the principle that conscious intention plays a rather humble role in human affairs, for Hume disputes the official Whig line that limited government emerged in England as the intended result of the struggle against royal prerogative. See Miller, p. 171. Bernard Mandeville, the scandal of moral minds, laughs at those systems of morality that "bestowed a thousand encomiums on the rationality of our souls, by the help of which we were capable of performing the most noble achievements" (*Fable of the Bees*, p. 22). See also the theory of the abbé Du Bos that sympathy is natural, does not conform to "the ways of reasoning," and provides the foundation of society; discussed in David Marshall, *The Surprising Effects of Sympathy: Marivaux, Diderot, Rousseau, and Mary Shelley* (Chicago: University of Chicago Press, 1988), chap. 1. In our own time the Smithian position has been taken up by F.A. Hayek, who stresses "the limitations of the powers of individual reason" (*The Counter-Revolution of Science: Studies on the Abuse of Reason* [Glencoe, Ill.: Free Press, 1952], p. 86).

25. It is a commonplace of eighteenth-century prescriptive literature that women possess "less capacity for reason than the other sex." Felicity Nussbaum, *The Brink of All We Hate: English Satires on Women, 1660–1750* (Lexington: University Press of Kentucky, 1984), p. 146. Cf. Bloch, "Gendered Meanings of Virtue in Revolutionary America," p. 42: Traditionally, "men were

deemed more rational than women." Cf. Sarah Ellis, *The Women of England, Their Social Duties and Domestic Habits* (London, 1839[?]), p. 302: "it requires more able reasoning than the generality of women are capable of."

26. Cf. Viner, *Role of Providence*, p. 78.

27. *TMS*, p. 128n. and *Wealth of Nations*, p. 755.

28. See also J. Ralph Lindgren, *The Social Philosophy of Adam Smith* (The Hague: Martinus Nijhoff, 1973), p. 145: "the short-sighted and impotent efforts of men." Cf. Burke, *Reflections on the Revolution in France*, p. 39: "the fallible and feeble contrivances of our reason."

29. See Lindgren, *Social Philosophy of Adam Smith*, p. 77. See also Donald Winch, *Adam Smith's Politics: An Essay in Historiographic Revision* (Cambridge: Cambridge University Press, 1978), p. 167. See also Rosenberg, "Adam Smith, Consumer Tastes, and Economic Growth." Simply by quoting from Smith, Rosenberg puts beyond doubt the former's sense of the sheer inanity of the love of luxury and display—the very motive that drives commercial society. Cf. La Rochefoucauld's opinion that self-love "is capricious, struggling at times with vast zeal and boundless effort to obtain things of no use to it, indeed of positive harm, but which it is driven to by desire." *The Maxims of La Rochefoucauld,* trans. Louis Kronenberger (New York: Random House, 1959), p. 141. (Smith linked La Rochefoucauld and Mandeville as corrupters of thought [*TMS*, p. 308], but his own moral vision resembles theirs more than he liked to admit.) I think it significant that for centuries women had been chastised precisely for their luxury, love of display, sensational capriciousness, and unruly desires.

30. In a sense, sympathy is Smith's answer to the question of how to go back to a precritical state once tradition has been put into question. F. A. Hayek, in his defense of the free market, opposes conscious design but does not say how we are to go back into unconsciousness. On "unreflective" as opposed to modern or polemical conservatism, see Karl Mannheim, *Essays on Sociology and Social Psychology* (New York: Oxford University Press, 1953), chap. 2.

31. Lindgren, *Social Philosophy of Adam Smith*, p. 107. Cf. Defoe, *Complete English Tradesman*, vol. 1, p. 162: "Every part of this discourse shows how much a tradesman's welfare depends upon the justice and courtesy of his neighbours, and how nice and critical a thing reputation is. This, well considered, would always keep a tradesman humble, and show him what need he has to behave courteously and obligingly among his neighbours."

32. Cf. Bloom and Bloom, *Addison's Sociable Animal*, p. 25: "The task before Addison and other Englishmen was to salvage the wholesome traditions of the past and blend them with a modernity purified of rawness and greed." Adam Smith attempted just this task. As I will argue, the *Spectator* essays wherein Addison plays the censor of society anticipate the Smithian spectator watching over social performances.

33. Benjamin Barber, *The Conquest of Politics: Liberal Philosophy in Democratic Times* (Princeton: Princeton University Press, 1988), p. 35.

34. "Nature has wisely judged that the distinction of ranks, the peace and order of society, would rest more securely upon the plain and palpable difference of birth and fortune, than upon the invisible and often uncertain difference of wisdom and virtue" (*TMS*, p. 226). Cf. *Wealth of Nations*, p. 671. In a world of disagreement on fundamentals, Smith looks for something indisputable. Sympa-

thy, the binding force of the Smithian universe exercising an undoubted pull on our sentiments, is such a thing. And it is because we sympathize with our masters that we don't dispute with them (*TMS*, p. 53). Smith's defense of a class system he knows to be corrupt bears out rather ironically the observation that "liberalism presupposed a morality inherited from the pre-enlightened past," meaning that liberalism lived on inherited moral capital. Christopher Lasch, "The Fragility of Liberalism," *Salmagundi*, Fall 1991, p. 16.

35. Smith, *Wealth of Nations*, p. 128. On the "impertinent jealousy," "mean rapacity," and "interested sophistry" of merchants and manufacturers, see *WN*, pp. 460–61.

36. This aspect of sentimentality is skillfully analyzed in Ann Douglas, *The Feminization of American Culture* (New York: Avon, 1977).

37. Burke, *The Sublime and the Beautiful*, p. 46; on the bond between Smith's thought and Burke's, see J. T. Boulton's introduction to this volume, p. xlii. Cf. the observation of Du Bos that people "run toward the objects most fit to break their hearts," cited in Marshall, *The Surprising Effects of Sympathy*, p. 23.

38. Marilyn Butler, *Jane Austen and the War of Ideas* (Oxford: Clarendon Press, 1975), p. 17. The author brings out Mackenzie's rejection of system (a bond with Burke) and his small opinion of the artificial ways of reason (a bond with Smith).

39. Butler, *Jane Austen and the War of Ideas*, p. 23.

40. On this subject, see also Terry Eagleton, *The Ideology of the Aesthetic* (Oxford: Basil Blackwell, 1990), chaps. 2 and 3. Early in the *Theory of Moral Sentiments* Smith remarks that sympathetic passions sometimes arise in us without our even knowing what we are sympathizing with: "The passions, upon some occasions, may be transfused from one man to another, instantaneously, and antecedent to any knowledge of what excited them in the person principally concerned" (p. 11). At times Smith speaks of sympathy withheld or reluctantly given, or given "at last" (*TMS*, p. 9), as though it were in fact under our control. See David Marshall, *The Figure of Theater: Shaftesbury, Defoe, Adam Smith, and George Eliot* (New York: Columbia University Press, 1986), p. 183. Finally, however, nature underwrites the operation of sympathy, not only in that it disposes us to take the part of others but in that it prompts those others to modulate their passions to ease the flow of sympathy (*TMS*, p. 22). Sympathy will flow naturally to the actor once he sets his passions to just the right frequency. A. L. Macfie, in chapters 3 and 4 of *The Individual in Society* makes a case for the reasoned character of Smithian sympathy. I find his argument overstated and woefully repetitive, but would agree that out of the originally instinctive response of sympathy (which makes us "naturally shrink" when we see a blow about to fall [*TMS*, p. 10]), Smith refines something more elaborate. Macfie generally ignores Smith's depreciations of reason and does not seem to recognize the all-importance of sheer habit, conformity, and error (none of them especially rational) in Smithian society. Smith himself goes out of his way to emphasize the perfectly irrational nature of the bonds of sympathy binding subjects to rulers and the many to the elite. See, e.g., *TMS*, pp. 50–53.

41. Butler, *Jane Austen and the War of Ideas*, p. 26.

42. For example, we "naturally writhe and twist" when watching the slack-

rope walker (*TMS*, p. 10). This example occurs in the opening section of the *Moral Sentiments*, where Smith lays the foundation of his theory.

43. See Northrop Frye, *Anatomy of Criticism: Four Essays* (New York: Atheneum, 1967), p. 35.

44. On this point, see Garry Wills, *Inventing America: Jefferson's Declaration of Independence* (Garden City: Doubleday, 1978), p. 282.

45. On changes in the theory of child rearing during the reign of Sympathy and Benevolence, see J. H. Plumb, "The New World of Children" in Neil McKendrick, John Brewer, and J. H. Plumb, *The Birth of a Consumer Society: The Commercialization of Eighteenth-Century England* (Bloomington: Indiana University Press, 1982).

46. Albert Hirschman, *The Passions and the Interests: Political Arguments for Capitalism before Its Triumph* (Princeton: Princeton University Press, 1977). Cf. Joseph Addison's argument in *Spectator* No. 255 (1711) that unless men were prompted to perform good actions despite themselves, the world would never have improved.

47. On this usage, see Hirschman, *The Passions and the Interests*, p. 58.

48. See *Spectator* No. 262 in *The Spectator*, ed. Donald F. Bond (Oxford: Clarendon Press, 1965), vol. 2, p. 519. On the links between spectatorship, quiet contemplation, and the hushing of political passions, see Winch, *Adam Smith's Politics*, pp. 25–26.

49. Bloom and Bloom, *Addison's Sociable Animal*, pp. 4–5. There was some disingenuousness in Addison's stance as a sympathetically impartial spectator free of political passions. He himself wrote Whig propaganda, for example, his melodramatic allegory of Public Credit in the *Spectator*. (On this see Bloom and Bloom, pp. 56–57.) Addison thus exemplifies the political speaker who pretends to be no politician—a common tactic today among those trying to turn the disrepute of the public realm to their own advantage.

50. This is equally true of Defoe, who finds "public affairs . . . run by parties and factions, by schisms and divisions in principles," in contrast to the civility of trade (*Complete English Tradesman*, vol. 2, p. 146). In his own way, the modest man protects the class structure against the assaults of impostors out to make their fortune. The modest tradesman of Adam Smith and Defoe makes his fortune by the imperceptibly slow accretion of wealth; he takes no impudent shortcuts.

51. Patricia Werhane, *Adam Smith and His Legacy for Modern Capitalism* (New York: Oxford University Press, 1991), p. 107.

52. Thomas Babington Macaulay, *Selected Writings*, eds. John Clive and Thomas Pinney (Chicago: University of Chicago Press, 1972), p. 237. David McNally is correct to note that only if property is secure does Adam Smith believe that the human drive to better one's circumstances will enrich society and prevail over obstacles; see *Political Economy and the Rise of Capitalism*, pp. 206–7, 250–51.

53. *Wealth of Nations*, p. 326. Cf. *Rasselas*: "Avarice is an uniform and tractable vice." Samuel Johnson, Rasselas, *Poems and Selected Prose*, ed. Bertrand Bronson (New York: Holt, Rinehart and Winston, 1958), p. 586.

54. Fordyce, *Sermons to Young Women*, vol. 1, p. 20.

55. On the prudent man's aversion to public life, see *TMS,* pp. 215–16. On the homebound woman as the arbiter of "the fate of nations," see the popular prescriptive work, *Woman's Mission* by Sarah Lewis, as cited in Elizabeth Helsinger, Robin Lauterbach Sheets, and William Veeder, eds., *The Woman Question,* vol. 1: *Defining Voices* (Chicago: University of Chicago Press, 1983), p. 13.

56. Cited in Hirschman, *The Passions and the Interests,* p. 17.

57. On French diatribes against public women, see Joan Landes, *Women and the Public Sphere in the Age of the French Revolution* (Ithaca: Cornell University Press, 1988).

58. See *Spectator* No. 257 (1711). Cf. *Spectator* No. 317: "I do not suppose that a Man loses his Time, who is not engaged in Publick Affairs, or in an Illustrious Course of Action. On the contrary, I believe our Hours may very often be more profitably laid out in such Transactions as make no figure in the World, than in such as are apt to draw upon them the Attention of Mankind. One may become wiser and better by several Methods of Employing ones Self in Secrecy and Silence." Addison goes on to recommend the kind of spiritual bookkeeping that was also dear to Benjamin Franklin.

59. Butler, *Jane Austen and the War of Ideas,* p. 34.

60. Poovey, *The Proper Lady and the Woman Writer,* p. 18.

61. See the manuscript of Reid's critique of Smith as reproduced by J. C. Stewart-Robertson and David Fate Norton, "Thomas Reid on Adam Smith's Theory of Morals," *Journal of the History of Ideas* 45 (1984): 320.

62. See Reid as reproduced by Stewart-Robertson and Norton, "Reid on Adam Smith's Theory of Morals," p. 315. On the emphasis on stoicism in the last edition of *TMS,* see the introduction, pp. 5–10.

63. A point stressed in Anthony Long's article on the "Ethics of Stoicism" in the *Dictionary of the History of Ideas* (New York: Scribner's, 1973), vol. 4, pp. 319–22.

64. See Long, "Ethics of Stoicism," p. 321: the stoic "and he alone, acts always and only from right intentions."

65. Reid in Stewart-Robertson and Norton, "Thomas Reid on Adam Smith's Theory of Morals," p. 314. Reid insists that involuntary feelings like sympathy are nothing to base a moral theory on.

66. On the pliancy of men, see David Spadafora, *The Idea of Progress in Eighteenth-Century Britain* (New Haven: Yale University Press, 1990), chap. 4; pp. 333–54.

67. David Hume, *A Treatise of Human Nature* (Harmondsworth, Middlesex: Penguin, 1985), p. 623.

68. D. A. Reisman, *Adam Smith's Sociological Economics* (London: Croom Helm, 1976), p. 94.

69. I refer to Edmund Burke's philosophical essay on the sublime and the beautiful, whose second edition appeared the same year as the first edition of the *Theory of Moral Sentiments.* The discourse of the sublime sometimes uses metaphors that are masculine to the point of grotesquery, as in John Baillie's account of the sublime as something that "extends" man's being, "elevates" the soul, and makes for the "Enlargement" of the mind. Early readers of Burke recognized, too, that he had in mind feminine beauty when he descanted on the beautiful. See J. T. Boulton's introduction to Burke's *The Sublime and the Beautiful,* pp. lii, lxxv.

70. On traditional virtues, see Ian Maclean, *The Renaissance Notion of Woman: A Study in the Fortunes of Scholasticism and Medical Science in European Intellectual Life* (Cambridge: Cambridge University Press, 1980), p. 55. On the "demolition of the hero," see Hirschman, *The Passions and the Interests,* p. 11. On the difference between the best and the second-best virtues, see Norbert Waszek, "Two Concepts of Morality: A Distinction of Adam Smith's Ethics and Its Stoic Origin," *Journal of the History of Ideas* 45 (1984), e.g., p. 596: "The justice of Solomon, the self-command of Cato cannot be expected, but to abstain from infringing upon other people's rights and to confine the bodily appetites within the limits of modesty is certainly required." By locating the distinction between excellence and propriety (the best and the second best) within the tradition of stoicism itself, the author is able to argue that Adam Smith successfully carries forward ancient stoicism into a modern commercial society. In my view this reading smooths over the incompatibility between stoic values and the envious emulation, conspicuous consumption, and sheer vanity that lie just beneath the propriety of bourgeois life, even in Smith's own view.

71. Bloch, "Gendered Meanings of Virtue in Revolutionary America," p. 38. Cf. Mary Poovey, *Uneven Developments: The Ideological Work of Gender in Mid-Victorian England* (Chicago: University of Chicago Press, 1988), p. 5. Mandeville argues that just because the sexual appetites of men are "more violent and ungovernable" than women's, it is all right for them to have amours (*Fable of the Bees,* p. 42); thus the traditional double standard survives changes in the gender code brought about by commercial society.

72. The "general tendency" of stoicism was to "animate [men] to actions of the most heroic magnanimity and most extensive benevolence" (*TMS,* p. 293).

73. On these matters, see chapter 3.

74. Bloch, "The Gendered Meanings of Virtue in Revolutionary America," p. 50. Cf. Jane Rendall, "Virtue and Commerce: Women in the Making of Adam Smith's Political Economy," in Ellen Kennedy and Susan Mendus, eds., *Women in Western Political Philosophy: Kant to Nietzsche* (New York: St. Martin's, 1987), p. 45: "Inseparably associated with . . . [the] changing view of the public sphere, was the relocation of the pursuit of virtue within the private sphere, at its heart the life of the family and the moral inspiration of women."

75. Judith Shklar, *Ordinary Vices* (Cambridge: Harvard University Press, 1984), p. 197.

76. *TMS,* p. 214. On Addison's commendation of thrift as a kind of modern stoicism, see Bloom and Bloom, *Addison's Sociable Animal,* p. 37.

77. Nietzsche, *Beyond Good and Evil: Prelude to a Philosophy of the Future,* trans. Walter Kaufmann (New York: Vintage, 1966), p. 109.

78. *Rambler* No. 6 in *The Works of Samuel Johnson,* eds. W. J. Bate and Albrecht Strauss (New Haven: Yale University Press, 1969), vol. 3, p. 31. Cf. Johnson's skeptical treatment of the sounding doctrines of stoicism in chap. 18 of *Rasselas.* Cf. Burke, *Reflections on the Revolution in France,* p. 117: "Strong instances of self-denial operate powerfully on our minds, and a man who has no wants has obtained great freedom and firmness and even dignity. But . . . the mass of any description of men are but men."

79. David Kettler, *The Social and Political Thought of Adam Ferguson* (Columbus, Ohio: Ohio State University Press, 1965), p. 159.

80. Laurence Sterne, *A Sentimental Journey* (London: Oxford University Press, 1968), p. 94.

81. Robert Adams, *The Roman Stamp: Frame and Facade in Some Forms of Neo-Classicism* (Berkeley: University of California Press, 1974), p. 203.

82. On the eschewing of political transformation, see M. H. Abrams, *Natural Supernaturalism: Tradition and Revolution in Romantic Literature* (New York: Norton, 1973), e.g., p. 356f.

83. McKendrick, *Birth of a Consumer Society*, p. 41. Cf. Defoe, *Complete English Tradesman*, vol. 1, p. 81: expensive dress "particularly respects the ladies . . . yet, to do justice to them, it must be acknowledged that men have their share in it." On imitation of the consumer habits of the rich, see also Stuart Ewen, *All Consuming Images: The Politics of Style in Contemporary Culture* (New York: Basic, 1988), chap. 2.

84. On Hume's worries over the bubble of credit, see Miller, *Philosophy and Ideology in Hume's Political Thought*, e.g., p. 132. Burke takes a catastrophic view of public debt in his *Reflections on the Revolution in France*. On Adam Smith's own forebodings, see *Wealth of Nations*, p. 863.

85. Hume's stoic pictures the temple of wisdom as "seated on a rock" of "sublime" height, possessing solidity indeed. See *Essays Moral, Political, and Literary*, p. 150.

86. "Awful gravity"; "manly freedom": Burke, *Reflections on the Revolution in France*, p. 39. Cf. p. 43: "a system of . . . austere and masculine morality."

87. Cited in Poovey, *Proper Lady and the Woman Writer*, p. 26. (The quoted words seem like an expurgated version of the old refrain that women are masters of deceit—on which, see chap. 3.) See also Mandeville, *Fable of the Bees*, p. 42: "A young lady of refined education keeps a strict guard over her looks as well as her actions."

88. John Mullan, *Sentiment and Sociability: The Language of Feeling in the Eighteenth Century* (Oxford: Clarendon Press, 1988), p. 94; cf. p. 5.

89. See Penelope Corfield's review of David Castronovo's *The English Gentleman: Images and Ideals in Literature and Society* in *Eighteenth-Century Studies* 21 (1988): 378–82. On the throwing open of the category of "gentleman," cf. a remark of Fielding's cited in McKendrick et al., *Birth of a Consumer Society*, p. 25: "While the Nobleman will emulate the Grandeur of a Prince and the Gentleman will aspire to the proper state of a Nobleman; the Tradesman steps from behind his Counter into the vacant place of the Gentleman. Nor doth the confusion end there."

90. *On Liberty*, p. 65.

91. Before Adam Smith, Joseph Addison—an improver—toyed with the idea that nonconformists in matters like dress should be sent to the madhouse. (See *Spectator* No. 576.) Mill considers this no laughing matter.

92. Wolin, *Politics and Vision*, p. 301.

93. Eagleton, *The Ideology of the Aesthetic*, p. 38.

94. Eagleton, *Ideology of the Aesthetic*, p. 41.

95. Cf. Hume, *Treatise of Human Nature*, p. 643: "This principle of sympathy is of so powerful and insinuating a nature, that it enters into most of our sentiments and passions." A critic of liberal political theory inverts Adam

Smith's theory of sympathy, arguing that it is the "festive spectacle of violence inflicted on another" that affirms the political community. "The knowledge . . . that something causes pain to another is dependent on an identification with that other, on the belief that the other feels what one would feel oneself in the same circumstances. Cruelty thus marks community." The onlookers rejoice that they are not suffering like the one marked out for violence: what is this but a kind of "devil's parody" of the liberalism of Adam Smith? See Anne Norton, *Reflections on Political Identity* (Baltimore: Johns Hopkins University Press, 1988), p. 183. An updated theory of moral sentiments would perhaps feature the principle of numbing—the blocking of feeling—as Smith and Hume feature sympathy. I take the term "numbing" from Robert Jay Lifton.

96. On the injustice of the status quo, see, for example, Lindgren, *Social Philosophy of Adam Smith*, p. 91.

97. Judith Shklar, "Jean-Jacques Rousseau and Equality," *Daedalus,* Summer 1978, p. 18. Cf. *Wealth of Nations*, p. 672: in the hunting phase, "universal poverty establishes . . . universal equality." See also Shklar, *Men and Citizens: A Study of Rousseau's Social Theory* (Cambridge: Cambridge University Press, 1985), p. 29: "The division of labor, the vehicle of progress, was evidently nothing but an infernal engine in Rousseau's eyes." A sharply different attitude toward the division of labor is that of Charlotte Perkins Gilman, who looks to higher forms of specialized labor (for example, professional cooks in place of housewives performing primitive labor) to liberate women from an archaic sexual economy and raise both them and men above their present corruption and meanness. Gilman's cure for amour-propre is socialized childrearing. See *Women and Economics* (1898).

98. See Norton, *Reflections on Political Identity,* p. 81. On the heroic magnanimity of "savages," see *TMS*, pp. 206–7.

99. Hirschman, *The Passions and the Interests*, p. 52.

100. The pebble-in-a-bag figure appears in Sterne, *Sentimental Journey*, p. 54, in a discourse on the female shopkeepers of Paris. Later Yorick speaks of shillings worn smooth by long use, contending, however, that the English still preserve their "distinct variety and originality of character" (p. 90). On the process of mutual polishing, cf. Shaftesbury as cited by Peter Gay, *The Enlightenment: An Interpretation* (New York: Knopf, 1966), p. 177.

101. Jacques Savary, cited by Hirschman, *The Passions and the Interests,* pp. 59–60. Date is 1675; emphasis in the original handbook, widely known in many translations in the eighteenth century. On the Puritan concept of a divinely instituted division of labor, see Max Weber, *The Protestant Ethic and the Spirit of Capitalism,* trans. Talcott Parsons (New York: Scribners, 1930), p. 161.

102. On the history behind the idea of the providential ordering of commerce, see Viner, *Role of Providence,* chap. 2. On farfetched luxuries, see also Pope, *The Rape of the Lock,* vol. 1, pp. 133–34: "This casket India's glowing gems unlocks, / And all Arabia breathes from yonder box." In Pope, *Poetical Works,* ed. Herbert Davis (London: Oxford University Press, 1966). In his "Modest Proposal," written in the language of political economy, Swift mocks the proposition that commerce employs the poor, spreads civility, raises the level of taste, and promotes elegance.

103. Thomas Babington Macaulay, *Critical and Historical Essays* (New York: Dutton, 1967), vol. 2, p. 483. (Macaulay does insist, though, that Addison was "manly" in his dying: p. 519.) Edward and Lillian Bloom consider that the "strong steady masculine piety" eulogized in *Spectator* No. 201 is a sounding phrase with little meaning; it implies all at once courage, submission to superiors, "modest joy," and the pleasure taken in amassing capital. (See *Addison's Sociable Animal*, pp. 162–64.) Addison is a figure in the history of taste, and his principle of "masculine piety" (a notion characteristic of him) is no more rationally explicable than a taste. Like-minded readers at the time would presumably have had a taste for what Addison meant.

104. Terry Eagleton, *The Function of Criticism: From* The Spectator *to Post-Structuralism* (London: Verso, 1984), p. 24. Mandeville likens the sweet rhetoric of Steele to "the tricks made use of by the women that would teach children to be mannerly" (*Fable of the Bees*, p. 28).

105. Defoe, *Complete English Tradesman*, vol. 1, p. 151.

106. Norbert Elias, *Power and Civility*, trans. Edmund Jephcott (New York: Pantheon, 1982), p. 241. Orig. pub. 1939. *Power and Civility* is vol. 2 of Elias's study of *The Civilizing Process*.

107. Elias, *Power and Civility*, p. 243. Max Weber, too, studies the process in which life is brought under close, even, and intense regulation.

108. Fordyce, *Sermons to Young Women*, vol. 1, pp. 22–23. Fordyce's good woman possesses perfect social pitch. Her mind is "seldom wrought up to ecstasy, and seldom overwhelmed by terror" (vol. 2, p. 22). She is neither too reserved nor too unreserved (vol. 2, p. 71).

109. Fordyce, *Sermons to Young Women*, p. 23.

110. In *On Liberty* Mill remarks on the close resemblance between Christian principles and those of Marcus Aurelius.

111. Jean-Jacques Rousseau, *Emile or on Education*, trans. Allan Bloom (New York: Basic, 1979), p. 456.

112. Lindgren, *Social Philosophy of Adam Smith*, p. 107.

113. See McKendrick et al., *Birth of a Consumer Society*. Smith's understanding of luxury as a badge of distinction for others to gawk at and imitate is shared by Fernand Braudel, *Civilization and Capitalism, 15th-18th Century*, vol. 1: *The Structures of Everyday Life: The Limits of the Possible*, trans. Siân Reynolds (New York: Harper and Row, 1979), p. 324: "I have always thought that fashion resulted to a large extent from the desire of the privileged to distinguish themselves, whatever the cost, from the masses who followed them." (Braudel takes a lighter view of human folly than Smith, however.) The author leaves no doubt that the eighteenth century marks the turning point in the history of consumption.

114. On satires on the vanity of women, see Nussbaum, *The Brink of All We Hate*, particularly its discussions of the motif of women dressing, lost in the contemplation of their imaginary glory; cf. Lady Mary Wortley Montagu's censure of "the unusual vanity" of the female sex, cited on p. 125. See also Mandeville, *Fable of the Bees*, pp. 89–90: "The youthful fair, in a vast concern of being overlooked, by the continual change of her posture betrays a violent desire of being observed, and, catching as it were at every body's eyes, courts with obliging looks the admiration of her beholders." On mercantilist complaints about the vanity and luxury of women, see Louis Landa, *Essays in*

Eighteenth-Century English Literature (Princeton: Princeton University Press, 1980), pp. 32–33. Swift reprehends the vanity of women in his "Modest Proposal." On Swift on "the vanity and pride, and luxury of . . . women, and of the fops who admire them," see Landa, p. 203. Cf. *The Rape of the Lock,* part II, line 6: "ev'ry eye was fix'd on her alone." In his teasing essay "Of Love and Marriage" Hume rates women's vanity, their love of show, as second only to their love of power. Dr. Johnson refers to women whose "desire of admiration makes them sacrifice their principles to the poor pleasure of worthless praise" (*Rambler* No. 71). Mary Wollstonecraft censures the vanity of women. The vanity of David Copperfield's mother is noted by Poovey, *Uneven Developments,* p. 91. At the center of Guy de Maupassant's well-known story "The Necklace" is the vanity of a woman. Of Natasha in *War and Peace* Tolstoy says, "She was . . . happy because she had someone to adore her: the adoration of others was a lubricant the wheels of her machine needed to make them run freely" (*War and Peace,* trans. Louise and Aylmer Maude [New York: Oxford University Press, 1991], p. 911). Nietzsche on women's vanity: "It is 'the slave' in the blood of the vain person, a residue of the slave's craftiness—and how much 'slave' is still residual in woman, for example!—that seeks to *seduce* him to good opinions about himself" (*Beyond Good and Evil,* p. 209). In *Luxury and Capitalism,* one of the highest expressions of traditional antifeminism, Werner Sombart alleges that the vanity and luxury of woman preside over the capitalist order.

115. Mary Beth Norton, *Liberty's Daughters: The Revolutionary Experience of American Women, 1750–1800* (Boston: Little, Brown, 1980), p. 115.

116. Ellis, *Women of England,* p. 300. Emphasis in the original.

117. Sekora, *Luxury,* pp. 44–45.

118. Werner Sombart, *Luxury and Capitalism,* trans. W. R. Dittmar (Ann Arbor: University of Michigan Press, 1967), p. 95. Sombart also alleges that women were the guiding spirit behind sugar consumption in Europe, although he offers nothing like evidence for the claim (p. 99).

119. On the vanity of "weak men," see *TMS,* p. 117.

120. On effeminacy, see, e.g., E. A. J. Johnson, *Predecessors of Adam Smith: The Growth of British Economic Thought* (New York: Prentice-Hall, 1937), pp. 289–97. A characteristic sentiment is that of William Wood, cited on p. 291: "The truth of the matter is that where riot and luxuries are not discountenanc'd, the inferior rank of men, become presently infected, and grow lazy, effeminate, impatient of labour, and expensive, and consequently cannot thrive by trade, tillage and planting." Sekora, *Luxury,* stresses the fear of insubordination that is written into statements like this.

121. Marshall, *Figure of Theater,* p. 185.

122. On Mandeville and the *Female Tatler,* see M. M. Goldsmith, "Mandeville and the Spirit of Capitalism," *Journal of British Studies,* 17 (Fall 1977): 63–81, esp. pp. 75 and 80.

123. What is more, the *Persian Letters* deny the reader the comfort of saying that our European style of subordinating women is rational, in contrast to the Persian style. Whatever the author's intention, the whole effect of this work is to throw into question sheer prejudices like the one that declares the European position of women an institution of nature and the Persian a wild-minded inven-

tion of men. On Montesquieu on showy women, see Landes, *Women and the Public Sphere in the Age of the French Revolution*, p. 36; cf. Letter 106, with its sketch of a woman of imperious vanity, determined to figure at a ball.

124. See *Wealth of Nations*, p. 172; Lindgren, *Social Philosophy of Adam Smith*, pp. 104–5; *The Early Writings of Adam Smith*, ed. J. Ralph Lindgren (New York: Augustus Kelley, 1967), pp. 143–44. On vanity in men, see *TMS*, p. 255f. Unlike Hume, who tends to slur vanity and pride, Smith draws out a distinction between the two; in his terms, Darcy in *Pride and Prejudice* would be proud, Wickham vain.

125. That Josiah Wedgwood consciously prompted the middle ranks to imitate the fashions of court is fully documented in McKendrick, *Birth of a Consumer Society*.

126. Eagleton, *The Function of Criticism*, p. 10.

127. *Wealth of Nations*, pp. 734–35.

128. See Keith Thomas, "The Double Standard," *Journal of the History of Ideas* 20 (1959): 195–216.

129. "To act indirectly": Poovey, *Proper Lady and the Woman Writer*, p. 33.

130. Adam Smith, *Lectures on Justice, Police, Revenue and Arms* (New York: Kelley and Millman, 1956), p. 259.

131. *Wealth of Nations*, p. 739.

132. *Wealth of Nations*, pp. 659–60.

133. *Wealth of Nations*, p. 734.

134. Adam Smith probably believed that the common laborer received benefits from commercial society, such as a better standard of living, that offset the crippling effects of the division of labor, as grave as they are. It is certain that he believed that the "sole use and end" of government is to promote the happiness of the people. See *TMS*, p. 185.

135. Cited in Kettler, *Social and Political Thought of Adam Ferguson*, p. 200.

136. Cited in Kettler, *Social and Political Thought of Adam Ferguson*, p. 205.

137. On the imagistic nature of the social universe in the commercial order, see again Lindgren, *Social Philosophy of Adam Smith*, p. 104. The universe of images that we now seem to inhabit is prefigured in Adam Smith.

138. Hume, "The Stoic," *Essays Moral, Political, and Literary*, p. 148.

139. Clearly Adam Smith had his differences with stoic doctrine as well; one of these, concerning the question of suicide, will come up for discussion later. On Smith's reservations about stoicism, see *TMS*, p. 292; introduction to *TMS*, pp. 9–10; Lindgren, *Social Philosophy of Adam Smith*, p. 61, etc.

140. Cf. Istvan Hont and Michael Ignatieff, "Needs and Justice in the *Wealth of Nations*: An Introductory Essay" in *Wealth and Virtue: The Shaping of Political Economy in the Scottish Enlightenment*, eds. Hont and Ignatieff (Cambridge: Cambridge University Press, 1983), p. 8: "Certainly, Smith attached immense positive significance to the plain facts of a modern labourer's material abundance and he dissented strongly from the civic moralist jeremiad on the impact of luxury upon the morals and industry of the poor. Yet it is notorious, from his contemptuous references in the *Wealth of Nations* to the medieval lord's fascination for the 'baubles and trinkets' of trade goods, and from his sardonic strictures in the *Theory of Moral Sentiments* on men's passion for accumulating

objects of 'frivolous utility,' that he believed material prosperity was purchased, more often than not, at the price of a measure of what he himself called 'deception.'" Smith's position is close to that of Imlac in Samuel Johnson's *Rasselas*, who holds that "some desire is necessary to keep life in motion, and he, whose real wants are supplied, must admit those of fancy" (*Rasselas*, p. 522), an example of a fanciful good being the pyramids of Egypt, which Imlac sees as temples to vanity, or monumental trinkets. While despising the common objects of desire, both Smith and Imlac seem to believe that it is for the best that men busy themselves pursuing things of no worth. The argument that the production and consumption of fanciful goods keeps commercial society busy was developed most fully by Mandeville.

141. See Mary Wollstonecraft, *A Vindication of the Rights of Woman* (New York: Norton, 1988), p. 44: "in order to preserve [women's] innocence, as ignorance is courteously termed, truth is hidden from them." The duty to lie to women is notably expressed in Conrad's *Heart of Darkness*: "They—the women I mean—are out of it—should be out of it. We must help them to stay in that beautiful world of their own, lest ours gets worse." Joseph Conrad, *Heart of Darkness* (New York: Norton, 1971), p. 49. Marlow accordingly lies to Kurtz's Intended.

142. *Moral Discourses of Epictetus*, p. 216. Cf. p. 22: "Why should any one person envy another? Why should he be struck with awful admiration of those who have great possessions, or are placed in high rank?" Adam Smith views the strivings of the poor man's son in just this spirit of disenchantment, and, like Epictetus, he prizes "greatness of soul and a manly spirit" (p. 23). The stoic goes on to argue that freedom does not consist in the enjoyment of our desires, but in overcoming those desires. Adam Smith's defense of negative liberty thus rests squarely on the discourse of positive liberty.

143. *Moral Discourses of Epictetus*, p. 103.

144. Lindgren, *Social Philosophy of Adam Smith*, p. 46. McNally, *Political Economy and the Rise of Capitalism*, p. 184. Hume believed that many do not suffer from ambition (the lust for a higher rank), but that people generally do seek status. See Miller, *Philosophy and Ideology in Hume's Political Thought*, pp. 110, 118. Rosenberg, "Adam Smith, Consumer Tastes, and Economic Growth," 364–65, reads the poor man's son as I do. Mandeville holds that in commercial society all ape their superiors. "We all look above ourselves, and, as fast as we can, strive to imitate those that some way or other are superior to us" (*Fable of the Bees*, pp. 87–88). For the argument that emulation runs through "all the several stations and conditions"—through all of society—see McKendrick, *Birth of a Consumer Society*, p. 11; cf. p. 95. Fielding laments that "an infinite number of lower people aspire to the pleasures of the fashionable" (cited in McKendrick, p. 54). Defoe finds that "young beginners" like the poor man's son "rather ape the gaeities of the court than appear like what the grave and sober citizens of the last century were willing to be." In language close to Adam Smith's, Defoe observes that "there seems to be a general corruption of manners throughout the kingdom"; some way must be found "to curb that spirit of luxury and extravagance that seems to have seized on the minds of almost all ranks of men." *Complete English Tradesman*, vol. 2, p. 71. On Samuel Fawconer's complaint (evidently unoriginal) against the universal emulation of "pomp and parade,"

see Sekora, *Luxury,* pp. 98–99. If Smithian man were not an emulator himself, he would not be so disposed to fashion his conduct to the social pattern.

145. Smith, *Wealth of Nations,* p. 766. My emphasis.

146. The poor man's son loses the end (felicity) in the means (drudgery). The counterimage of the poor man's son would be the miser who finds his felicity in slaving away for wealth rather than in using his money. Mandeville's "Laborio" is one of these. He knows of no pleasure "so great as getting of Money," the description playing, perhaps, on the old image of the avaricious merchant as a sort of sexual pervert who begets money. See M. M. Goldsmith, "Liberty, Luxury and the Pursuit of Happiness" in *The Languages of Political Theory in Early-Modern Europe,* ed. Anthony Pagden (Cambridge: Cambridge University Press, 1987), pp. 242–43.

147. A Mandevillian argument made by the anonymous author of "A Vindication of Commerce and the Arts" (1758), reprinted in *A Select Collection of Scarce and Valuable Tracts on Commerce,* ed. John McCulloch (New York: Augustus Kelley, 1966). The pamphleteer speaks of "imaginary" rather than false goods.

148. *Wealth of Nations,* p. 508. Dickens's Pip, his head filled with romantic ambition, bears comparison with the poor man's son.

149. Shklar, *Men & Citizens,* p. 77: "Each person becomes so obsessed with the possibility of rising in the social scale that he forgets his actual misery. Ambition blinds men to their real situation as their eyes are fixed upon higher spheres. Even the artisans in Paris dress up on Sundays so that people on the street will think that they are employed at court."

150. See G. J. Barker-Benfield, "Mary Wollstonecraft: Eighteenth-Century Commonwealthwoman," *Journal of the History of Ideas* 50 (1989): 95–115.

151. William Cobbett, the highly influential journalist, opens his *Advice to Young Men* with a homily on the depraving effects of contracting artificial wants, aspiring above one's station, and courting the great—the very syndrome of the poor man's son.

152. Fordyce, *Sermons to Young Women,* vol. 2, p. 228; vol. 2, p. 26; vol. 1, p. 110. In her *Letters on the Female Mind* (1793) Laetitia Hawkins castigates "the thirsty vanity of young women." (Cited in Poovey, *Proper Lady and the Woman Writer,* p. 31.) In the tradition of Fordyce, the popular Victorian homilist Sarah Lewis censures women's "vain attempts to excite the admiration of strangers" and their desire for the "gilded toys" of wealth and status. (See Helsinger, Sheets and Veeder, *Woman Question,* p. 9.) Adam Smith's social actor is motivated by vanity and yearns for gilded toys.

153. On this point, see Mullan, *Sentiment and Sociability,* pp. 97–98.

154. Patricia Meyer Spacks, "Ev'ry Woman is at Heart a Rake," *Eighteenth-Century Studies* 8 (1974): 33. Of Eliza Haywood's heroines the author says that they "have trouble waking up" (p. 33); so too the poor man's son, who reflects Adam Smith's interest in the tricks that the appetite for luxury plays on us (both "appetite" and "luxury" having sexual undermeanings). On the association of women and the tricks of the sexual imagination, cf. La Rochefoucauld, maxim no. 277: "Women often falsely imagine they are in love. The excitement of an intrigue, the emotions aroused by sex, the instinctive enjoyment of being wooed and the difficulties of saying no, all give them an illusion of passion where nothing exists beyond coquetry."

155. "And it is well that nature imposes upon us in this manner. It is this deception which rouses and keeps in continual motion the industry of mankind" (*TMS*, p. 183).

156. Wollstonecraft, *Vindication of the Rights of Woman*, p. 61. Smith might well cavil over calling human beings rational creatures, and in the poor man's son he illustrates defective rationality.

157. Fordyce, *Sermons to Young Women*, p. 25; Wollstonecraft, *Vindication of the Rights of Woman*, p. 93. Wollstonecraft does find British society effeminate—corrupted by women, whom it corrupts in turn.

158. Jean-Jacques Rousseau, *A Discourse on Inequality,* trans. Maurice Cranston (Harmondsworth, Middlesex: Penguin, 1984), p. 66. Adam Smith is known to have read this work.

159. *Early Writings of Adam Smith,* p. 27. By contrast, Mandeville derides stoicism and gives a woman the argument that it makes sense "to Slave part of [one's] life to make the rest more happy," the ambition of the poor man's son. See Goldsmith, "Mandeville and the Spirit of Capitalism," 78.

160. Benjamin Barber, "Rousseau and the Paradoxes of the Dramatic Imagination," *Daedalus,* Summer 1978, p. 83. On the disrepute of theater, see also *Wealth of Nations,* p. 107.

161. Barber, "Rousseau and the Paradoxes of the Dramatic Imagination," p. 83. On Hume on the multiplication of "imaginary wants," see Miller, *Philosophy and Ideology in Hume's Political Thought,* p. 109. Those who "feel new wants" are rebuked in a 1777 work on the habits of luxury cited by McKendrick, *Birth of a Consumer Society,* p. 51; cf. p. 71.

162. Reprinted in McCulloch, *Select Collection of Scarce and Valuable Tracts on Commerce.*

163. Mandeville, *Fable of the Bees,* p. 73. A higher version of Mandeville's thesis that men possess insatiable appetites is Hume's thesis that reason is unable to yoke, restrain, or master the passions. I take these terms from Wolin, "Hume and Conservatism," 1002–3. On unbounded desires, see also *Wealth of Nations,* p. 164. That society sets a standard of propriety for the expenditures of the various classes (thus fencing in the desires of men) is the argument of Reisman, *Smith's Sociological Economics,* p. 119.

164. Smith, *Wealth of Nations,* p. 391. Men consume their patrimony, Smith says, "for trinkets and baubles, fitter to be the play-things of children than the serious pursuits of men" (p. 391).

165. Reisman, *Smith's Sociological Economics,* p. 105.

166. *Wealth of Nations,* p. 625.

167. Fordyce, *Sermons to Young Women,* vol. 1, p. 78. Mandeville insists on the "unbounded" nature of men's appetite for showy things.

168. J. G. A. Pocock, *Virtue, Commerce, and History: Essays on Political Thought and History, Chiefly in the Eighteenth Century* (Cambridge: Cambridge University Press, 1985), pp. 112–13. On the seeming effeminacy of economic man, see p. 114. Considering that the good fruits of the commercial way of life are the "unintended consequence of the pursuit of vanity by the barons coupled with the cupidity of the merchants" (Winch, *Adam Smith's Politics,* p. 78), it figures that the economic actor doesn't know what he is doing.

In a characteristically wry section of the *Wealth of Nations,* the author discourses on the financial fantasy that makes men buy lottery tickets and generally miscalculate their chances of success and failure (pp. 107–9).

169. See, e.g., Reisman, *Smith's Sociological Economics,* chap. 2.

170. Kettler, *Social and Political Thought of Adam Ferguson,* p. 142. Cf. Smith's letter to Gilbert Elliot, 10 October 1759: in spite of our dependence on others, "real magnanimity and conscious virtue can support itselfe under the disapprobation of all mankind." *Correspondence of Adam Smith,* eds. Mossner and Ross, p. 49. In the same letter Smith speaks of "the great lesson of Stoical magnanimity and firmness" (p. 56).

171. *Moral Discourses of Epictetus,* p. 193.

172. See Stewart-Robertson and Norton, "Thomas Reid on Adam Smith's Theory of Morals," p. 320.

173. Cited in Kettler, *Social and Political Philosophy of Adam Ferguson,* p. 143.

174. Compare Guy de Maupassant's description in "The Necklace" of Mme. Loisel, her moral sentiments corrupted by envious love of the rich and elegant: "She would so have liked to please, to be envied, to be charming, to be sought after."

175. Cf. *TMS,* p. 226: "The undistinguishing eyes of the great mob of mankind . . ."

176. Cf. La Rochefoucauld, maxim no. 43: "We think we lead when we are being led, and while making for one goal with our minds, are unconsciously drawn to another by our hearts." Also no. 460: "We far from realize all that our passions make us do." Although Adam Smith was scandalized by La Rochefoucauld, many of the aphorist's insights still apply to Smith's moral theory, suggesting perhaps that Smithian man carries on the habits of deference and envy of a hierarchical age. The doctrine that history is made by those who don't know what they are doing, and that only "unconscious activity bears fruit," found its highest expression in Tolstoy; see Isaiah Berlin's discussion of that writer in *Russian Thinkers* (Harmondsworth, Middlesex: Penguin, 1978), esp. p. 34.

177. "Airy good": "Vanity of Human Wishes," line 10.

178. See the discussion of "The Dangerous Prevalence of Imagination," chap. 44 of *Rasselas.*

179. Kettler, *Social and Political Thought of Adam Ferguson,* p. 163.

180. Hont and Ignatieff, "Needs and justice in the *Wealth of Nations,*" p. 10. Like Adam Smith, Rousseau responded deeply to the stoic ideal—the ideal of a man independent of Fortune and opinion—but he would have kept Corsica "undeveloped, at any cost" (Shklar, *Men & Citizens,* p. 28).

181. Dr. Johnson remarks that it is good for the world that women are taught to busy themselves with little things. "Perhaps, the most powerful fancy might be unable to figure the confusion and slaughter that would be produced by so many piercing eyes and vivid understandings, turned loose at once upon mankind, with no other business than to sparkle and intrigue, to perplex and destroy." See *Rambler* No. 85. Adam Smith's moral theory implies that if the eyes of men pierced through to the folly of things, commercial society would be finished.

182. On the disastrous economic results of "complete resignation to the

Divine will," a sort of stoicism gone mad, see R. H. Campbell, "The Enlightenment and the Economy" in *The Origins and Nature of the Scottish Enlightenment,* eds. R. H. Campbell and Andrew Skinner (Edinburgh: John Donald, 1982), p. 13.

183. Wolin, *Politics and Vision,* p. 324. Compare Wolin's "unrelenting activity" with Adam Smith's "uniform, constant, and uninterrupted effort of every man to better his condition" (*Wealth of Nations,* p. 326). Cf. Reisman's analysis of the "fundamental insecurity" of Smith's capitalist, in *Smith's Sociological Economics,* p. 94.

184. Adams, *Roman Stamp,* p. 202.

185. See *Moral Discourses of Epictetus,* p. 245: "What is my own is safe." Cf. *TMS,* p. 213: "Security . . . is the first and the principal object of prudence." The prudent man, in turn, is the principal actor in the *Theory of Moral Sentiments.* Defoe describes a thriving tradesman who has achieved the independence of the stoic without incurring the rigors of the stoic ideal: *Complete English Tradesman,* vol. 2, p. 90.

186. Wolin, *Politics and Vision,* p. 329. Cf. Max Weber's thoughts on the calculability of things in modern society.

187. Cited in Hirschman, *Passions and the Interests,* p. 17.

188. Pope writes in his epistle "To a Lady": "But grant, in Public Men sometimes are shown, / A Woman's seen in Private life alone. / Our bolder Talents in full light display'd; / Your Virtues open fairest in the shade." Women, being "bred to disguise," dissimulate and "hide" in public. (See lines 199f.) I think it significant that Pope himself hides the identity of the women he caricatures, by means of a kind of teasing diaphanous veil.

189. Macfie, *The Individual in Society,* p. 58; cf. pp. 68, 91. On the influence of Adam Ferguson on Schiller, see Abrams, *Natural Supernaturalism,* pp. 210–11.

190. *Kant's Political Writings,* ed. Hans Reiss, trans. H. B. Nisbet (Cambridge: Cambridge University Press, 1971), p. 41.

191. *Kant's Political Writings,* p. 45. Cf. Schiller's statement, "If the manifold potentialities in man were ever to be developed, there was no other way but to pit them against each other." Cited in Charles Taylor, *Hegel and Modern Society* (Cambridge: Cambridge University Press, 1979), p. 7.

192. Mandeville, *Fable of the Bees,* p. 132. Cf. Abrams, *Natural Supernaturalism,* p. 206: "Kant's secular theodicy is therefore one of private evils, public benefits."

193. Lindgren, *Social Philosophy of Adam Smith,* p. 148.

194. ". . . all those frivolous nothings which fill up the void of human life" (*TMS,* p. 41).

195. Wollstonecraft, *Vindication of the Rights of Woman,* p. 45.

196. *Kant's Political Writings,* p. 112. The source is "Perpetual Peace."

197. *Wealth of Nations,* pp. 744–45.

198. *Kant's Political Writings,* p. 112.

199. *Kant's Political Writings,* p. 71. "On the Common Saying: 'This May be True in Theory, but it does not Apply in Practice.'"

200. On Kant's notions of autonomy and struggle, see Taylor, especially pp. 3–5. According to one view, Kant holds that almost all of us are autonomous but that a lot of us fail our autonomy and do not carry it out in action. See Thomas

Hill, "The Kantian Concept of Autonomy" in *The Inner Citadel: Essays on Individual Autonomy,* ed. John Christman (New York: Oxford University Press, 1989), pp. 91–105. Mary Wollstonecraft might easily have said that women *have* rationality, they just fail it.

201. *Kant's Political Writings,* p. 54. "An Answer to the Question: 'What is Enlightenment?'" (1784).

202. *Kant's Political Writings,* p. 54.

203. See Mitzi Myers, "Impeccable Governesses, Rational Dames, and Moral Mothers: Mary Wollstonecraft and the Female Tradition in Georgian Children's Books," *Children's Literature* 14 (1986): 43: empathy is "culturally associated with women."

204. I quote from a collection of stoic teachings translated into English in 1675 and quoted in turn by R. S. Crane, "Suggestions Toward a Genealogy of the 'Man of Feeling,'" *ELH* 1 (1934): 216.

205. The spectator's sympathy gives rise to the "soft, the gentle, the amiable virtues." The actor's self-command gives rise to "the great, the awful and respectable" virtues of "self-government" (*TMS,* p. 23).

206. Eagleton, *Ideology of the Aesthetic,* p. 75.

207. "Unconscious imitation": see Sarah Lewis, *Woman's Mission,* in Helsinger, Sheets, and Veeder, *Defining Voices,* p. 6.

208. Fordyce, *Sermons to Young Women,* vol. 1, pp. 35, 36. Cf. Eagleton's analysis of the disappearance of "heteronomous law" in the aesthetic ideal: *Ideology of the Aesthetic,* e.g., p. 28. On the superiority of influence to precept, see also Poovey, *Uneven Developments,* p. 8.

209. See Mullan, *Sentiment and Sociability,* pp. 143–44; the author quotes *The Sentimental Magazine.* Cf. Pope's "Essay on Criticism," line 574: "Men must be taught as if you taught them not." An analogy between the "invisible" work of the writer and the also invisible work of the housewife is unfolded by Poovey, *Uneven Developments,* pp. 122–23. The principle that people respond to images more than precepts passed into romantic thought.

210. *Spectator* No. 57. Cf. Fordyce, *Sermons to Young Women,* vol. 1, p. 208: the role of women is to "improve our pleasures and soothe our pains." Hume observes that in cities the sexes "meet in an easy and sociable manner; and the tempers of men, as well as their behaviour, refine apace" (*Essays Moral, Political, and Literary,* p. 271). While Adam Smith worried that city people would lose themselves in crowds and so escape surveillance (*Wealth of Nations,* p. 747), Hume imagines the city as a great Spectator club. J. S. Mill, seen by some (for example, A. L. Macfie) as a member of the Scottish tradition, offers a bitterly ironic interpretation of the "improving" effects of surveillance.

211. *Spectator* No. 16.

212. Eighteenth-century Edinburgh "saw a proliferation of Spectatorial clubs and societies, practising the virtues of polite conversation and enlightened taste while discussing the economic, cultural and even—given an age in which manners seemed no unimportant part of morality—the moral improvement of Scottish life." J. G. A. Pocock, "Cambridge Paradigms and Scotch Philosophers: A Study of the Relations Between the Civic Humanist and the Civil Jurisprudential Interpretation of Eighteenth-Century Social Thought," in *Wealth and Virtue,*

eds. Hont and Ignatieff, p. 240. Spectatorship also figures in the thought of Smith's own preceptor, Francis Hutcheson.

213. Butler, *Jane Austen and the War of Ideas,* p. 36.

214. Helsinger, Sheets, and Veeder, *The Women Question,* p. 11. The theme is a commonplace.

215. Ellis, *Women of England,* p. 53.

216. Sarah Hale, cited in Douglas, *Feminization of American Culture,* p. 86. Compare Barber's description of the consumption of "vicarious emotions," "Rousseau and the Paradoxes of the Dramatic Imagination," p. 85.

217. See Lindgren, *Social Philosophy of Adam Smith,* p. 91.

218. Wollstonecraft, *Vindication of the Rights of Woman,* pp. 58, 90.

219. Wollstonecraft, *Vindication of the Rights of Woman,* p. 9. The author refers to the middle class.

220. Pocock, "Cambridge Paradigms and Scotch Philosophers," in *Wealth and Virtue,* eds. Hont and Ignatieff, p. 242.

221. Pocock, "Cambridge Paradigms and Scotch Philosophers," in *Wealth and Virtue,* eds. Hont and Ignatieff, p. 241.

222. Pocock, "Cambridge Paradigms and Scotch Philosophers," p. 237.

223. Introduction to the *Theory of Moral Sentiments,* p. 5.

224. Hont and Ignatieff resolve the question of Smith's loyalties in favor of the liberal paradigm: "For all of his undoubted sympathy for the civic ideal of undivided personality and his advocacy of martial education to combat the stupefying and privatizing effects of the division of labour, Smith was convinced that it was impossible to restore human beings to an integrated identity as productive labourers and soldier-citizens" ("Needs and justice in the *Wealth of Nations,* in *Wealth and Virtue,* p. 8). Cf. Donald Winch, *Adam Smith's Politics,* p. 175: "It is . . . possible to appreciate the insight into Smith's position contained in John Pocock's view that the interest of the Scottish historians of civil society in progress, and their recognition of the enlarged role played by economic factors in modern commercial society, did not lead to a complete abandonment of the humanist criteria. . . . Having registered this insight, however, it is important not to exaggerate its significance for an understanding of Smith's politics."

225. Pocock, "Cambridge Paradigms and Scotch Philosophers" in *Wealth and Virtue,* eds. Hont and Ignatieff, p. 244.

226. See Jonas Barish, "Ovid, Juvenal, and *The Silent Woman,*" *PMLA* 71 (1956): 214. On the association of Juvenal with manliness, rugged virtue, incorruption, and disdain for courtly elegance, see Howard Weinbrot, "History, Horace, and Augustus Caesar: Some Implications for Eighteenth-Century Satire," *Eighteenth-Century Studies* 7 (1974): 391–414.

227. Pocock, "Cambridge Paradigms and Scotch Philosophers," p. 243.

228. Pocock, "Cambridge Paradigms and Scotch Philosophers," p. 243.

229. Contrast the debunking of Cato in La Rochefoucauld's *Maxims,* no. 504. The author's attitude toward stoicism is intimated by maxim no. 22: "Philosophy triumphs with ease over misfortunes past and to come, but present misfortunes triumph over it." On Cato, see Sekora, *Luxury,* e.g., p. 37.

230. See M. M. Goldsmith, "Liberty, Luxury, and the Pursuit of Happiness" in *Languages of Political Theory in Early-Modern Europe,* ed. Pagden, pp. 228–29.

231. Pocock, "Cambridge Paradigms and Scotch Philosophers," p. 235.

232. Mill, *On Liberty*, p. 8.

233. Myers, "Impeccable Governesses, Rational Dames, and Moral Mothers," p. 43. Cf. Marshall, *Figure of Theater*, p. 184: "One might expect Smith to have more to say about women in a treatise on moral sentiments written in an age that closely associated both sympathy and sentiment with 'feminine' sensibilities." Indeed, the first edition of the *Theory of Moral Sentiments* appeared during the vogue of male sensibility, men being pictured as tenderhearted, sweetly benevolent, and given to "moral weeping." See Crane, "Suggestions Toward a Genealogy of the 'Man of Feeling,' " p. 205. Women were advised, correspondingly, "to melt into affectionate sorrow." See Fordyce, *Sermons to Young Women*, vol. I, p. 185.

234. Wollstonecraft, *Vindication of the Rights of Woman*, pp. 57–58.

235. For example, Fordyce, *Sermons to Young Women*, vol. I, p. 78. But this is a commonplace.

236. Sheila Delany, "Sex and Politics in Pope's 'Rape of the Lock' " in *Weapons of Criticism: Marxism in America and the Literary Tradition*, ed. Norman Rudich (Palo Alto: Ramparts Press, 1976), p. 182.

237. Jeremy Bentham, *An Introduction to the Principles of Morals and Legislation* (Darien: Hafner, 1970), p. 59: a woman's "affections are apt to be less enlarged [than a man's]: seldom expanding themselves so much as to take in the welfare of her country in general." Cf. Jean Bethke Elshtain, *Public Man, Private Woman: Women in Social and Political Thought* (Princeton: Princeton University Press, 1981), p. 132. The argument that women are prone to ignore what is remote from themselves is given an interesting twist by the nineteenth-century feminist William Thompson. He argues that women must be accorded political rights precisely to counteract "the *tendency* to attach too great relative importance to domestic and selfish over social and sympathetic affections, to immediate over remote objects and enjoyments," a tendency that follows from their physical confinement. See Helsinger, Sheets, and Veeder, *The Woman Question*, p. 34.

238. On this point, see Russell Nieli, "Spheres of Intimacy and the Adam Smith Problem," *Journal of the History of Ideas* 47 (1986): 623.

239. See Hume, *Treatise of Human Nature*, p. 652; and Miller, *Philosophy and Ideology in Hume's Political Thought*, pp. 106–7. Cf. Defoe, *Complete English Tradesman*, vol. I, p. 26: "He that will be a complete tradesman should principally confine himself within his own sphere." Hume expects us to "confine our view to that narrow circle, in which any person moves" (p. 652); John Stuart Mill is dismayed to find people (men and women) caged in "the narrow circle of personal and family selfishness" (*On Liberty*, p. 101).

240. Fernand Braudel, cited by McKendrick in *Birth of a Consumer Society*, p. 33.

241. Lindgren, *Social Philosophy of Adam Smith*, p. 129.

242. As noted in my introduction, this prejudice in men's favor appears with rare clarity in Hume's *Treatise of Human Nature*. Indeed, Hume's description of *men* as endowed with "extensive sympathy" but "limited generosity" matches Adam Smith's description of *women* as possessing plenty of fellow-feeling but lacking the strength of character that real generosity requires. See *TMS*, pp. 190–91.

243. Eagleton, *Ideology of the Aesthetic*, p. 50.

Chapter 3

1. Introduction to *TMS*, p. 21.

2. *Spectator* No. 397. See *The Spectator,* ed. Donald Bond (Oxford: Clarendon Press, 1965), vol. 3. The idea of the amicability of trade dates back to the fourth century. See Jacob Viner, *The Role of Providence in the Social Order: An Essay in Intellectual History* (Philadelphia: American Philosophical Society, 1972), chap. 2.

3. The author is one Baptist Goodall, writing in 1630; cited in Louis Landa, *Essays in Eighteenth-Century English Literature* (Princeton: Princeton University Press, 1980), p. 212. Cf. The *Encyclopedia* article on "Commerce" written by Forbonnais, included in *Encyclopedia Selections,* eds. and trans. Nelly Hoyt and Thomas Cassirer (Indianapolis: Library of Liberal Arts, 1965), p. 49: "The Supreme Being forged the bonds of commerce in order to incline the peoples of the earth to keep peace with each other and to love each other, and in order to gather to himself the tribute of their praise." The theme is a commonplace.

4. Adam Smith, *An Inquiry into the Nature and Causes of the Wealth of Nations* (New York: Modern Library, 1937), p. 460.

5. See J. G. A. Pocock, "Cambridge Paradigms and Scotch Philosophers: A Study of the Relations Between the Civic Humanist and the Civil Jurisprudential Interpretation of Eighteenth-Century Social Thought" in *Wealth and Virtue: The Shaping of Political Economy in the Scottish Enlightenment,* eds. Istvan Hont and Michael Ignatieff (Cambridge: Cambridge University Press, 1983).

6. Elizabeth Helsinger, Robin Lauterbach Sheets, and William Veeder, eds., *The Woman Question: Society and Literature in Britain and America, 1837–1883,* vol. 1: *Defining Voices* (Chicago: University of Chicago Press, 1983), p. 8. On the "almost religious scrupulosity" of the prudent man, see *TMS,* p. 214. The figurative identity of the prudent man and his wife is hinted at in an observation of Yorick in Sterne's *Sentimental Journey:* "In London a shopkeeper and a shopkeeper's wife seem to be one bone and one flesh: in the several endowments of mind and body, sometimes the one, sometimes the other has it, so as in general to be upon a par, and to tally with each other as nearly as man and wife need to do." Laurence Sterne, *A Sentimental Journey* (London: Oxford University Press, 1968), p. 54.

7. Smith, *Wealth of Nations,* p. 745.

8. J. Ralph Lindgren, *The Social Philosophy of Adam Smith* (The Hague: Martinus Nijhoff, 1973), p. 107.

9. Istvan Hont and Michael Ignatieff, "Needs and Justice in the *Wealth of Nations:* An Introductory Essay" in *Wealth and Virtue,* eds. Hont and Ignatieff, pp. 8–9. Cf. D. A. Reisman, *Adam Smith's Sociological Economics* (London: Croom Helm, 1976), p. 18: "Certain it is that Smith, a serious-minded academic rather than an entrepreneur or a gambler, did not personally share that love of hedonistic commodity-utility or aggressive profit-maximisation that one would expect from the ideologue of a society comprised of salesmen." The paradox Smith confronted, as a man of conservative temper committed to a market economy that undoes traditional values, looked like this a hundred years later: "How could the modern economic imperative to multiply needs be reconciled

with the moral tradition inherited from Christian and non-Christian antiquity, which counseled self-discipline and restraint of desire?" See Rosalind Williams, *Dream Worlds: Mass Consumption in Late-Nineteenth Century France* (Berkeley: University of California Press, 1982), p. 224. By means of the language of stoicism, Smith imports the ancient tradition of self-command into an analysis of modern commercial society.

10. Hont and Ignatieff, "Needs and justice in the *Wealth of Nations*," in *Wealth and Virtue*, p. 10.

11. On this point, see the Introduction to *TMS*, p. 9.

12. Adam Smith's notion of women emerges in a passage in the *Wealth of Nations* commending their education. "They are taught what their parents or guardians judge it necessary or useful for them to learn; and they are taught nothing else. Every part of their education tends evidently to some useful purpose; either to improve the natural attractions of their person, or to form their mind to reserve, to modesty, to chastity, and to oeconomy; to render them both likely to become the mistresses of a family, and to behave properly when they have become such." See *Wealth of Nations*, p. 734.

13. On this issue, cf. Knud Haakonssen, "What Might Properly Be Called Natural Jurisprudence?" in *The Origins and Nature of the Scottish Enlightenment*, eds. R. H. Campbell and Andrew Skinner (Edinburgh: John Donald, 1982), pp. 205–225.

14. See Norbert Elias, *The History of Manners* and *Power and Civility*, both translated by Edmund Jephcott. *Manners* (New York: Pantheon, 1978); *Power* (New York: Pantheon, 1982). Both originally published 1939. These two volumes constitute *The Civilizing Process*.

15. Charles Lamb, "Imperfect Sympathies" in *The Complete Works and Letters of Charles Lamb* (New York: Modern Library, 1935), pp. 51, 54. The text has "variest thrall." "Jews christianizing—Christians judaizing—puzzle me. I like fish or flesh," writes Lamb in the same essay where he declares his distaste for the positivity of the Scots. Lamb claims a kind of antirational license.

16. H. L. A. Hart, "Immorality and Treason" in the Norton Critical Edition of John Stuart Mill, *On Liberty*, ed. David Spitz (New York: Norton, 1975), pp. 246–52. Lindgren, *Social Philosophy of Adam Smith*, emphasizes Smith's loyalty to the community's feelings of sympathy and aversion.

17. Christopher Hill, "Clarissa Harlowe and her Times," *Essays in Criticism* 5 (1955): 332. Compare Kant, *Foundations of the Metaphysics of Morals*, trans. Lewis White Beck (New York: Macmillan, 1990), p. 10: "The good will is not good because of what it effects or accomplishes or because of its competence to achieve some intended end; it is good only because of its willing (i.e., it is good in itself)."

18. An interesting section of the *Theory of Moral Sentiments* is devoted to describing and in fact justifying our habit of judging by outcomes and not strictly by intentions (*TMS*, pp. 97–108). The doctrine of unintended outcomes moots intention entirely. On chastity as an absolute, see Jane Rendall, "Virtue and Commerce: Women in the Making of Adam Smith's Political Economy" in *Women in Western Political Philosophy*, eds. Ellen Kennedy and Susan Mendus (New York: St. Martin's, 1987), pp. 60, 62–64.

19. "Still, I know that it will require a considerable length of time to eradicate the firmly rooted prejudices which sensualistis have planted." Mary Wollstonecraft, *A Vindication of the Rights of Woman,* ed. Carol Poston (New York: Norton, 1988), p. 47.

20. See M. H. Abrams, *Natural Supernaturalism: Tradition and Revolution in Romantic Literature* (New York: Norton, 1973), pp. 390–99. Wordsworth clashes with the norm of propriety that received its most stately expression from Adam Smith; moreover, as Abrams makes clear, his thought is nourished by evangelical influences of the kind Smith distrusted.

21. Reisman, *Smith's Sociological Economics,* p. 74.

22. See Introduction to *TMS,* p. 16. If morality is so much a matter of the correct presentation of the passions—so much a matter of appearance—how are we to distinguish morality from mere semblance? On Jane Austen's handling of the issue, see Alasdair MacIntyre, *After Virtue: A Study in Moral Theory* (Notre Dame: University of Notre Dame Press, 1981), p. 224. The expedient figure of the man within resolves this problem for Adam Smith. The argument that women are not in fact inferior just because they have come to seem so (just because public opinion says they are) was made with clarity by François Poulain de la Barre (1647–1723); see Michael Seidel, "Poulain de la Barre's *The Woman as Good as the Man," Journal of the History of Ideas* 35 (1974): 499–508.

23. On this point, see Reisman, *Smith's Sociological Economics,* p. 76.

24. Jean-Jacques Rousseau, *Emile,* trans. Allan Bloom (New York: Basic, 1979), p. 364. Cf. Sarah Ellis, *The Women of England, Their Social Duties and Domestic Habits* (London, 1839[?]), p. 303: "With regard to the love of admiration, it is much to be regretted that all women who make this one of the chief objects of their lives, do not at the same time evince an equal solicitude to be admired for what is really praiseworthy."

25. Lindgren, *Social Philosophy of Adam Smith,* p. 48. In order to win praise (or any other social good), we need not possess virtue; the appearance of virtue will do. "Honesty is useful, because it assures us credit; so are punctuality, industry, frugality, and that is the reason they are virtues. A logical deduction from this would be that where, for instance, the appearance of honesty serves the same purpose, that would suffice." Max Weber, *The Protestant Ethic and the Spirit of Capitalism,* trans. Talcott Parsons (New York: Scribners, 1930), p. 52. The stoic loves virtue for its own sake and not for the social gains it brings; thus he saves the Smithian actor from imputations of dishonesty and playacting.

26. Cf. David McNally, *Political Economy and the Rise of Capitalism: A Reinterpretation* (Berkeley: University of California Press, 1988), pp. 183–84. McNally is unconvinced by Smith's attempt to secure the individual against the corrupting effects of public opinion.

27. John Mullan, *Sentiment and Sociability: The Language of Feeling in the Eighteenth Century* (Oxford: Clarendon Press, 1988), p. 85. Mullan refers to Grandison as "a strangely absent apparition" (p. 85).

28. There seems to be a note of futility in Adam Smith's statement that even the exceptional man will fail to "conquer the rooted prejudices of the people" (*TMS,* p. 233) with superior arguments.

29. Lindgren, *Social Philosophy of Adam Smith,* p. 80.

30. See, e.g., Haakonssen, "What Might Properly Be Called Natural Jurisprudence," pp. 220–21. The point is "overwhelmingly important," says Haakonssen.

31. See the manuscript of Reid's critique of Smith as reproduced by J. C. Stewart-Robertson and David Fate Norton, "Thomas Reid on Adam Smith's Theory of Morals," *Journal of the History of Ideas* 45 (1984), 317–18.

32. Max Scheler, *The Nature of Sympathy,* trans. Peter Heath (New Haven: Yale University Press, 1954), p. 6. First edition, 1912.

33. "The popular fear of engrossing and forestalling may be compared to the popular terrors and suspicions of witchcraft. The unfortunate wretches accused of this latter crime were not more innocent of the misfortunes imputed to them, than those who have been accused of the former" (*Wealth of Nations,* p. 500).

34. Reisman, *Smith's Sociological Economics,* p. 112. The phrase has a fittingly tautological air.

35. Originally Smith's, this profundity is the refrain of Reisman's study of *Smith's Sociological Economics.*

36. Says Hume, men, "guided more by custom than by reason, follow, without inquiry, the manners which are prevalent in their own time." Cited in David Miller, *Philosophy and Ideology in Hume's Political Thought* (Oxford: Clarendon Press, 1981), p. 103; see also p. 113.

37. *The Poetry and Prose of William Blake,* ed. David Erdman (Garden City: Doubleday, 1970), p. 479.

38. On Francis Hutcheson, see Caroline Robbins, *The Eighteenth-Century Commonwealthman: Studies in the Transmission, Development and Circumstance of English Liberal Thought from the Restoration of Charles II until the War with the Thirteen Colonies* (New York: Atheneum, 1968), pp. 185–96; Rendall, "Virtue and Commerce," pp. 53–54. On Mary Wollstonecraft as Commonwealthwoman, see G. J. Barker-Benfield, "Mary Wollstonecraft: Eighteenth-Century Commonwealthwoman," *Journal of the History of Ideas* 50 (1989): 95–115.

39. Again, see *Wealth of Nations,* p. 734. Even Fordyce despised boarding-school accomplishments—French and other fripperies. On the attitudes of eighteenth-century literati toward women's education and the woman question generally, see Katherine Clinton, "Femme et Philosophe: Enlightenment Origins of Feminism," *Eighteenth-Century Studies* 8 (1975): 283–99.

40. Wollstonecraft, *Vindication of the Rights of Woman,* p. 135.

41. Wollstonecraft, *Vindication of the Rights of Woman,* p. 45.

42. Analyzed to a nicety by David Marshall, *The Figure of Theater: Shaftesbury, Defoe, Adam Smith, and George Eliot* (New York: Columbia University Press, 1986), chap. 7. On the sociology of imitation, see Neil McKendrick, John Brewer, and J. H. Plumb, *The Birth of a Consumer Society* (Bloomington: Indiana University Press, 1982), e.g., p. 11: "In imitation of the rich the middle ranks [of eighteenth-century England] spent more frenziedly than ever before, and in imitation of them the rest of society joined in as best they might."

43. An interesting portrayal of a stoic woman is Dr. Johnson's *Rambler* No. 75, in *The Works of Samuel Johnson,* eds. W. J. Bate and Albrecht Strauss (New Haven: Yale University Press, 1969), vol. 4, pp. 28–33.

44. On Mary Wollstonecraft's "manly" ideal of the rights of man and her

contempt for Burke's womanish "sensibility," see Terry Eagleton, *Ideology of the Aesthetic* (Oxford: Basil Blackwell, 1990), p. 61. In his repudiation of the idea of new-modeling the constitution and his reliance on mysterious agencies like sympathy, Adam Smith bears comparison with Burke (himself an advocate of free trade).

45. J. G. A. Pocock, *Virtue, Commerce, and History: Essays on Political Thought and History, Chiefly in the Eighteenth Century* (Cambridge: Cambridge University Press, 1985), p. 112. On the multiplication of "imaginary wants," so suggestive of our own consumer society, see Hume as discussed in Miller, *Philosophy and Ideology in Hume's Political Thought*, p. 109.

46. See *TMS*, p. 115.

47. *TMS*, p. 191. In Henry Mackenzie's *Man of Feeling*, this distinction is criticized as spurious, scholastic, unnatural. Miss Walton's "beneficence was unbounded; indeed the natural tenderness of her heart might have been argued, by the frigidity of a casuist, as detracting from her virtue in this respect, for her humanity was a feeling, not a principle: but minds like Harley's are not very apt to make this distinction." Henry Mackenzie, *The Man of Feeling* (London: Cassell, 1893), p. 27. Mill's *On Liberty* was to be criticized in its own time on the similar grounds that the distinction between self-regarding and other-regarding acts is entirely artificial and legalistic, the kind of invention that would not occur to a healthy mind. The inarguable claim that "right-thinking (natural, healthy) minds don't think that way" can evidently be brought against anything you choose. Adam Smith himself appeals to the natural force of sympathy, and shares Mackenzie's sense that Nature's bonds are deeper than reason and her designs wiser than our designs; indeed, in the spirit of Mackenzie he claims that if only we consult conscience, we "shall stand in need of no casuistic rules" (*TMS*, p. 227).

48. See, for example, Smith's recognition that class society rests on nothing but a trick of the imagination and that habits of submission keep men from trying "to reason and dispute" with their masters (*TMS*, pp. 52–53).

49. Wollstonecraft, *Vindication of the Rights of Woman*, p. 47.

50. Mary Poovey, *The Proper Lady and the Woman Writer: Ideology as Style in the Works of Mary Wollstonecraft, Mary Shelley, and Jane Austen* (Chicago: University of Chicago Press, 1984), p. 70. On the affinities of men and women, see, e.g., *Vindication of the Rights of Woman*, p. 45: "in descanting on the folly of the [female] sex, let him not overlook his own."

51. Wollstonecraft, *Vindication of the Rights of Woman*, p. 86.

52. On Max Weber on reason, see Rogers Brubaker, *The Limits of Rationality: An Essay on the Social and Moral Thought of Max Weber* (London: George Allen and Unwin, 1984).

53. See *TMS*, p. 180n.

54. Max Horkheimer, *Eclipse of Reason* (New York: Seabury, 1974), p. 3. Cf. Paul Tillich, "The Lost Dimension of Religion," reprinted in *The Educated Reader*, ed. Gerald Levin (San Diego: Harcourt Brace Jovanovich, 1988), pp. 218–19: modern man "transforms everything he touches into a tool; and in doing so he himself becomes a tool. But if he asks, a tool for what, there is no answer." Cf. Richard Flathman on Erving Goffman in *The Philosophy and Politics of Freedom* (Chicago: University of Chicago Press, 1987), p. 176: "As Goffman

describes us, we modern Westerners regularly display a quite impressive instrumental rationality. We are skillful, clever, even ingenious in our pursuit of the objectives we happen to have. But we have little capacity to assess the merits of those objectives." Adam Smith noted the tendency of institutions to drift from the purposes they were intended to serve, as though means took on a life of their own and superseded ends. See *TMS*, p. 185. See also Lindgren's remarks on this subject, *Social Philosophy of Adam Smith*, e.g., p. 75.

55. Horkheimer, *Eclipse of Reason*, p. 7. Cf. Paul Corcoran, *Political Language and Rhetoric* (Austin: University of Texas Press, 1979), p. 173: "In a culture which values 'hard data' and rewards those who produce and work with them—a culture which claims to accept only objective, empirical and scientific data in conformity with its dominant epistemology—it is peculiar that there is a pervasive assumption that such knowledge can have no bearing upon public discourse in general and the substance of political rhetoric in particular." Analogously, I have questioned whether masculine epistemology is really as "hard" and "objective" as commonly supposed.

56. Horkheimer, *Eclipse of Reason*, p. 10. Tillich criticizes our "competitive and conformist" society in the article just cited. An eighteenth-century writer like Mandeville would call competition-and-conformity by the single name of "emulation."

57. Lindgren, *Social Philosophy of Adam Smith*, p. 131.

58. Mill, *On Liberty*, p. 8.

59. A. L. Macfie, *The Individual in Society: Papers on Adam Smith* (London: George Allen and Unwin, 1967), p. 54.

60. See Werner Sombart, *Luxury and Capitalism*, trans. W. R. Dittmar (Ann Arbor: University of Michigan Press, 1967), p. 84.

61. *On Liberty*, p. 58. By a swift descent, Adam Smith's all-seeing spectator becomes the sort of spy who, as Charlotte Perkins Gilman says, "watch[es] over and comment[s] upon" every move in the relation of unmarried men and women. Gilman, *Women and Economics* (Boston: Small, Maynard and Company, 1898), p. 312.

62. See *Wealth of Nations*, p. 633. Smith's stringently skeptical attitude toward men of commerce is discussed by McNally, *Political Economy and the Rise of Capitalism*.

63. Mill, *On Liberty*, p. 58.

64. See the article on "Commerce" contained in *Encyclopedia Selections*, eds. and trans. Hoyt and Cassirer, p. 49.

65. See, for example, Lindgren, *Social Philosophy of Adam Smith*, p. 107. In his 1836 essay on "Civilization," however, Mill remarks on the salutary effect of public opinion in small towns; by reminding people that they have a reputation to lose, it keeps them honest. The same point is made in the *Wealth of Nations* (p. 747).

66. See the Introduction to *TMS*, p. 9.

67. On Smith's aestheticizing of the loveliness and propriety of men, see also Reisman, *Smith's Sociological Economics*, pp. 52–53.

68. Smith, *Wealth of Nations*, p. 633.

69. See Stewart Justman, *The Hidden Text of Mill's* Liberty (Savage, Md.: Rowman and Littlefield, 1990).

70. Mill, *On Liberty*, pp. 47–48. A similar disdain for the craven precepts of

Christianity is seen in Adam Smith's comment that Hume faced death "with more real resignation to the necessary course of things, than any Whining Christian ever dyed with pretended resignation to the will of God." Cited in Introduction to *TMS*, p. 19.

71. See, e.g., Haakonssen, "What Might Properly Be Called Natural Jurisprudence?"

72. See, e.g., John Brown, *An Estimate of the Manners and Principles of the Times* (London, 1757), vol. 1, p. 18: "We have not the Virtue to secure our Freedom. The Spirit of Liberty is now struggling with the Manners and Principles as formerly it struggled with the Tyrants of the Time. But the Danger is now greater, because the Enemy is within; working secretly and securely, and destroying all those internal Powers, from which alone an effectual Opposition can arise." No reader of *On Liberty* can miss the similarities.

73. A case in point is Gibbon's thesis that the Septennial Act had a "vicious" origin but evolved into the bedrock of liberty. See Edward Bloom and Lillian Bloom, *Joseph Addison's Sociable Animal* (Providence: Brown University Press, 1971), p. 130. A perhaps-related example is Smith's own thesis that in some cases standing armies end up securing our liberties, by making the sovereign feel so strong that he can afford to be tolerant (*Wealth of Nations*, p. 668). Again, the British policy of restraining colonial manufacture had the unintended effect of forwarding the Americans' progress toward "wealth and greatness" by confining them to the most productive of all economic pursuits, agriculture (*Wealth of Nations*, pp. 347–48; cf. p. 549). The colonies were planted in the first place not by farseeing wisdom of the mother country but by exiles from the mother country (p. 555). Indeed, the whole mercantile system is a bungle. Smith contemplates results like these with a kind of Olympian irony; that is, he sees what the actors themselves do not. (And if men are apt to act blindly, that is the more reason for them not to attempt to act in public ways.) On Smith's belief in an "Author of Nature" who works through men in ways they don't perceive, producing effects they never intend, see Reisman, *Smith's Sociological Economics*, pp. 84–85. On unintended consequences, see also La Rochefoucauld, maxim no. 57: "Though men take pride in their noble deeds, the deeds themselves often derive, not from noble intentions, but from simple chance." Also no. 519: "Evil results from good, and good from evil." *The Maxims of La Rochefoucauld*, trans. Louis Kronenberger (New York: Random House, 1959). Cf. Edmund Burke, *Reflections on the Revolution in France* (Indianapolis: Library of Liberal Arts, 1955), p. 201: in a well-settled polity, "we often see the end best obtained where the means seem not perfectly reconcilable to what we may fancy was the original scheme." Arguing in the introduction to *On Liberty* that the spiritual slavery of his contemporaries is the ironic outcome of a historic struggle for freedom, Mill inverts the doctrine of unintended good.

74. See the *Encyclopedia* article on "Luxury," contained in *Encyclopedia Selections*, p. 229. The author is Charles-François de Saint-Lambert. This richly interesting article bears comparison with the thinking of Adam Smith.

75. Mill, *On Liberty*, p. 101.

76. John Stuart Mill, *The Subjection of Women* in Mill and Harriet Taylor Mill, *Essays on Sex Equality*, ed. Alice Rossi (Chicago: University of Chicago Press, 1970), p. 222.

77. Mill, *The Subjection of Women*, p. 226.

78. A progressive journal wrote in 1865 that a "sense of duty towards the public good . . . is rarely found" in wives. *Victoria Magazine* 6, cited in Helsinger, Sheets, and Veeder, *The Woman Question*, p. 101.

79. Mill, *Subjection of Women*, p. 225. Cf. Adam Smith's distinction between the amiable and the awful virtues: *TMS*, p. 23.

80. David Hume, *A Treatise of Human Nature* (Harmondsworth, Middlesex: Penguin, 1985), p. 480.

81. Poovey, *Proper Lady and the Woman Writer*, p. 205.

82. Phillipson, "Adam Smith as civic moralist" in *Wealth and Virtue*, eds. Hont and Ignatieff, p. 182n. Phillipson's comment that "it is interesting that [Smith] regarded his collection of homely Addisonian illustrations as a strong enough foundation on which to raise [his] central argument" hints rather broadly at the weak foundation of the *Theory of Moral Sentiments,* a point I have made with a different emphasis. On the serene irony of Adam Smith, see Donald Winch, *Adam Smith's Politics: An Essay in Historiographic Revision* (Cambridge: Cambridge University Press, 1978), p. 180.

83. Claudia Johnson, *Jane Austen: Women, Politics and the Novel* (Chicago: University of Chicago Press, 1988), cogently challenges the received opinion that Austen is on the conservative side of the political divide, and in particular disputes the findings of Marilyn Butler in *Jane Austen and the War of Ideas* (Oxford: Clarendon Press, 1975).

84. Ellis, *Women of England*, p. 122.

85. Gerald Bruns, *Inventions: Writing, Textuality, and Understanding in Literary History* (New Haven: Yale University Press, 1982), p. 118.

86. Jane Austen, *Pride and Prejudice* (New York: Norton, 1966), p. 77.

87. *Pride and Prejudice*, p. 76.

88. Wollstonecraft, *Vindication of the Rights of Woman*, p. 94.

89. *Pride and Prejudice*, p. 262. The word "roused" possibly carries an erotic charge.

90. *Pride and Prejudice*, p. 142.

91. Cf. the pronouncement of Mary, "who piqued herself upon the solidity of her reflections," that " 'Vanity and pride are different things, though the words are often used synonimously. A person may be proud without being vain. Pride relates more to our opinion of ourselves, vanity to what we would have others think of us' " (p. 13). Adam Smith draws out a lengthy distinction between pride and vanity along just these lines.

92. Austen, *Pride and Prejudice*, p. 255.

93. According to Thomas Reid, if "unjust imputations are thrown upon" a man of integrity, "he flings them off with a noble disdain. . . . We may call this the Pride of Virtue, but it is not a vicious but a Noble, a Magnanimous Disposition." (See Stewart-Robertson and Norton, "Thomas Reid on Adam Smith's Theory of Morals," p. 319.) The parallels to Darcy are clear.

94. On Smith's agrarian bias, see McNally's excellent study, *Political Economy and the Rise of Capitalism.*

95. Robert Adams, *The Land and Literature of England* (New York: Norton, 1983), p. 367. The author hears in Jane Austen "the lucid and assured voice of the eighteenth century" (p. 367), or in other words, Adam Smith. A passing com-

parison of Smith and Austen appears in Rendall, "Virtue and Commerce," p. 72.

96. See *Wealth of Nations,* p. 668.

97. Butler, *Jane Austen and the War of Ideas,* p. 294. Johnson, *Jane Austen,* situates Austen on the progressive side of the war of ideas.

98. Letter from Adam Smith to Andreas Holt, 26 Oct. 1780, in *The Correspondence of Adam Smith,* eds. Ernest Campbell Mossner and Ian Simpson Ross (Oxford: Clarendon Press, 1977), p. 250. Cf. Jean Bethke Elshtain, "Feminist Discourse and Its Discontents: Language, Power, and Meaning" in *Feminist Theory: A Critique of Ideology* (Chicago: University of Chicago Press, 1982), p. 133: "For Hobbes, the power of language was so great and its potential for promoting sedition so high that language must be stripped of that power." Perhaps the extreme propriety of Adam Smith's own language can be understood as an attempt to discredit dangerous abuses of language like those that worried Hobbes.

99. Rather similarly, Addison, voice of gentleness and civility, may have been repelled by the fury of the partisan politics he himself lived. Benjamin Franklin is another political man who offered counsels of modesty and mildness.

100. Viner, *Role of Providence,* p. 85.

101. See chap. 5 of McKendrick et al., *Birth of a Consumer Society.*

102. As Wordsworth in fact did with his turn to quietism following the defeat of his hopes for the French Revolution. Abrams, *Natural Supernaturalism,* p. 338.

103. MacIntyre, *After Virtue,* pp. 157–58.

104. See Epictetus, *Moral Discourse of Epictetus,* trans. Elizabeth Carter (London: J. M. Dent, 1910), p. 21: "If what philosophers say of the kindred between God and man be true, what has any one to do, but, like Socrates, when he is asked what countryman he is, never to say that he is a citizen of Athens, or of Corinth, but of the world?" On this point, cf. MacIntyre, *After Virtue,* p. 157: "The good man is a citizen of the universe; his relation to all other collectivities, to city, kingdom or empire is secondary and accidental." Cf. Charles Taylor, *Hegel and Modern Society* (Cambridge: Cambridge University Press, 1979), p. 92. On the stoic ideal and the collapse of the public realm, see Karl Mannheim, *Essays on Sociology and Social Psychology* (New York: Oxford University Press, 1953), pp. 292–93.

105. See *Wealth of Nations,* p. 800, on the merchant as "a citizen of the world." Smith's merchants—conspiratorial, rapacious, stateless—bear the traditional image of the Jew.

106. "He that will be a complete tradesman should principally confine himself within his own sphere; never was the Gazette so full of bankruptcies as since our shopkeepers have so much engaged in parties, formed into clubs to hear news and study politics. The known story of the upholsterer is very instructive, who, in his abundant concern for the public, ran himself out of his business into a jail." Daniel Defoe, *The Complete English Tradesman* (New York: Burt Franklin, 1970), vol. 1, p. 26.

107. *Wealth of Nations,* p. 587.

108. Smith's respect for "established powers and privileges," tolerance of abuses, and wariness of innovation (*TMS,* pp. 232–33) degrade into the kind of obstructionism that angered Jeremy Bentham. While an antimonopolist, Smith

left it for others to battle the monopolists of political power, much as the enthusiasts of technological innovation in Smith's time left it to others (like Bentham) to contend for political innovation. On the enthusiasm for invention, see David Spadafora, *The Idea of Progress in Eighteenth-Century Britain* (New Haven: Yale University Press, 1990), p. 60.

109. Bloom and Bloom, *Addison's Sociable Animal*, pp. 4–5.

110. Cited in Ernst Cassirer, *The Myth of the State* (New Haven: Yale University Press, 1946), p. 178.

111. On this point, see McNally, *Political Economy and the Rise of Capitalism*, p. 207.

112. "He never assumes impertinently over any body, and, upon all common occasions, is willing to place himself rather below than above his equals" (*TMS*, p. 214).

113. On Hume on politics, see Miller, *Philosophy and Ideology in Hume's Political Thought*, pp. 96–97.

114. Johnson, *Jane Austen*, pp. 78–79. Cf. Peter Gay, *The Enlightenment: An Interpretation* (New York: Knopf, 1966), p. 299: "In the rebellious Netherlands, the center of learning and religious controversy, educated men turned to Stoicism as a cure for the diseases of civil war." And so it was throughout Western Europe. Adam Smith's stoicism thus comports with his distrust of sects and their "enthusiasm."

115. Abrams, *Natural Supernaturalism*, p. 365.

116. Abrams, *Natural Supernaturalism*, pp. 338, 134. The author opposes Carlyle's "economic activism" and Wordsworth's quietism. On Carlyle's exhortations to work, see *Sartor Resartus* in *A Carlyle Reader*, ed. G. B. Tennyson (New York: Modern Library, 1969), p. 260.

117. Sarah Lewis, *Woman's Mission*, as cited in Helsinger, Sheets, and Veeder, *The Woman Question*, p. 12.

118. The manic quality of the attacks on luxury and commerce comes out clearly in the many excerpts from eighteenth-century polemics cited by John Sekora, *Luxury: The Concept in Western Thought, Eden to Smollett* (Baltimore: Johns Hopkins University Press, 1977).

119. Johnson, *Jane Austen*, p. 24.

120. Cf. Defoe's pamphlet "A Plan of the English Commerce" (2nd ed. 1730), reprinted in *A Select Collection of Scarce and Valuable Tracts on Commerce*, ed. John McCulloch (New York: Augustus Kelley, 1966), p. 137: "Thus money raises armies, and trade raises money; and so it may be truly said of trade, that it makes princes powerful, nations valiant, and the most effeminate people that can't fight for themselves, if they have but the money, and can hire other people to fight for them, they become as formidable as any of their neighbours." Defoe preserves the old language of valor and effeminacy even while outmoding it.

121. M. M. Goldsmith, "Liberty, Luxury and the Pursuit of Happiness" in *The Languages of Political Theory in Early-Modern Europe*, ed. Anthony Pagden (Cambridge: Cambridge University Press, 1987), p. 251.

122. James Fordyce, *Sermons to Young Women* (London, 1766), vol. 1, p. 54. When J. S. Mill rejects consenting slavery in *On Liberty*, does this reflect on a corrupt sexual morality?

123. One version of the old theme that patience vanquishes: the good woman "Charms by accepting, by submitting sways, / Yet has her humor most when she obeys" (Pope's Epistle II: To a Lady, lines 263–64). Cf. Edward Young, cited by Felicity Nussbaum, *The Brink of All We Hate: English Satires on Women, 1660–1750* (Lexington: University Press of Kentucky, 1984), p. 132: "How have I seen a gentle nymph draw nigh, / Peace in her air, persuasion in her eye; / Victorious tenderness! it all o'ercame, / Husbands look'd mild, and savages grew tame."

124. On romance, guile, and women, see Northrop Frye, *The Secular Scripture: A Study of the Structure of Romance* (Cambridge: Harvard University Press, 1976), chap. 3.

125. Fordyce, *Sermons to Young Women,* vol. 1, p. 88. Cf. p. 118: "That women who, having families of their own, go much abroad, and affect to shine any where but in their proper sphere, are peculiarly to blame, must, I think, be acknowledged." On female virtue shunning the light, cf. Nussbaum, *The Brink of All We Hate,* pp. 117–18.

126. Fordyce, *Sermons to Young Women,* vol. 1, p. 108. Smith's prudent man is so averse to the more active virtues that the author appears to find him cowardly. Smith's precursor Addison, for all of his partiality for the bourgeois virtues, felt that prudence is too often another name for timidity. See Bloom and Bloom, *Addison's Sociable Animal,* pp. 18–19. Cf. La Rochefoucauld, maxim no. 169: "When laziness and timidity yoke us to our duties, we often give virtue the credit for it." Also no. 578: "Justice is but a lively fear of losing what belongs to us: hence our consideration and respect for our neighbor's rights and our great care not to cause him damage. Because of such fear, men stay within the bounds set for them by birth and fortune, where otherwise they would continually prey upon others." For Adam Smith's discussion of "mere justice," see *TMS,* p. 82; for his disapproval of La Rochefoucauld, see *TMS,* p. 308.

127. On this matter, see Lindgren, *Social Philosophy of Adam Smith,* p. 119.

128. "Both in his conduct and conversation, he is an exact observer of decency, and respects with an almost religious scrupulosity, all the established decorums and ceremonials of society" (*TMS,* p. 214).

Chapter 4

1. Cf. David Hume, *A Treatise of Human Nature* (Harmondsworth, Middlesex: Penguin, 1945), p. 531: "When any virtuous motive or principle is common in human nature, a person, who feels his heart devoid of that motive, may hate himself upon that account, and may perform the action without the motive, from a certain sense of duty."

2. *TMS,* p. 214. Noted on the same page are the prudent man's distaste for "convivial societies" and his generally unconvivial manner.

3. "Dominant" here doesn't mean that the view was held by the largest number of people but that it was culturally ascendant and spread by men who controlled the pen. On Smith as an adumbrator of the Victorian ideal, see Jane Rendall, "Virtue and Commerce: Women in the Making of Adam Smith's

Political Economy" in *Women in Western Political Philosophy: Kant to Nietzsche,* eds. Ellen Kennedy and Susan Mendus (New York: St. Martin's, 1987), p. 72: "There were important elements in [Smith's] treatment of the role of women, though largely unnoticed, which were fundamental themes in what has come to be thought of as the 'Victorian' concept of womanhood."

4. Joan Landes, *Women and the Public Sphere in the Age of the French Revolution* (Ithaca: Cornell University Press, 1988), p. 38.

5. See Sheila Delany, "Sex and Politics in Pope's 'Rape of the Lock'" in *Weapons of Criticism: Marxism in America and the Literary Tradition,* ed. Norman Rudich (Palo Alto: Ramparts Press, 1976), pp. 173–90. On Belinda as the cynosure of the world, see Louis Landa, *Essays in Eighteenth-Century English Literature* (Princeton: Princeton University Press, 1980), pp. 178–98.

6. Landa, *Essays in Eighteenth-Century English Literature,* p. 197.

7. The celebration of trade could have accidentally obscene overtones, as in the personification of trade as a sort of public woman, "the universal mistress of mankind courted and caressed by all civilized nations." Cited in Edward and Lillian Bloom, *Joseph Addison's Sociable Animal* (Providence: Brown University Press, 1971), p. 59. Thus Milton's Dalila, "courted by all the winds" (*Samson Agonistes,* line 719). The consuming woman is the world's courtesan. In "The Rape of the Lock" the caress of a "universal" woman is transformed into the image of sylphs fussing over "their darling care" (part I, line 145). A certain prurience hovers about Pope's description of Belinda awakening to her lapdog's tongue and performing her private rites.

8. As in James Fordyce's statement, "How often have I seen a company of men who were disposed to be riotous, checked all at once into decency by the accidental entrance of an amiable woman" (*Sermons to Young Women* [London, 1766], vol. 1, p. 21). Here a woman performs the chastening role that in the *Theory of Moral Sentiments* is assigned to the impartial spectator. Tocqueville sees American women, similarly, as the guardians of morality.

9. See Felicity Nussbaum, *The Brink of All We Hate: English Satires on Women, 1660–1750* (Lexington: University Press of Kentucky, 1984), pp. 121, 136, 162–63. Cf. Marlene LeGates, "The Cult of Womanhood in Eighteenth-Century Thought," *Eighteenth-Century Studies* 10 (1976): 21: "The misogyny which had characterized traditional satire and philosophic thought from the ancient Greeks through the seventeenth century was replaced by the eighteenth-century version of the Cult of True Womanhood." The author finds, however, that "the traditional view of the female as a sexual threat" survived (p. 26). On the displacement of the libidinous woman by the domestic ideal, see also Mary Poovey, *Uneven Developments: The Ideological Work of Gender in Mid-Victorian England* (Chicago: University of Chicago Press, 1988), p. 10.

10. See Linda Woodbridge, *Women and the English Renaissance: Literature and the Nature of Womankind, 1540–1620* (Urbana: University of Illinois Press, 1984); and Francis Lee Utley, *The Crooked Rib: An Analytical Index to the Argument About Women in English and Scots Literature to the End of the Year 1568* (Columbus: Ohio State University Press, 1944).

11. The image of woman as a danger to men lives on, for example in the figure of the femme fatale and the woman who spends her husband's money feeding her

shopping habit. I believe these images do not have the cultural authority they once did.

12. See Nietzsche, *Beyond Good and Evil,* trans. Walter Kaufmann (New York: Vintage, 1966), e.g., p. 169: "What inspires respect for woman, and often enough even fear, is her *nature,* which is more 'natural' than man's, the genuine, cunning suppleness of a beast of prey, the tiger's claw under the glove, the naiveté of her egotism, her uneducability and inner wildness." On the "tuning down of the affects," see p. 109.

13. See Bernard Mandeville, *The Fable of the Bees* (Edinburgh, 1772). See also M. M. Goldsmith, "Liberty, Luxury and the Pursuit of Happiness" in *The Languages of Political Theory in Early-Modern Europe,* ed. Anthony Pagden (Cambridge: Cambridge University Press, 1987), p. 247.

14. Woodbridge, *Women and the English Renaissance,* p. 168.

15. Norbert Elias, *The Loneliness of the Dying* (Oxford: Basil Blackwell, 1985), p. 7.

16. Adam Smith, *An Inquiry into the Nature and Causes of the Wealth of Nations* (New York: Modern Library, 1937), p. 389.

17. See Gervase Mathew, "Marriage and *Amour Courtois* in Late Fourteenth-Century England" in *Chaucer and His Contemporaries: Essays on Medieval Literature and Thought,* ed. Helene Newstead (New York: Fawcett, 1968).

18. On the shift from appetite to sentiment, see John Mullan, *Sentiment and Sociability: The Language of Feeling in the Eighteenth Century* (Oxford: Clarendon Press, 1988), p. 24. By its title, the *Theory of Moral Sentiments* sets us in a world of tamed passions. On the licit passion for consumer goods, see the anonymous "Vindication of Commerce and the Arts" (1758): "To want what may be innocently acquired is no crime. To be in pursuit of what is innocent, to strongly desire it, and to have a moral certainty of attaining it, is one of the highest degrees of human felicity. It is no hurt to have wants and desires, but to indulge and gratify irregular and vicious ones." Reprinted in *A Select Collection of Scarce and Valuable Tracts on Commerce,* ed. John McCulloch (New York: Augustus Kelley, 1966), p. 506.

19. On the effort to control the reputedly riotous appetites of the many (as by sumptuary laws) and to legislate their position in a rigidly stratified order, see John Sekora, *Luxury: The Concept in Western Thought, Eden to Smollett* (Baltimore: Johns Hopkins, 1977). The author sees the obsession with "luxury"—a vice pictured as a woman in male typology (pp. 44-45)—as defining Western thought.

20. Daniel Defoe, *The Complete English Tradesman* (New York: Burt Franklin, 1970), vol. 1, p. 151.

21. I quote from one Mr. Day, himself cited by Mary Wollstonecraft in *A Vindication of the Rights of Woman* (New York: Norton, 1988), p. 41n. Inevitably, Mr. Day also scourges women's love of display.

22. On corrupt imitation, fashion, and the vanity of men, see *TMS,* p. 64.

23. Neil McKendrick, John Brewer, and J. H. Plumb, *The Birth of a Consumer Society: The Commercialization of Eighteenth-Century England* (Bloomington: Indiana University Press, 1982), p. 12.

24. "For the sake of that little enhancement of price which . . . monopoly

might afford our producers, the home-consumers have been burdened with the whole expence of maintaining and defending [an] empire. For this purpose, and for this purpose only, in the last two wars, more than two hundred millions have been spent, and a new debt of more than a hundred and seventy millions has been contracted over and above all that had been expended for the same purpose in former wars." Smith, *Wealth of Nations,* p. 626. Smith finds the entire mercantile system to be monstrously illogical and expensive.

25. Sarah Ellis, *The Women of England, Their Social Duties and Domestic Habits* (London, 1839[?]), p. 257. The female consumer demands such things as silk cloaks and satin shoes. The root of the evil, says Ellis, somewhat in the manner of Mary Wollstonecraft, is "the system of false refinement which now prevails in this country" (p. 257). On the vanity and luxury of women, see also Eliza Lynn Linton's "The Girl of the Period," reprinted in *The Woman Question: Society and Literature in Britain and America, 1837–1883,* vol. 1: *Defining Voices,* eds. Elizabeth Helsinger, Robin Lauterbach Sheets, and William Veeder (Chicago: University of Chicago Press, 1983). The editors report that most commentators were unpersuaded by Linton's diatribe. On the attribution of insatiability to women in British moral literature of the eighteenth and nineteenth centuries, see Mary Poovey, *The Proper Lady and the Woman Writer: Ideology as Style in the Works of Mary Wollstonecraft, Mary Shelley, and Jane Austen* (Chicago: University of Chicago Press, 1984), chap. 1; also p. 189. The author reads propriety as a defense against the presumedly all-devouring nature of women's desire.

26. "After himself, the members of his own family, those who usually live in the same house with him, his parents, his children, his brothers and sisters, are naturally the objects of [a man's] warmest affections" (*TMS,* p. 219). Cf. *TMS,* p. 227: "Not only we ourselves, but all the objects of our kindest affections, our children, our parents, our relations, our friends, our benefactors, all those whom we naturally love and revere the most, are commonly comprehended within [the state]."

27. "Weaken and tame": Albert Hirschman, *The Passions and the Interests: Political Arguments for Capitalism before Its Triumph* (Princeton: Princeton University Press, 1977), p. 20. On weak passions defeating strong ones, see, e.g., pp. 63–66.

28. Merchant's Tale, lines 1338–46 in *The Works of Geoffrey Chaucer,* ed. F. N. Robinson (Boston: Houghton Mifflin, 1957).

29. Merchant's Tale, line 1429.

30. "And al myn heritage, toun [town] and tour [tower], / I yeve [give] it yow, maketh chartres [deeds] as yow leste [as you like]; / This shal be doon to-morwe er [before] sonne reste." Thus January to May. See Merchant's Tale, lines 2172–74.

31. Merchant's Tale, line 1303.

32. It may be that the teller of the Merchant's Tale was intended to be the Monk, in which case the antifeminism of the tale would accord well with the clerical custom of abusing women for tempting men away from holy things.

33. See Eliza Lynn Linton's indictment of "The Girl of the Period" (1868), reprinted in Helsinger, Sheets, and Veeder, *The Woman Question,* p. 109.

34. "It is impossible to discuss and condemn the follies of 'modern women' apart from those of modern men. . . . We are all of us extravagant, superficial, and luxurious together." Cited in Helsinger, Sheets, and Veeder, *The Woman Question,* pp. 122–23. On James's concern for "the masculine character," see Lionel Trilling, *Freud and the Crisis of Our Culture* (Boston: Beacon Press, 1955), p. 27.

35. On whores as handmaidens of virtue, see Keith Thomas, "The Double Standard," *Journal of the History of Ideas* 20 (1959): 197.

36. In the early years of the eighteenth century, angry Englishmen depicted the Catholic Church as a flashy harlot given to "vulgar display." See Bloom and Bloom, *Addison's Sociable Animal,* pp. 155–56. The image of the biblical harlot is remarkably constant and durable.

37. See Sekora, *Luxury,* pp. 44–49. On the power of luxury-woman to devour men's estates, see p. 49: "When it strikes a man, it has the fatal power to dissolve his character and to destroy his estate—that is, his social position and financial well-being." The domestic woman improves her husband's character and secures his estate.

38. Excerpts from Eustache Deschamps and Richard de Bury, as well as other antifeminist sources, appear in Robert P. Miller, ed., *Chaucer: Sources and Backgrounds* (New York: Oxford University Press, 1977), pp. 397–473.

39. Cited in Miller, *Chaucer: Sources and Backgrounds,* p. 413.

40. Within the *Odyssey* itself Penelope is antithetically paired with Clytemnestra, the wife, betrayer and murderer of Agamemnon.

41. Thus, for example, Hamlet accuses woman of cuckolding men, painting their faces, and playing tricks with words. "You nickname God's creatures and make your wantonness your ignorance" (*Hamlet,* 3.1.144–146).

42. Alan Macfarlane, *The Culture of Capitalism* (Oxford: Basil Blackwell, 1987), p. 39.

43. See Thomas, "The Double Standard," pp. 204, 211.

44. Defoe, *Complete English Tradesman,* vol. 1, pp. 81–82. Cf. p. 94: "Let tradesmen say what they will, and endeavour to excuse themselves as much as they will, by loading their wives with the blame of their miscarriage, as I have known some do, and as old father Adam in another case did before them, I must say so much in the woman's behalf . . . that if her husband truly and timely represented his case to her, and how far he was or was not able to maintain the expense of their way of living, I have not the least doubt but she would comply with her husband's circumstances, and retrench her expenses rather than go on for awhile and come to poverty and misery." Defoe judges "very few" women to be "so unreasonable" as to deliberately spend their husbands to ruin (pp. 97–98). He does argue that to thrive one must not wive too soon—not, however, because of the riotous nature of women but because the beginner in trade isn't yet in a position to support the ordinary expenses of married life.

45. Like beauty, the steady amassing of wealth is an idealization. Economic crises in eighteenth-century England seemed "exceptionally arbitrary and cruel," striking unpredictably and ruining men who possessed prudence and the other Smithian virtues. See John Brewer, "Commercialization and Politics" in McKendrick et al., *Birth of a Consumer Society,* p. 212.

46. Defoe, *Complete English Tradesman,* vol. 2, p. 88.

47. Louis Wright, *Middle-Class Culture in Elizabethan England* (Ithaca: Cornell University Press, 1965), p. 465.

48. Ian Maclean, *The Renaissance Notion of Woman: A study in the Fortunes of Scholasticism and Medical Science in European Intellectual Life* (Cambridge: Cambridge University Press, 1980), pp. 22, 26.

49. Woodbridge, *Women and the English Renaissance*, p. 18. Cf. Alan Macfarlane, *Marriage and Love in England: Modes of Reproduction, 1300–1840* (Oxford: Basil Blackwell, 1986), chap. 9.

50. Swetnam is cited in Woodbridge, *Women and the English Renaissance*, p. 83.

51. Macfarlane, *Culture of Capitalism*, p. 140.

52. See lines 214, 314, and 801 of the Wife of Bath's Prologue.

53. Wife of Bath's Tale, line 1168. In her own defense the Wife even cites Juvenal, king of the antifeminists.

54. See Macaulay's speech on Jewish Disabilities in Thomas Babington Macaulay, *Selected Writings*, eds. John Clive and Thomas Pinney (Chicago: University of Chicago Press, 1972), p. 190. In his *Reflections on the Revolution in France* Edmund Burke rails against Jews and complains of the adulteration of real wealth (gold, silver, land) by paper money. For Smith himself, merchants who can always pack up and leave if they find more favorable terms elsewhere stand in a "natural" opposition to landholders with a permanent interest in the country.

55. Werner Sombart, *Luxury and Capitalism,* trans. W. R. Dittmar (Ann Arbor: University of Michigan Press, 1967), p. 97. It is not entirely surprising to read that Sombart bought into Nazism in the early 1930s (p. xxv).

56. Smith's attacks on the conspiracies of merchants are legendary. Less well-known, perhaps, is his view that merchants feel no loyalty to their host country and are perfectly willing to ruin others by leaving: "The proprietor of stock is properly a citizen of the world, and is not necessarily attached to any particular country. He would be apt to abandon the country in which he was exposed to a vexatious inquisition, in order to be assessed to a burdensome tax. . . . By removing his stock he would put an end to all the industry which it had maintained in the country which he left." *Wealth of Nations,* p. 800; cf. p. 395.

57. Smith, *Wealth of Nations,* p. 461. Merchants and their co-conspirators are given to "sneaking arts," "impertinent jealousy," "mean rapacity" (p. 460).

58. Edmund Burke, *Reflections on the Revolution in France* (Indianapolis: Library of Liberal Arts, 1955), p. 110. The association of women with shifting caprice, moral ruin, ungovernable appetites, and commercial dealings is vividly realized in Grushenka in *The Brothers Karamazov.* Grushenka possesses business cunning; her detractors say that she is as bad as a Jew. See book 7, chapter 3. It is interesting that Father Zossima explicitly denies a tenet of Adam Smith: that in a commercial society the poor are better able to satisfy their wants. In his mind commerce possesses none of the beneficent, civilizing properties that it has in the mind of Adam Smith.

59. See Fernand Braudel, *Civilization and Capitalism, 15th–18th Century,* vol. 2: *The Wheels of Commerce,* tr. Siân Reynolds (New York: Harper and Row, 1979), p. 563.

60. On the rising reputation of women in the seventeenth century, see Roberta Hamilton, *The Liberation of Women: A Study of Patriarchy and Capitalism* (London: George Allen and Unwin, 1978), p. 20.

61. On men's habit of imputing to women all that besets them, see Poovey, *Proper Lady and the Woman Writer,* p. 5: "Because sexual desire momentarily undermines self-control, women are voracious; because the future is uncertain, they are inconstant; because life is full of contradictions, women are irrational." This habit of attribution underlies men's complaints about Fortune's female nature.

62. Adam Smith, *Wealth of Nations,* p. 325. But a little of the old image of Fortune as a perverse female, a scandal to reason, shows through in a passage in the *Theory of Moral Sentiments:* "Fortune has . . . great influence over the moral sentiments of mankind, and, according as she is either favourable or adverse, can render the same character the object, either of general love and admiration, or of universal hatred and contempt" *(TMS,* pp. 252–53).

63. Hume, *Treatise of Human Nature,* p. 647.

64. Hume, *Treatise of Human Nature,* p. 274. Unless the "changeable, weak, and irregular"—Fortune-like—principles of the mind are brought under control, "human nature must immediately perish and go to ruin."

65. Boethius, *The Consolation of Philosophy,* tr. Richard Green (Indianapolis: Library of Liberal Arts, 1962), p. 21. Cf. Dr. Johnson's "Vanity of Human Wishes," line 75: "Delusive Fortune . . ." On the genealogy of the image of Fortune, see Howard Patch, *The Goddess Fortuna in Mediaeval Literature* (Cambridge: Harvard University Press, 1927).

66. Maxwell Luria and Richard Hoffman, eds., *Middle English Lyrics* (New York: Norton, 1974), p. 9.

67. *King Lear,* 2.4.52.

68. *Hamlet,* 2.2.235–36.

69. See Ruth Bottigheimer, *Grimms' Bad Girls and Bold Boys: The Moral and Social Vision of the Tales* (New Haven: Yale University Press, 1987), p. 126: "In *Grimms' Tales* work generally bears no measurable or logical relationship to the success that follows." The author speculates that the antifeminist tradition that viewed labor as the penalty of Eve's sin could not envision labor yielding good fruits (p. 170). In this sense, too, Adam Smith's notion of diligence rewarded entails the displacement of traditional antifeminism.

70. In the *Wealth of Nations* Smith likens irrational economic theories to "the popular terrors and suspicions of witchcraft" (p. 500).

71. The opposition of Fortune and virtue is legible in Adam Smith's statement, "The candidates for fortune too frequently abandon the paths of virtue" *(TMS,* p. 64). On Smith and republicanism, see the Introduction to *TMS,* p. 19; Hirschman, *Passions and the Interests,* p. 106; Alasdair MacIntyre, *After Virtue: A Study in Moral Theory* (Notre Dame: University of Notre Dame Press, 1981), p. 220; Donald Winch, *Adam Smith's Politics: An Essay in Historiographic Revision* (Cambridge: Cambridge University Press, 1978); Hiram Caton, "The Preindustrial Economics of Adam Smith," *Journal of Economic History* 45 (1985): 853. On Francis Hutcheson (Smith's teacher) as republican, see Caroline Robbins, *The Eighteenth-Century Commonwealthman: Studies in the Transmission, Development and Circumstance of English Liberal Thought from the Resto-*

ration of Charles II until the War with the Thirteen Colonies (New York: Atheneum, 1968), pp. 185-96. On subduing Fortune, see J. G. A. Pocock, *The Machiavellian Moment: Florentine Political Thought and the Atlantic Republican Tradition* (Princeton: Princeton University Press, 1975). On Machiavelli and stoicism, see Sebastian de Grazia, *Machiavelli in Hell* (Princeton: Princeton University Press, 1989), p. 210. If Adam Smith and others of the civic humanist tradition despised the court as a center of false values, even corruption, Fortune was traditionally thought to inhabit the court. "As Fortuna is very much at home at court, so she deals particularly in royal favors, bestowing kingship, empire, and crown, and taking them back again." Patch, *Goddess Fortuna in Mediaeval Literature*, p. 59.

72. Niccolò Machiavelli, *The Prince,* trans. Robert Adams (New York: Norton, 1977), p. 72. See also Hanna Fenichel Pitkin, *Fortune Is a Woman: Gender and Politics in the Thought of Niccolò Machiavelli* (Berkeley: University of California Press, 1984).

73. *The Spectator,* ed. Donald F. Bond (Oxford: Clarendon Press, 1965), vol. 4.

74. Cited in Macfarlane, *Marriage and Love in England,* p. 149. Pope broadly hints that the widow weeps for show: "Not louder shrieks to pitying heav'n are cast, / When husbands, or when lapdogs breathe their last." *The Rape of the Lock* part III, lines 157-58, in Pope, *Poetical Works,* ed. Herbert Davis (London: Oxford University Press, 1966).

75. Anthony Trollope, *The Eustace Diamonds* (Oxford: Oxford University Press, 1983).

76. Like Machiavelli's prince, Boethius is to withstand Fortune's changes, in fact do battle against Fortune. "Indeed, virtue gets its name from that virile strength which is not overcome by adversity. . . . You [must] fight manfully against any fortune, neither despairing in the face of misfortune nor becoming corrupt in the enjoyment of prosperity." *Consolation of Philosophy,* p. 99. We might say that Mill's *On Liberty* (itself disdainful of opinion) accuses Victorians of becoming corrupt in their prosperity.

77. Cf. *TMS,* p. 115: "ignorant and groundless praise."

78. *Wealth of Nations,* p. 740. On the threat to trade posed by "whim, hearsay, fantasy, and rumour"—all of them intimately and habitually associated with women—see John Brewer, "Commercialization and Politics" in McKendrick et al., *Birth of a Consumer Society,* p. 214.

79. Ben Jonson, *Epicoene,* part IV.iii, lines 22-23; cf. part I.iii, line 35.

80. See, for example, Max Weber, *The Protestant Ethic and the Spirit of Capitalism,* trans. Talcott Parsons (New York: Scribners, 1930), p. 58: In traditional societies, free enterprise "has not generally been ethically justified and encouraged, but only tolerated as a fact. And this fact has been treated either as ethically indifferent or as reprehensible, but unfortunately unavoidable." The enterprising Wife of Bath seizes on St. Paul's grudging tolerance of marriage as a merchant might seize on the Church's grudging endorsement of profit.

81. Weber, *Protestant Ethic and the Spirit of Capitalism,* p. 73.

82. "The Western moral tradition displays an astonishing unity and solidarity in the uneasiness and mistrust it evinces towards money as the medium of exchange. Because so many of the components of the good life can be had for

money, we are under a constant temptation to mistake money for the *summum bonum.*" J. G. A. Pocock, *Virtue, Commerce, and History: Essays on Political Thought and History, Chiefly in the Eighteenth Century* (Cambridge: Cambridge University Press, 1985), pp. 103–4. For the argument that even Addison mistrusted the commercial way of life, see M. M. Goldsmith, "Mandeville and the Spirit of Capitalism," *Journal of British Studies* 17 (Fall 1977): 63–81. The conventional image of wealth as a kind of public woman who circulates among men, tempting them to ruin, appears with clarity in the late medieval morality play *Everyman*.

83. Defoe censures the urge to make "a show and ostentation of figure in the world" as the vice of a decadent age. See *Complete English Tradesman*, vol. 1, p. 75.

84. Cited in E. A. J. Johnson, *Predecessors of Adam Smith: The Growth of British Economic Thought* (New York: Prentice-Hall, 1937), p. 297. With a bold stroke, Hume neutralizes the meaning of the word "luxury" in his essay on "Refinement in the Arts." Attempts to efface the sensational meaning of terms like "luxury" anticipate Bentham's effort to neutralize the meaning of alarmist political terms. On the obsessive rant against luxury in eighteenth-century Britain, see Sekora, *Luxury*.

85. Even Defoe, no enemy of trade, wishes that "we ourselves were less corrupted by . . . superfluities in which we trade, and that we could be (like those quakers who deal in finery and ornament but never wear them themselves) content to bring them home, but to re-export them to more effeminate nations, than we would have ours to be." *Complete English Tradesman*, vol. 2, p. 230.

86. Cited in G. R. Owst, *Literature and Pulpit in Medieval England* (Oxford: Blackwell, 1961), p. 401.

87. *The Book of Margery Kempe* (London: Early English Text Society, 1940), p. 9.

88. Mandeville, *Fable of the Bees,* p. 273. On women as patrons of commerce, see also p. 165: "The variety of work that is performed, and the number of hands employed, to gratify the fickleness and luxury of women, is prodigious," as though the traditional appetites of woman had turned into social benefactors. See also M. M. Goldsmith, "Liberty, Luxury and the Pursuit of Happiness" in *The Languages of Political Theory in Early-Modern Europe,* p. 238. On the identification of women with "overconsumption and luxury" in France during the Old Regime, see Landes, *Women and the Public Sphere in the Age of the French Revolution,* p. 23. On the image of the adorned woman, see Proverbs 7:10–11: "And, behold, there met him a woman with the attire of an harlot, and subtil of heart. She is loud and stubborn; her feet abide not in her house." (Cunning, wandering, loudness of voice all belong to the Wife of Bath, who wears scarlet hose.)

89. Again, Margery Kempe condemns herself in just these terms: in her unregenerate condition she "euyr [ever] desyryd mor & mor" (*Book of Margery Kempe,* p. 9).

90. Mandeville, *Fable of the Bees,* p. 13. Cf. Fernand Braudel's characterization of luxury as "contradictory" and "constantly changing": *Civilization and Capitalism, 15th–18th Century,* vol. 1: *The Structures of Everyday Life: The Limits of the Possible,* trans. Siân Reynolds (New York: Harper and Row, 1979),

p. 183. The high importance that Braudel assigns to what moralists would call fickleness and frivolity (if not corruption) emerges on pp. 323-24.

91. Braudel, *Structures of Everyday Life,* pp. 323-24.

92. Mandeville, *Fable of the Bees,* p. 283.

93. In the General Prologue we learn that the Wife of Bath makes her offerings first and in style, and does not enjoy being upstaged. Clearly she likes to be in the public eye—"to be observed." On women and emulation, see also Defoe, *Complete English Tradesman,* vol. 1, p. 60: "It is observable, that the buyers, or retail customers, especially the ladies, follow one another as sheep follow the flock," a comment that fructifies in *On Liberty,* with its attack on the sheepishness and petty copying. In the nineteenth century Ruskin still rails against the woman who "play[s] at precedence with her next-door neighbour!" (John Ruskin, *Sesame and Lilies* [New York: Crowell, n. d.], p. 137) and Eliza Lynn Linton against the creature of fashion whose "main endeavour is to outvie her neighbours" in dress (Helsinger, Sheets, and Veeder, *The Woman Question,* p. 109). The figure of the vain woman is a cultural constant.

94. *Wealth of Nations,* p. 172. Fordyce's pet complaint is women's love of show and forwardness to display themselves. He rails against the "wandering" woman much as medieval preachers did, another sign that traditional anti-feminism lies not too far behind the polite ideal of the domestic woman. While celebrating the woman of "oeconomy" who faithfully cares for her husband's wealth, he also warns against wasteful women—as we might say, consumers. All men "dread a woman of expense" (*Sermons to Young Women,* vol. 1, p. 141). On the censure of female vanity and love of show in the Victorian age, see Helsinger, Sheets, and Veeder, *The Woman Question,* pp. 3-13.

95. McKendrick, *Birth of a Consumer Society,* p. 63. On the figure of the male housewife, or "cott-quean," see Joseph Addison's *Spectator* No. 482. Another effeminate male, the "woman's man" (as we now say, ladies' man), is sketched in *Spectator* No. 536, "vapours" and all. Cf. Hume's remarks on "women's men" in the *Treatise,* p. 664.

96. Nussbaum, *The Brink of All We Hate,* p. 161. Cf. LeGates, "Cult of Womanhood in Eighteenth-Century Thought," p. 30: "It is remarkable that the family, religion, and the state are now identified with woman rather than seen as being threatened by her." Related too, perhaps, is the transformation of sentiment itself from something reputedly "light, trivial, and shifting" (attributes notoriously identified with women) to something decent, wise, and stable (as in a theory of moral sentiments); see Garry Wills, *Inventing America: Jefferson's Declaration of Independence* (Garden City: Doubleday, 1978), p. 279.

97. Hutcheson insists that our moral sense judges of rightness and wrongness the way our sense of taste judges of food, and that the one has as little to do with reason as the other. On women as archetypal consumers, see Sekora on Cato's attack on the riotous appetites (and unreason) of women clamoring for the repeal of sumptuary laws: *Luxury,* p. 37. The figure of Cato was culturally authoritative.

98. The good woman "would regard her husband as her 'lord,' would not try to dress as richly as a lady, and would be content to stay at home instead of running about . . . where people might mistake her for a strumpet." Sylvia Thrupp, *The Merchant Class of Medieval London, 1300-1500* (Chicago: University of Chicago Press, 1948), p. 172.

99. "A considerable portion of what the prosperity of London, and trade in general, and consequently the honour, strength, safety, and all the worldly interest of the nation consist in, depends entirely on the deceit and vile stratagems of women, and . . . humility, content, meekness, obedience to reasonable husbands, frugality, and all the virtues together if they were possessed of them in the most eminent degree, could not possibly be a thousandth part so serviceable to make an opulent, powerful, and what we call *a flourishing kingdom,* than [sic] their most hateful qualities" (*Fable of the Bees,* p. 167). Thus Mandeville inverts and yet preserves the tradition of antifeminism, as the theorists of the domestic woman, frugal and obedient, do in their own fashion.

100. Smith, *Wealth of Nations,* p. 649.

101. Wife of Bath's Prologue, line 820.

102. Woodbridge, *Women and the English Renaissance,* p. 83.

103. See *Wealth of Nations,* p. 668. The mobs share with women the quality of "impertinent wantonness" (p. 668).

104. See, e.g., *Wealth of Nations,* pp. 328–29: "In the midst of all the exactions of government, . . . capital has been silently and gradually accumulated by the private frugality and good conduct of individuals, by their universal, continual, and uninterrupted effort to better their own condition." The force of gravity might be described as universal, continual, and uninterrupted.

105. Fordyce, *Sermons to Young Women,* vol. 1, p. 212. By "public business" Fordyce probably means private business.

106. Sarah Lewis, *Woman's Mission,* as cited by Helsinger, Sheets, and Veeder, *The Woman Question,* pp. 12–13: "Removed from the actual collision of political contests, and screened from the passions which such engender, she brings party questions to the test of the unalterable principles of reason and religion. . . . The blindness which sees not how [woman's] influence would be lessened by taking her out of the sphere assigned by Providence, if voluntary, is wicked,—if real, is pitiable. As well might we desire the earth's beautiful satellite to give place to a second sun, thereby producing the intolerable and glaring continuity of perpetual day."

107. Edmund Burke, *A Philosophical Enquiry into the Origin of Our Ideas of the Sublime and the Beautiful* (London: Routledge and Kegan Paul, 1958), p. 115.

108. Eve Kosofsky Sedgwick, *Between Men: English Literature and Male Homosocial Desire* (New York: Columbia University Press, 1985), p. 82.

109. On women of leisure: "But now there are many young ladies, whose situation does not supply a sphere of domestic exercise sufficient to fill up that part of their time, which is not necessarily appropriated to female occupations and idle amusements." Fordyce, *Sermons to Young Women,* vol. 2, pp. 9–10.

110. See, e.g., Helsinger, Sheets, and Veeder, *The Woman Question,* p. 11: "The principle of divided labor seems to be a maxim of the divine government, as regards the creature. It is only by a concentration of powers to one point [cf. Smith's example of the pin factory] that so feeble a being as man can achieve great results." The popular prescriptive writer Sarah Lewis is quoted.

111. See *Rambler* No. 85 in *The Works of Samuel Johnson,* eds. W. J. Bate and Albrecht Strauss (New Haven: Yale University Press, 1969), vol. 4, p. 86: unless women are kept busy with crafts, no one could "figure the confusion and

slaughter" caused by so many women "turned loose at once upon mankind, with no other business than to sparkle and intrigue, to perplex and to destroy." This statement clearly reveals the ancestral image of woman, as destroyer of men, behind the domestic woman.

112. Terry Eagleton, *The Ideology of the Aesthetic* (Oxford: Basil Blackwell, 1990), p. 28. Fittingly, the good mother was thought to rule noncoercively—to teach her children by the force of example and sweet influence rather than by precept. Says James Fordyce, preceptor of women: the good mother is skilled "in moulding the behaviour [of her children] without constraint" (*Sermons to Young Women*, vol. 1, p. 35). Growing up under a good mother is thus like moving under the influence of an invisible hand that does not feel coercive.

113. In the *Wealth of Nations* Smith does remark one case in which children pay. In colonies where land is abundant but the hands to work it few (as in America), high wages encourage marriage. "The children, during the tender years of infancy, are well fed and properly taken care of, and when they are grown up, the value of their labour overpays their maintenance" (p. 532). In Britain, where land is scarce and population high, the case is presumably different.

114. Macfarlane, *Marriage and Love in England*, p. 66. Cf. Defoe, *Complete English Tradesman*, p. 93: When a man in trade "brings home a wife, besides the furnishing his house, he must have formal housekeeping, even at the very first; and as children come on, more servants, that is, maids and nurses, that are as necessary as the bread he eats, especially if he multiplies apace, as he ought to suppose he may. In this case let the wife be frugal and managing, let her be unexceptionable in her expense, yet the man finds his charge mount high." Not the wife so much as children, or the family condition itself, is a tax on the husband. An exception to the rule is the high value of children in America, owing to the scarcity of labor there; see *Wealth of Nations*, p. 70.

115. Macfarlane, *Marriage and Love in England*, p. 75.

116. On children and consumer culture in eighteenth-century England, see J. H. Plumb, "The New World of Children" in McKendrick et al., *Birth of a Consumer Society*.

117. For Hume, wives are under a sacred obligation to be chaste, in part because children as so expensive that men need to be sure they are their own. See *Treatise of Human Nature*, p. 621.

118. Raymond Williams, *Keywords: A Vocabulary of Culture and Society* (New York: Oxford University Press, 1976), p. 69. The Wife of Bath falsely accuses her old husbands of likening women's love "to wilde fyr; / The moore it brenneth [burns], the moore it hath desir / To consume every thyng that brent [burnt] wole be." Wife of Bath's Prologue, lines 373–75.

119. Plumb, "The Acceptance of Modernity" in McKendrick et al., *Birth of a Consumer Society*, p. 316.

120. On "consume," see Rosalind Williams, *Dream Worlds: Mass Consumption in Late Nineteenth-Century France* (Berkeley: University of California Press, 1982), p. 6. On "luxury," see again Johnson, *Predecessors of Adam Smith*, p. 297; Sekora, *Luxury*.

121. Charlotte Perkins Gilman, *Women and Economics* (Boston: Small, Maynard and Company, 1898), pp. 118–19).

122. Gilman, *Women and Economics*, p. 121.

123. Gilman, *Women and Economics,* p. 120.

124. Thus, for example, the often-cited lines of Tennyson's "The Princess": "Man for the field and woman for the hearth: / Man for the sword and for the needle she."

125. Walter Houghton, *The Victorian Frame of Mind* (New Haven: Yale University Press, 1957), p. 202. Cf. Edmund Burke's devotion to hereditary relations (including a chivalric manliness), commerce or no commerce.

126. Martin Pernick, "The Calculus of Suffering in 19th-Century Surgery" in *Sickness and Health in America: Readings in the History of Medicine and Public Health,* eds. Judith Walzer Leavitt and Ronald Numbers (Madison: University of Wisconsin Press, 1985), p. 107. In the case of the royal household in England, the domestic angel seems to have been Albert. See Helsinger, Sheets, and Veeder, *The Woman Question,* pp. 74–75. On the hypertrophy of gender distinctions in the thought of Leslie Stephen, see Noel Annan, *Leslie Stephen: His Thought and Character in Relation to his Time* (London: Macgibbon and Kee, 1951), pp. 224–27. On the pronounced binarism of Victorian attitudes toward gender, see Poovey, *Uneven Developments,* chap. 1.

127. Joseph Conrad, *Heart of Darkness* (New York: Norton, 1971), p. 18. According to Edward and Lillian Bloom, Joseph Addison recognized that prudence—the cardinal virtue of commercial society—covered up sheer timidity on the one hand and on the other "allowed greed without audacity and cruelty without courage." This is an unattributed quotation of *Heart of Darkness.* See Bloom and Bloom, *Addison's Sociable Animal,* p. 19.

Chapter 5

1. J. G. A. Pocock, *Virtue, Commerce, and History: Essays on Political Thought and History, Chiefly in the Eighteenth Century* (Cambridge: Cambridge University Press, 1985), p. 114.

2. Edmund Burke, *Reflections on the Revolution in France* (Indianapolis: Library of Liberal Arts, 1955), p. 86.

3. Burke, *Reflections on the Revolution in France,* p. 87.

4. Burke, *Reflections on the Revolution in France,* p. 42.

5. On Smithian man's defect of rationality, see, e.g., J. Ralph Lindgren, *The Social Philosophy of Adam Smith* (The Hague: Martinus Nijhoff, 1973), p. 77; and Donald Winch, *Adam Smith's Politics: An Essay in Historiographic Revision* (Cambridge: Cambridge University Press, 1978), p. 167.

6. William Hazlitt, *Selected Writings* (New York: Oxford University Press, 1991), p. 55.

7. Sarah Ellis, *The Women of England, Their Social Duties and Domestic Habits* (London, 1839 [?]), p. 19.

8. Ellis, *Women of England,* p. 13.

9. Charles Taylor, *Hegel and Modern Society* (Cambridge: Cambridge University Press, 1979), p. 71.

10. See Rogers Brubaker, *The Limits of Rationality: An Essay on the Social and Moral Thought of Max Weber* (London: George Allen and Unwin, 1984).

11. "Areopagitica" in John Milton, *Paradise Lost and Selected Poetry and Prose*, ed. Northrop Frye (New York: Holt, Rinehart and Winston, 1964), p. 479. Cf. *Paradise Lost* book III, line 108. In contrast to Milton's apocalyptic hopes, voiced in "Areopagitica," stands Adam Smith's belief in gradualism. In post-Renaissance Europe, "for the first time men seemed to have developed ways to achieve . . . plenty and happiness gradually and peacefully instead of abruptly and catastrophically, and by human and material means, without the need for a sudden relief expedition from the sky." M. H. Abrams, *Natural Supernaturalism: Tradition and Revolution in Romantic Literature* (New York: Norton, 1973), p. 59. Smith's censure of enthusiasm, his naturalistic idea of causation, his warning against revolution in the *Moral Sentiments,* his vision of the gradual increase of "plenty"—all identify him as being of the antiprophetic, or anti-Miltonic school.

12. "Demanding consumer": Louis Landa, *Essays in Eighteenth-Century English Literature* (Princeton: Princeton University Press, 1980), p. 204. The identification of women with overconsumption in France: Joan Landes, *Women and the Public Sphere in the Age of the French Revolution* (Ithaca: Cornell University Press, 1988), p. 23. "Creatures of consumption par excellence": Rosalind Williams, *Dream Worlds: Mass Consumption in Late Nineteenth-Century France* (Berkeley: University of California Press, 1982), p. 307.

13. *Wealth of Nations,* p. 625. In our century Paul Tillich has objected to the model of society as a pin-factory that turns out goods endlessly and mechanizes persons themselves. "The immense mechanism, set up by man to produce objects for his use, transforms man himself into an object used by the same mechanism of production and consumption." See "The Lost Dimension in Religion" in *The Educated Reader,* ed. Gerald Levin (San Diego: Harcourt Brace Jovanovich, 1988), p. 219. Smith hoped in effect that stoicism would preserve the autonomy here described as lost.

14. On the democratization of consumer style, see Stuart Ewen, *All Consuming Images: The Politics of Style in Contemporary Culture* (New York: Basic, 1988), chap. 2.

15. Karl Mannheim, *Essays on Sociology and Social Psychology* (New York: Oxford University Press, 1953), p. 86. In one form or another, Mannheim's thesis is widely accepted.

16. Burke, *Reflections on the Revolution in France,* p. 99.

17. Paul Corcoran, *Political Language and Rhetoric* (Austin: University of Texas Press, 1979), p. 157. Corcoran argues, surely correctly, that political advertisers are interested in the viewer's sympathies "and not his conscious command of a body of information" (p. 166).

18. Kenneth Burke, *A Rhetoric of Motives* (Berkeley: University of California Press, 1969), p. 98.

19. This is not to say that Mary Wollstonecraft opposes conventional morality at all points. She concedes that the stuffy Fordyce makes some good arguments, and even the proper Sarah Ellis was to share her revulsion at women's over-refinement and affectation of delicacy; indeed, Ellis thought lower-middle-class women ought to be able to enter trades like engraving and millinery.

20. R. M. Janes, "On the Reception of Mary Wollstonecraft's *A Vindication*

of the Rights of Woman" reprinted in *A Vindication of the Rights of Woman*, ed. Carol Poston (New York: Norton, 1988), pp. 297–307.

21. See Peter Gay, *The Enlightenment: An Interpretation* (New York: Knopf, 1966), pp. 107, 109.

22. Such is the curiously tangled relation between the thought of Mary Wollstonecraft and Smith's, that she herself befriends stoicism; see her sentimental portrait of a widow who teaches her children "to endure adversity" (*Vindication of the Rights of Woman*, p. 51).

23. Cited in Abrams, *Natural Supernaturalism*, p. 396.

24. Isaac Kramnick, *Republicanism and Bourgeois Radicalism: Political Ideology in Late Eighteenth-Century England and America* (Ithaca: Cornell University Press, 1990), pp. 13–14.

25. See Garry Wills, "Ross Perot and the Immaculate Election," *Washington Post Weekly,* June 1–7, 1992, p. 23.

Select Bibliography

Abrams, M. H. *Doing Things with Texts: Essays in Criticism and Critical Theory.* New York: Norton, 1989.

———. *Natural Supernaturalism: Tradition and Revolution in Romantic Literature.* New York: Norton, 1973.

Adair, Douglass. " 'That Politics May Be Reduced to a Science': David Hume, James Madison, and the Tenth *Federalist.*" *Huntington Library Quarterly* 20 (1957): 343–60.

Adams, Robert. *The Land and Literature of England.* New York: Norton, 1983.

———. *The Roman Stamp: Frame and Facade in Some Forms of Neo-Classicism.* Berkeley: University of California Press, 1974.

Addison, Joseph, et al. *The Spectator.* Edited by Donald F. Bond. Oxford: Clarendon Press, 1965.

Annan, Noel. *Leslie Stephen: His Thought and Character in Relation to his Time.* London: Macgibbon and Kee, 1951.

Austen, Jane. *Emma.* Harmondsworth, Middlesex: Penguin, 1972.

———. *Pride and Prejudice.* New York: Norton, 1966.

Barber, Benjamin. "Rousseau and the Paradoxes of the Dramatic Imagination." *Daedalus,* Summer 1978, 79–92.

Barish, Jonas. "Ovid, Juvenal, and *The Silent Woman.*" *PMLA* 71 (1956): 213–24.

Barker-Benfield, G. J. "Mary Wollstonecraft: Eighteenth-Century Commonwealthwoman." *Journal of the History of Ideas* 50 (1989): 95–115.

Berlin, Isaiah. *Four Essays on Liberty.* New York: Oxford University Press, 1969.

Blake, William. *The Poetry and Prose of William Blake.* Edited by David Erdman. Garden City: Doubleday, 1970.

Bloch, Ruth. "The Gendered Meanings of Virtue in Revolutionary America." *Signs* 13 (1987): 37–58.

Bloom, Edward, and Lillian Bloom. *Joseph Addison's Sociable Animal.* Providence: Brown University Press, 1971.

Bibliography

Boethius. *The Consolation of Philosophy.* Translated by Richard Green. Indianapolis: Library of Liberal Arts, 1962.

Bottigheimer, Ruth. *Grimms' Bad Girls and Bold Boys: The Moral and Social Vision of the Tales.* New Haven: Yale University Press, 1987.

Braudel, Fernand. *Civilization and Capitalism, 15th–18th Century.* Vol. 1: *The Structures of Everyday Life: The Limits of the Possible;* Vol. 2: *The Wheels of Commerce.* Translated by Siân Reynolds. New York: Harper and Row, 1979.

Bridenthal, Renate, and Claudia Koonz, eds. *Becoming Visible: Women in European History.* Boston: Houghton Mifflin, 1977.

Brown, John. *An Estimate of the Manners and Principles of the Times.* 2 vols. London, 1757–58.

Bruns, Gerald. *Inventions: Writing, Textuality, and Understanding in Literary History.* New Haven: Yale University Press, 1982.

Burke, Edmund. *A Philosophical Enquiry into the Origin of our Ideas of the Sublime and the Beautiful.* London: Routledge and Kegan Paul, 1958.

———. *Reflections on the Revolution in France.* Indianapolis: Library of Liberal Arts, 1955.

Burke, Kenneth. *A Rhetoric of Motives.* Berkeley: University of California Press, 1969.

Butler, Marilyn. *Jane Austen and the War of Ideas.* Oxford: Clarendon Press, 1975.

Campbell, Colin. *The Romantic Ethic and the Spirit of Modern Consumerism.* Oxford: Basil Blackwell, 1987.

Campbell, R. H., and Andrew Skinner, eds. *The Origins and Nature of the Scottish Enlightenment.* Edinburgh: John Donald, 1982.

Cassirer, Ernst. *The Myth of the State.* New Haven: Yale University Press, 1946.

Caton, Hiram. "The Preindustrial Economics of Adam Smith." *Journal of Economic History* 45 (1985): 833–53.

Christman, John, ed. *The Inner Citadel: Essays on Individual Autonomy.* New York: Oxford University Press, 1989.

Cicero, Marcus Tullius. *Brutus; On the Nature of the Gods; On Divination; On Duties.* Translated by Hubert Poteat. Chicago: University of Chicago Press, 1950.

Clifford, James, ed. *Man Versus Society in Eighteenth-Century Britain: Six Points of View.* Cambridge: Cambridge University Press, 1968.

Clinton, Katherine. "Femme et Philosophe: Enlightenment Origins of Feminism." *Eighteenth-Century Studies* 8 (1975): 283–99.

Cole, Lucinda. "(Anti)feminist Sympathies: The Politics of Relationship in Smith, Wollstonecraft, and More." *ELH* 58 (Spring 1991): 107–40.

Conrad, Joseph. *Heart of Darkness.* New York: Norton, 1971.

Corfield, Penelope. Review of David Castronovo, *The English Gentleman: Images and Ideals in Literature and Society* in *Eighteenth-Century Studies* 21 (1988): 378–82.

Crane, R. S. "Suggestions Toward a Genealogy of the 'Man of Feeling.'" *ELH* 1 (1934): 205–30.

Cropsey, Joseph. *Polity and Economy: An Interpretation of the Principles of Adam Smith.* The Hague: Martinus Nijhoff, 1957.

Bibliography

Defoe, Daniel. *The Complete English Tradesman.* New York: Burt Franklin, 1970.

Douglas, Ann. *The Feminization of American Culture.* New York: Avon, 1977.

Eagleton, Terry. *The Function of Criticism: From* The Spectator *to Post-Structuralism.* London: Verso, 1984.

———. *The Ideology of the Aesthetic.* Oxford: Basil Blackwell, 1990.

Elias, Norbert. *The History of Manners.* Translated by Edmund Jephcott. New York: Pantheon, 1939. Orig. pub. 1939.

———. *The Loneliness of the Dying.* Oxford: Basil Blackwell, 1985.

———. *Power and Civility.* Translated by Edmund Jephcott. New York: Pantheon, 1982. Orig. pub. 1939.

Ellis, Sarah. *The Women of England, Their Social Duties and Domestic Habits.* London, 1839(?).

Elshtain, Jean Bethke. *Public Man, Private Woman: Women in Social and Political Thought.* Princeton: Princeton University Press, 1981.

Epictetus. *The Moral Discourses of Epictetus.* Translated by Elizabeth Carter. London: J. M. Dent, 1910.

Ewen, Stuart. *All Consuming Images: The Politics of Style in Contemporary Culture.* New York: Basic, 1988.

Fordyce, James. *Sermons to Young Women.* London, 1766.

Franklin, Benjamin. *Autobiography.* Edited by J. A. Leo Lemay and P. M. Zall. New York: Norton, 1986.

Frye, Northrop. *The Secular Scripture: A Study of the Structure of Romance.* Cambridge: Harvard University Press, 1976.

Gilman, Charlotte Perkins. *Women and Economics.* Boston: Small, Maynard, and Company, 1898.

Goldsmith, M. M. "Mandeville and the Spirit of Capitalism." *Journal of British Studies* 17 (Fall 1977): 63–81.

Guest, Harriet. "A Double Lustre: Femininity and Sociable Commerce, 1730–60." *Eighteenth-Century Studies* 23 (1990): 479–501.

Hamilton, Roberta. *The Liberation of Women: A Study of Patriarchy and Capitalism.* London: George Allen and Unwin, 1978.

Helsinger, Elizabeth, Robin Lauterbach Sheets, and William Veeder, eds. *The Woman Question.* Vol. 1: *Defining Voices.* Chicago: University of Chicago Press, 1983.

Hill, Christopher. "Clarissa Harlowe and her Times." *Essays in Criticism* 5 (1955): 315–40.

Hirschman, Albert. *The Passions and the Interests: Political Arguments for Capitalism before Its Triumph.* Princeton: Princeton University Press, 1977.

Hont, Istvan, and Michael Ignatieff, eds. *Wealth and Virtue: The Shaping of Political Economy in the Scottish Enlightenment.* Cambridge, U.K.: Cambridge University Press, 1983.

Horkheimer, Max. *Eclipse of Reason.* New York: Seabury, 1974.

Houghton, Walter. *The Victorian Frame of Mind.* New Haven: Yale University Press, 1957.

Hoyt, Nelly and Thomas Cassirer, eds. and trans. *Encyclopedia Selections.* Indianapolis: Library of Liberal Arts, 1965.

Bibliography

Hume, David. *Essays Moral, Political, and Literary.* Indianapolis: Liberty Classics, 1987.

————. *A Treatise of Human Nature.* Harmondsworth, Middlesex: Penguin, 1985.

Johnson, Claudia. *Jane Austen: Women, Politics and the Novel.* Chicago: University of Chicago Press, 1988.

Johnson, E. A. J. *Predecessors of Adam Smith: The Growth of British Economic Thought.* New York: Prentice-Hall, 1937.

Johnson, Samuel. Rasselas, *Poems and Selected Prose.* Edited by Bertrand Bronson. New York: Holt, Rinehart and Winston, 1958.

————. *Works.* Edited by W. J. Bate and Albrecht Strauss. New Haven: Yale University Press, 1969.

Justman, Stewart. *The Hidden Text of Mill's Liberty.* Savage, Md.: Rowman and Littlefield, 1990.

Kant, Immanuel. *Kant's Political Writings.* Edited by Hans Reiss. Translated by H. B. Nisbet. Cambridge, U.K.: Cambridge University Press, 1971.

Kempe, Margery. *The Book of Margery Kempe.* London: Early English Text Society, 1940.

Kennedy, Ellen, and Susan Mendus, eds. *Women in Western Political Philosophy: Kant to Nietzsche.* New York: St. Martin's, 1987.

Keohane, Nannerl, Michelle Rosaldo, and Barbara Gelpi, eds. *Feminist Theory: A Critique of Ideology.* Chicago: University of Chicago Press, 1982.

Kettler, David. *The Social and Political Thought of Adam Ferguson.* Columbus: Ohio State University Press, 1965.

Kramnick, Isaac. *Republicanism and Bourgeois Radicalism: Political Ideology in Late Eighteenth-Century England and America.* Ithaca: Cornell University Press, 1990.

La Rochefoucauld, FranÇois. *The Maxims of La Rochefoucauld.* Translated by Louis Kronenberger. New York: Random House, 1959.

Landa, Louis. *Essays in Eighteenth-Century English Literature.* Princeton: Princeton University Press, 1980.

Landes, Joan. *Women and the Public Sphere in the Age of the French Revolution.* Ithaca: Cornell University Press, 1988.

Lasch, Christopher. *The Culture of Narcissism: American Life in an Age of Diminishing Expectations.* New York: Warner, 1979.

LeGates, Marlene. "The Cult of Womanhood in Eighteenth-Century Thought." *Eighteenth-Century Studies* 10 (1976): 21–39.

Lindgren, J. Ralph. *The Social Philosophy of Adam Smith.* The Hague: Martinus Nijhoff, 1973.

Long, Anthony. "Ethics of Stoicism." In vol. 4 of the *Dictionary of the History of Ideas.* New York: Scribners, 1973.

Macaulay, Thomas Babington. *Critical and Historical Essays.* New York: Dutton, 1967.

————. *Selected Writings.* Edited by John Clive and Thomas Pinney. Chicago: University of Chicago Press, 1972.

McCulloch, John, ed. *A Select Collection of Scarce and Valuable Tracts on Commerce.* New York: Augustus Kelley, 1966.

Macfarlane, Alan. *The Culture of Capitalism.* Oxford: Basil Blackwell, 1987.

Bibliography

————. *Marriage and Love in England: Modes of Reproduction, 1300–1840.* Oxford: Basil Blackwell, 1986.

Macfie, A. L. *The Individual in Society: Papers on Adam Smith.* London: George Allen and Unwin, 1967.

Machiavelli, Niccolò. *The Prince.* Translated by Robert M. Adams. New York: Norton, 1977.

MacIntyre, Alasdair. *After Virtue: A Study in Moral Theory.* Notre Dame: University of Notre Dame Press, 1981.

McKendrick, Neil, John Brewer, and J. H. Plumb. *The Birth of a Consumer Society: The Commercialization of Eighteenth-Century England.* Bloomington: Indiana University Press, 1982.

Maclean, Ian. *The Renaissance Notion of Woman: A Study in the Fortunes of Scholasticism and Medical Science in European Intellectual Life.* Cambridge, U.K.: Cambridge University Press, 1980.

McNally, David. *Political Economy and the Rise of Capitalism: A Reinterpretation.* Berkeley: University of California Press, 1988.

Mandeville, Bernard. *The Fable of the Bees; or, Private Vices, Publick Benefits.* Edinburgh, 1772.

Mannheim, Karl. *Essays on Sociology and Social Knowledge.* New York: Oxford University Press, 1953.

Marshall, David. *The Figure of Theater: Shaftesbury, Defoe, Adam Smith, and George Eliot.* New York: Columbia University Press, 1986.

————. *The Surprising Effects of Sympathy: Marivaux, Diderot, Rousseau, and Mary Shelley.* Chicago: University of Chicago Press, 1988.

Mill, John Stuart. *On Liberty.* Edited by David Spitz. New York: Norton, 1975.

———— and Harriet Taylor. *The Subjection of Women.* In *Essays on Sex Equality,* edited by Alice Rossi. Chicago: University of Chicago Press, 1970.

Miller, David. *Philosophy and Ideology in Hume's Political Thought.* Oxford: Clarendon Press, 1981.

Miller, Robert, ed. *Chaucer: Sources and Backgrounds.* New York: Oxford University Press, 1977.

Montesquieu, Charles-Louis de Secondat, Baron de. *The Persian Letters.* Translated by George R. Healy. Indianapolis: Library of Liberal Arts, 1964.

Mullan, John. *Sentiment and Sociability: The Language of Feeling in the Eighteenth Century.* Oxford: Clarendon Press, 1988.

Myers, Mitzi. "Impeccable Governesses, Rational Dames, and Moral Mothers: Mary Wollstonecraft and the Female Tradition in Georgian Children's Books." *Children's Literature* 14 (1986): 31–59.

Newstead, Helene, ed. *Chaucer and His Contemporaries: Essays on Medieval Literature and Thought.* New York: Fawcett, 1968.

Nieli, Russell. "Spheres of Intimacy and the Adam Smith Problem." *Journal of the History of Ideas* 47 (1986): 611–24.

Nietzsche, Friedrich. *Beyond Good and Evil: Prelude to a Philosophy of the Future.* Translated by Walter Kaufmann. New York: Vintage, 1966.

Norton, Mary Beth. *Liberty's Daughters: The Revolutionary Experience of American Women, 1750–1800.* Boston: Little, Brown, 1980.

Nussbaum, Felicity. *The Brink of All We Hate: English Satires on Women, 1660–1750.* Lexington: University Press of Kentucky, 1984.

Bibliography

Nye, Andrea. *Feminist Theory and the Philosophies of Man.* New York: Routledge, 1988.

Owst, G. R. *Literature and Pulpit in Medieval England.* Oxford: Blackwell, 1961.

Pagden, Anthony, ed. *The Languages of Political Theory in Early-Modern Europe.* Cambridge, U.K.: Cambridge University Press, 1987.

Pitkin, Hanna Fenichel. *Fortune Is a Woman: Gender and Politics in the Thought of Niccolò Machiavelli.* Berkeley: University of California Press, 1984.

Pocock, J. G. A. "Gibbon's *Decline and Fall* and the World View of the Late Enlightenment." *Eighteenth-Century Studies* 10 (1977): 287–303.

———. *The Machiavellian Moment: Florentine Political Thought and the Atlantic Republican Tradition.* Princeton: Princeton University Press, 1975.

———. *Virtue, Commerce, and History: Essays on Political Thought and History, Chiefly in the Eighteenth Century.* Cambridge, U.K.: Cambridge University Press, 1985.

Poovey, Mary. *The Proper Lady and the Woman Writer: Ideology as Style in the Works of Mary Wollstonecraft, Mary Shelley, and Jane Austen.* Chicago: University of Chicago Press, 1984.

———. *Uneven Developments: The Ideological Work of Gender in Mid-Victorian England.* Chicago: University of Chicago Press, 1988.

Pope, Alexander. *Poetical Works.* Edited by Herbert Davis. London: Oxford University Press, 1966.

Rae, John. *Life of Adam Smith.* New York: Augustus Kelley, 1965. Orig. pub. 1895.

Raphael, D. D. *British Moralists: 1650–1800.* Oxford: Clarendon Press, 1969.

Reisman, D. A. *Adam Smith's Sociological Economics.* London: Croom Helm, 1976.

Robbins, Caroline. *The Eighteenth-Century Commonwealthman: Studies in the Transmission, Development and Circumstance of English Liberal Thought from the Restoration of Charles II until the War with the Thirteen Colonies.* New York: Atheneum, 1968.

Rosenberg, Nathan. "Adam Smith, Consumer Tastes, and Economic Growth." *Journal of Political Economy* 76 (1968): 361–73.

Rousseau, Jean-Jacques. *Confessions.* Translated by J. M. Cohen. Harmondsworth, Middlesex: Penguin, 1953.

———. *A Discourse on Inequality.* Translated by Maurice Cranston. Harmondsworth, Middlesex: Penguin, 1984.

———. *Emile or On Education.* Translated by Allan Bloom. New York: Basic, 1979.

Rudich, Norman, ed. *Weapons of Criticism: Marxism in America and the Literary Tradition.* Palo Alto: Ramparts Press, 1976.

Schneider, Louis, ed. *The Scottish Moralists: On Human Nature and Society.* Chicago: University of Chicago Press, 1967.

Sedgwick, Eve Kosofsky. *Between Men: English Literature and Male Homosocial Desire.* New York: Columbia University Press, 1985.

Seidel, Michael. "Poulain de la Barre's *The Woman as Good as the Man.*" *Journal of the History of Ideas* 35 (1974): 499–508.

Sekora, John. *Luxury: The Concept in Western Thought, Eden to Smollett.* Baltimore: Johns Hopkins University Press, 1977.

Bibliography

Shklar, Judith. "Jean-Jacques Rousseau and Equality." *Daedalus,* Summer 1978, 13–25.

———. *Men and Citizens: A Study of Rousseau's Social Theory.* Cambridge, U.K.: Cambridge University Press, 1985.

———. *Ordinary Vices.* Cambridge, Mass.: Harvard University Press, 1984.

Skinner, A. S., and Thomas Wilson, eds. *Essays on Adam Smith.* Oxford: Clarendon Press, 1975.

Smith, Adam. *The Correspondence of Adam Smith.* Edited by Ernest Mossner and Ian Ross. Oxford: Clarendon Press, 1977.

———. *The Early Writings of Adam Smith.* Edited by J. Ralph Lindgren. New York: Augustus Kelley, 1967.

———. *An Inquiry into the Nature and Causes of the Wealth of Nations.* New York: Modern Library, 1937.

———. *Lectures on Justice, Police, Revenue and Arms.* New York: Kelley and Millman, 1956.

———. *The Theory of Moral Sentiments.* Edited by D. D. Raphael and A. L. Macfie. Indianapolis: Liberty Classics, 1982.

Sombart, Werner. *Luxury and Capitalism.* Translated by W. R. Dittmar. Ann Arbor: University of Michigan Press, 1967.

Spacks, Patricia Meyer. "Ev'ry Woman is at Heart a Rake." *Eighteenth-Century Studies* 8 (1974): 27–46.

Spadafora, David. *The Idea of Progress in Eighteenth-Century Britain.* New Haven: Yale University Press, 1990.

Sterne, Laurence. *A Sentimental Journey.* London: Oxford University Press, 1968.

Stewart-Robertson, J. C., and David Fate Norton. "Thomas Reid on Adam Smith's Theory of Morals." *Journal of the History of Ideas* 45 (1984): 309–21.

Taylor, Charles. *Hegel and Modern Society.* Cambridge, U.K.: Cambridge University Press, 1979.

Thomas, Keith. "The Double Standard." *Journal of the History of Ideas* 20 (1959): 195–216.

Trilling, Lionel. *Sincerity and Authenticity.* Cambridge, Mass.: Harvard University Press, 1972.

Viner, Jacob. *The Role of Providence in the Social Order: An Essay in Intellectual History.* Philadelphia: American Philosophical Society, 1972.

Waszek, Norbert. "Two Concepts of Morality: A Distinction of Adam Smith's Ethics and Its Stoic Origin." *Journal of the History of Ideas* 45 (1984): 591–606.

Weber, Max. *The Protestant Ethic and the Spirit of Capitalism.* Translated by Talcott Parsons. New York: Scribners, 1930.

Weinbrot, Howard. "History, Horace, and Augustus Caesar: Some Implications for Eighteenth-Century Satire." *Eighteenth-Century Studies* 7 (1974): 391–414.

Werhane, Patricia. *Adam Smith and His Legacy for Modern Capitalism.* New York: Oxford University Press, 1991.

Williams, Rosalind. *Dream Worlds: Mass Consumption in Late Nineteenth-Century France.* Berkeley: University of California Press, 1982.

Winch, Donald. *Adam Smith's Politics: An Essay in Historiographic Revision.* Cambridge, U.K.: Cambridge University Press, 1978.

Bibliography

Wolin, Sheldon. "Hume and Conservatism." *American Political Science Review* 48 (1954): 999–1016.

———. *Politics and Vision: Continuity and Innovation in Western Political Thought*. Boston: Little, Brown, 1960.

Wollstonecraft, Mary. *A Vindication of the Rights of Woman*. Edited by Carol Poston. New York: Norton, 1988.

Woodbridge, Linda. *Women and the English Renaissance: Literature and the Nature of Womankind, 1540–1620*. Urbana: University of Illinois Press, 1984.

Wright, Louis. *Middle-Class Culture in Elizabethan England*. Ithaca: Cornell University Press, 1965.

Index

Index

Index

Index